The Literary Agenda

The Digital Humanities and Literary Studies

T0003508

The Literary Agenda

The Digital Humanities and Literary Studies

MARTIN PAUL EVE

OXFORD
UNIVERSITY PRESS

OXFORD
UNIVERSITY PRESS

Great Clarendon Street, Oxford, OX2 6DP,
United Kingdom

Oxford University Press is a department of the University of Oxford.
It furthers the University's objective of excellence in research, scholarship,
and education by publishing worldwide. Oxford is a registered trade mark of
Oxford University Press in the UK and in certain other countries

© Martin Paul Eve 2022

First Edition published in 2022
Impression: 1

Enquiries concerning reproduction outside the scope of this licence
should be sent to the Rights Department, Oxford University Press, at the address above

Published in the United States of America by Oxford University Press
198 Madison Avenue, New York, NY 10016, United States of America

British Library Cataloguing in Publication Data
Data available

Library of Congress Control Number: 2021943566

ISBN 978–0–19–885048–9

Printed and bound by
CPI Group (UK) Ltd, Croydon, CR0 4YY

Links to third party websites are provided by Oxford in good faith and
for information only. Oxford disclaims any responsibility for the materials
contained in any third party website referenced in this work.

Series Introduction

The Crisis in, the Threat to, the Plight of the Humanities: enter these phrases in Google's search engine and there are 23 million results, in a great fifty-year-long cry of distress, outrage, fear, and melancholy. Grant, even, that every single anxiety and complaint in that catalogue of woe is fully justified—the lack of public support for the arts, the cutbacks in government funding for the humanities, the imminent transformation of a literary and verbal culture by visual/virtual/digital media, the decline of reading...And still, though it were all true, and just because it might be, there would remain the problem of the response itself. Too often there's recourse to the shrill moan of offended piety or a defeatist withdrawal into professionalism.

The Literary Agenda is a series of short polemical monographs that believes there is a great deal that needs to be said about the state of literary education inside schools and universities and more fundamentally about the importance of literature and of reading in the wider world. The category of 'the literary' has always been contentious. What *is* clear, however, is how increasingly it is dismissed or is unrecognized as a way of thinking or an arena for thought. It is sceptically challenged from within, for example, by the sometimes rival claims of cultural history, contextualized explanation, or media studies. It is shaken from without by even greater pressures: by economic exigency and the severe social attitudes that can follow from it; by technological change that may leave the traditional forms of serious human communication looking merely antiquated. For just these reasons this is the right time for renewal, to start reinvigorated work into the meaning and value of literary reading for the sake of the future.

It is certainly no time to retreat within institutional walls. For all the academic resistance to 'instrumentalism', to governmental measurements of public impact and practical utility, literature exists in and across society. The 'literary' is not pure or specialized or self-confined; it is not restricted to the practitioner in writing or the academic in studying. It exists in the whole range of the world which is its subject-matter: it consists in what non-writers actively receive from writings when, for example, they start to see the world more imaginatively as a result of reading novels and begin to think more carefully about human personality. It comes from literature making available much of human life that would not otherwise be existent to thought or recognizable as knowledge. If it is true that involvement in literature, so far from being a minority aesthetic, represents a significant contribution to the life of human thought, then that idea has to be argued at the public level without succumbing to a hollow rhetoric or bowing to a reductive world-view. Hence the effort of this series to take its place *between* literature and the world. The double-sided commitment to occupying that place and establishing its reality is the only 'agenda' here, without further prescription as to what should then be thought or done within it.

What is at stake is not simply some defensive or apologetic 'justification' in the abstract. The case as to why literature matters in the world not only has to be argued conceptually and strongly tested by thought, it should be given presence, performed and brought to life in the way that literature itself does. That is why this series includes the writers themselves, the novelists and poets, in order to try to close the gap between the thinking of the artists and the thinking of those who read and study them. It is why it also involves other kinds of thinkers—the philosopher, the theologian, the psychologist, the neuroscientist—examining the role of literature within their own life's work and thought, and the effect of that work, in turn, upon literary thinking. This series admits and encourages personal voices in an unpredictable variety of individual approach and expression, speaking wherever possible across countries and disciplines and temperaments. It aims for something more than intellectual assent: rather the literary sense of what it is like to feel the thought, to embody an idea in a person, to bring it to being in a narrative or in aid of adventurous reflection. If the artists refer to their own works, if other thinkers return to ideas that have marked much of their working life, that is not their vanity nor a failure of originality. It is what the series has asked of them: to speak out of what they know and care about, in whatever language can best serve their most serious thinking, and without the necessity of trying to cover every issue or meet every objection in each volume.

Philip Davis

For my mother, Gill Hinks,
who let me play on the computer more than I should have.

Acknowledgements

Work on this book was made possible through funding from a Philip Leverhulme Prize from the Leverhulme Trust.

Although there are many more people than it is ever possible properly to thank in an acknowledgement list, my thanks for this book go to Jacqueline Norton and Aimee Wright at Oxford University Press for commissioning the work and for overseeing its route to fruition; to Philip Davis, the series editor, for his support and encouragement; to James O'Sullivan for regenerating high-resolution images of his work on Flann O'Brien and for allowing reuse; to Peter Brennan for enlightening discussions of Wordsworth; to Ted Underwood and Leah Henrickson for generous guidance on the literature of NLG systems; to Bronač Ferran for illumination on the histories of concrete poetry; to Erik Ketzan for our joint work on Stephen King; to Simon Davies for his indexing; to my friend Joe Brooker for many entertaining discussions; to Caroline Edwards for comradeship and radical projects; to Carolyn Burdett, my head of department, for advocating for my time to work on this (and other) projects; to all at OLH and to my close collaborators at COPIM (Andy, Rose, Mauro, Paula, Eleanor, Tom, Toby) for keeping our open publishing dream alive; to my extended family, Nan, Mum, Rich, Alyce, Nova, Susan, Juliet, Lisa, Sam, Anthony, Julia, Carin, for ongoing support and love; to Toby, for interrupting all of my Zoom conference papers during the pandemic; and to Helen Eve, with all my love, for getting me through the bad times, and providing all the good ones.

Contents

List of Figures

List of Tables

Introduction

Words that Count

You may or may not have heard, but over the past two decades a secret and dangerous movement has been growing in humanities departments around the world. Sapping all of the conventional funding out of traditional humanistic pursuits, the so-called 'digital humanities' (or 'DH' to those in the know) brings a grim entrepreneurialism and technocratic mindset to English, history, classics, archaeology—and any other disciplinary space on which it can lay its hands. Seemingly charged with perverting the humanistic foundations of critical thinking and replacing them with techno-solutionist mindsets, the digital humanities are growing and thriving beneath our noses and many seem not even to have noticed the danger. As Roald Dahl wrote of his 'Great Automatic Grammatizator', we will need 'strength, Oh Lord', to resist the machine and the lure of such capital and technology. Dahl's narrator requests the courage to remain pure to art for art's sake, to resist the pull of technology. Contemporary literary critics also need the strength not to surrender to the promise of abundant riches in the digital domain. Give us the strength, Dahl posits, in spurning these new digital forms, 'to let our children starve'.[1]

I jest somewhat. But the study of literature with the aid of computers is undoubtedly controversial. Critics have derided digital methods in literary studies for being: useless (they tell us nothing that we did not already know); trivial (counting the word 'whale' in *Moby-Dick* can tell us only one thing: how often the word 'whale' is used in

---

[1] Roald Dahl, 'The Great Automatic Grammatizator', in *Someone Like You* (Harmondsworth: Penguin, 1986), pp. 190–209 (p. 209).

Moby-Dick); neoliberal (producing software is the Silicon Valley model of scholarship); and just plain wrong.[2] Proponents, by contrast, have pronounced forcefully on the possibilities for broad-scale literary history beyond the limitations on reading made by the finite human lifespan; on how we can better understand genre and form through visualization and spatialization; and even on the fresh perspectives such methods might bring for rethinking core theoretical assumptions about literature itself.[3] The digital humanities are certainly provocative and divisive.

However, one of the first misconceptions that requires a response lies in the equation of 'the digital humanities' with digital literary

---

[2] Timothy Brennan, 'The Digital-Humanities Bust', *The Chronicle of Higher Education*, 15 October 2017 <http://www.chronicle.com/article/The-Digital-Humanities-Bust/241424> [accessed 2 November 2017]; Daniel Allington, Sarah Brouillette, and David Golumbia, 'Neoliberal Tools (and Archives): A Political History of Digital Humanities', *Los Angeles Review of Books*, 2016 <https://lareviewofbooks.org/article/neoliberal-tools-archives-political-history-digital-humanities/> [accessed 29 May 2016]; Nan Z. Da, 'The Computational Case against Computational Literary Studies', *Critical Inquiry*, 45.3 (2019), 601–39 <https://doi.org/10.1086/702594>.

[3] For just a selection, see Lisa Samuels and Jerome J. McGann, 'Deformance and Interpretation', *New Literary History*, 30.1 (1999), 25–56 <https://doi.org/10.1353/nlh.1999.0010>; Franco Moretti, *Graphs, Maps, Trees: Abstract Models for Literary History* (London: Verso, 2007); Stephen Ramsay, *Reading Machines: Toward an Algorithmic Criticism*, Topics in the Digital Humanities (Urbana, IL: University of Illinois Press, 2011); Franco Moretti, *Distant Reading* (London: Verso, 2013); Matthew L. Jockers, *Macroanalysis: Digital Methods and Literary History*, Topics in the Digital Humanities (Urbana, IL: University of Illinois Press, 2013); Tanya E. Clement, 'Text Analysis, Data Mining, and Visualizations in Literary Scholarship', in *Literary Studies in the Digital Age: An Evolving Anthology*, 2013 <https://dlsanthology.mla.hcommons.org/text-analysis-data-mining-and-visualizations-in-literary-scholarship/> [accessed 6 September 2017]; Ray Siemens and Susan Schreibman, eds., *A Companion to Digital Literary Studies*, Blackwell Companions to Literature and Culture (New York: Wiley-Blackwell, 2013); Melissa M. Terras, Julianne Nyhan, and Edward Vanhoutte, eds., *Defining Digital Humanities: A Reader* (Farnham: Ashgate Publishing, 2013); David M. Berry and Anders Fagerjord, *Digital Humanities: Knowledge and Critique in a Digital Age* (Cambridge: Polity Press, 2017); Andrew Piper, *Enumerations: Data and Literary Study* (Chicago, IL: University of Chicago Press, 2018); Martin Paul Eve, *Close Reading With Computers: Textual Scholarship, Computational Formalism, and David Mitchell's* Cloud Atlas (Stanford, CA: Stanford University Press, 2019); Ted Underwood, *Distant Horizons: Digital Evidence and Literary Change* (Chicago, IL: University of Chicago Press, 2019). I will turn more thoroughly to examine these critiques later in this chapter.

studies. For digital approaches to the study of literature are not the same as '*the* digital humanities'. Indeed, as Eric Weiskott eloquently puts it, 'digital technology doesn't transform knowledge in one single way, programmatically, any more than print technology did'.[4] There is, then, really no such thing as a singular 'digital humanities'. As these technologies do not work systematically within any single epistemology in any single unified way on any single set of scholarly objects, it is essential to note that they also work across and within different disciplinary spaces. Historians, archaeologists, classicists, media scholars, ethnographers, theologians, and anthropologists are as likely to call themselves digital humanists as are the (in) famous advocates of distant reading in literary studies.[5] Those who speak of the digital humanities, in the singular, can all too often erase the specificity of disciplinary work outside of their own field. Those in literary studies can be among the worst culprits for this offence.

This is a book, then, that addresses specifically the questions in literary studies that computational methods and technological analyses may answer. I aim to deliver an introduction and overview of developing intersections between digital methods and literary studies to serve as a starting point for those who wish to learn more about the possibilities and the limitations of oft-touted digital humanities in the literary space. The volume intends to engage with the proponents of digital humanities and its detractors alike, aiming to offer a fair and balanced perspective on this controversial topic. This book fuses an introductory background approach and survey with original literary research. It should, therefore, be able to straddle the divide between seasoned digital experts and interested newcomers. That said, by way of a positional disclaimer: I am enthusiastic about the possibilities of

---

[4] Eric Weiskott, 'There Is No Such Thing as "The Digital Humanities"', *The Chronicle of Higher Education*, 1 November 2017 <https://www.chronicle.com/article/There-Is-No-Such-Thing-as/241633> [accessed 17 November 2018].

[5] For more on this and a range of examples, see Sarah E. Bond, Hoyt Long, and Ted Underwood, '"Digital" Is Not the Opposite of "Humanities"', *The Chronicle of Higher Education*, 1 November 2017 <http://www.chronicle.com/article/Digital-Is-Not-the/241634> [accessed 2 November 2017].

digital methods for literary studies even while recognizing the anxieties around their development.[6]

Many of the fears about digital humanities also stress the term *distant*—as in so-called 'distant reading', the quantitative study of literary texts—with disdain. They worry that the use of computers will take us further away from the joy of reading. As *my* provocation in this book, I instead argue that digital methods can bring us *closer* to literary texts; to give us a new viewport through which to observe their narratives. I even go so far here as to extend this to analogue counterparts of 'digital' approaches, such as tabulation and mapping. *Activities* associated with building databases and digital artefacts, even when conducted non-digitally, can be a way newly to engage with literary works. I attempt to demonstrate this argument through the novel case studies that appear in this book but also with reference to the extant work of others.

One of the most interesting things about literary studies, though, is that although it is now a core humanities subject in the Anglophone Global North, it is not, in fact, actually that old. A disruptive discipline that achieved ascendency to a central place in universities worldwide in just a century and a half, not coincidentally during the rise of the British Empire, 'English language and literature' was founded only in 1828 at University College London.[7] (Although, notably, Birkbeck, UCL's older sibling university, taught literary studies in a higher education context as early as 1823. Many Scottish institutions also had literary texts on their curricula before this date.) Over time English has undergone many mutations and methodological U-turns. Moreover, despite protests from revisionist historians of our discipline,

---

[6] This enthusiasm may stem from my background as a computer programmer. Conversely, the anxiety arises from my position within literary studies. Some might claim that my advocacy reflects a desire to bring a rare domain knowledge of quantification to the field. Am I merely bringing expertise that I have, but many others do not, to change the older field of literary studies for the worse? Although I would also note that I have conducted much non-digital literary critical work.

[7] Ted Underwood, *Why Literary Periods Mattered: Historical Contrast and the Prestige of English Studies* (Stanford, CA: Stanford University Press, 2013), p. 81; see also Franklin E. Court, *Institutionalizing English Literature: Culture and Politics of Literary Study, 1750–1900* (Stanford, CA: Stanford University Press, 1992); Gerald Graff, *Professing Literature: An Institutional History* (Chicago, IL: University of Chicago Press, 1989).

there have also long been quantitative practitioners within the space of literary studies.

For instance, Vernon Lee, the famed Victorian and Edwardian-era aesthetician, called for a quantitative analysis of literature—a 'statistical experiment'—in her *The Handling of Words* (1923) after a debate with Emil Reich.[8] The extension of literary mathematics into computational approaches also occurs far earlier in our disciplinary history than many credit. Dartmouth College, for one, offered a module to students entitled 'Literary Analysis by Computer' in 1969.[9] Certainly, a quantitative strain of literary studies—and its extension into computational modes—has been present for quite some time.

Admittedly, the digital era of mass access to computation and the internet—not even mentioning digitized texts—has accelerated the presence of this quantifying urge and brought with it a host of new possibilities but also challenges for literary studies. Among the drivers has been the proliferation of electronic literature, electronics within literature, and their study. For instance, Jessica Pressman notably examined how many contemporary e-literatures—that is, texts born and published digitally to take advantage of electronic affordances—re-work modernist texts to yield 'immanent critiques of their technocultural context'.[10] Further, other well-known scholars such as N. Katherine Hayles have joined the analysis of how contemporary print novels function as texts that emulate or anticipate the possibilities for digital literature, exemplified in Mark Z. Danielewski's *House of Leaves* (2000).[11] Zara Dinnen has also recently shown how digital technologies have become 'banal' in contemporary fiction, rendering us 'unaware of the ways we are co-constituted as subjects with

---

[8] Nicholas Dames, *The Physiology of the Novel: Reading, Neural Science, and the Form of Victorian Fiction* (Oxford: Oxford University Press, 2007), p. 188.

[9] Annette Vee, '"Literary Analysis by Computer" Offered at Dartmouth, Winter 1969, Working with Paradise Lost. #1960sComputing', *@anetv*, 2017 <https://twitter.com/anetv/status/919219418189660160/photo/1> [accessed 18 October 2017].

[10] Jessica Pressman, *Digital Modernism: Making It New in New Media*, Modernist Literature & Culture, 21 (New York: Oxford University Press, 2014), p. 156.

[11] See N. Katherine Hayles, *Writing Machines*, Mediawork Pamphlet (Cambridge, MA: MIT Press, 2002); Jessica Pressman, 'House of Leaves: Reading the Networked Novel', *Studies in American Fiction*, 34.1 (2006), 107–28 <https://doi.org/10.1353/saf.2006.0015>.

media'.[12] These 'distributed media systems' approaches to literature featuring the electronic, or literature that is born and read within the electronic environment, are of ever-increasing prominence.[13]

That said, some commentators have insisted that digital humanities are not 'to be understood as the study of digital artifacts, new media, or contemporary culture in place of physical artifacts, old media, or historical culture'.[14] I cannot agree entirely with this assessment. In this book, I do hone in on how digital methods—the 'methods of the medium' in Richard Rogers's phrasing—can be applied to literature, whether digital or print.[15] However, I also focus on how digital media condition the possibilities of those literatures. In other words, at various points in this book I read digital artefacts or works that contain digital elements, using more conventional literary critical methods. However, in conjunction with this, I will, of course, turn to how digital tools can bear on those literary artefacts. By necessity, this nonetheless involves some boundaries of exclusion. We *all* use digital technologies in our study of literature already: the ubiquitous Microsoft Word, for instance. Using such software can barely be said to make one a digital literary scholar, though.[16]

What Questions?

What could we include under such rhetoric of 'digital methods' and what types of question might such methods answer? There is, undeniably, a particular type of 'decompositional' thinking that is necessary to use digital approaches.[17] That is to say that computational methods require problems that can be broken into smaller solvable units of

[12] Zara Dinnen, *The Digital Banal: New Media and American Literature and Culture* (New York: Columbia University Press, 2018), p. 1.

[13] N. Katherine Hayles, *How We Think: Digital Media and Contemporary Technogenesis* (Chicago, IL: University of Chicago Press, 2012), p. 212.

[14] Anne Burdick et al., *Digital Humanities* (Cambridge, MA: MIT Press, 2012), p. 122.

[15] Richard Rogers, *Digital Methods* (Cambridge, MA: MIT Press, 2015), p. 1.

[16] That said, I do not intend to wade into the quagmire of defining the digital humanities, which has been addressed at great length in publications such as Terras et al.

[17] I borrow this terminology from D. L. Parnas, 'On the Criteria To Be Used in Decomposing Systems into Modules', *Communications of the ACM*, 15.12 (1972), 6; and David West, *Object Thinking* (Redmond, WA: Microsoft Press, 2004).

addressable and empirically verifiable hypotheses, to which some literary interpretative work is not suited.

An example may serve well to illustrate this decompositional—or, computational—thinking. Consider the genre of 'writers' advice'. This form seems almost as old as writing itself, with Plato advising in *Phaedrus* against the very act of writing: 'the man who thinks that he has left behind him a science in writing [...] in the belief that anything clear or certain will come from what is written down, would be full of simplicity'.[18] Writers have, indeed, always sought to advise other writers. My suspicion has long been, when encountering such guidance, that authors who dispense it might be hypocritical, that writers do not do as they say.

However, we could go further in breaking down (decomposing) this sample problem of 'writers' advice' into addressable components, as I have been doing in recent work with Erik Ketzan. Indeed, we cannot easily appraise some types of advice. If a writer advises us that the key to excellent writing is to 'write every day', or issues similar diktats, we must take his or her word for it. However, sometimes writers (ill-advisedly) dispense advice that is more susceptible to empirical analysis. The bestselling horror writer, Stephen King, is one such example. In his 2000 memoir, *On Writing*, King tells the reader that 'the adverb is not your friend'.[19] Specifically, King seems to exclude temporal adverbs and adverbial phrases.[20] In this instance, a set of addressable or decomposed problems for computational analysis might be: how frequently does Stephen King use adverbs and does this change throughout his career as his writing matures?[21] In general terms, with many caveats that I will not address here, but as shown in Figure I.1, the answer to this question is: yes. What the critic then goes on to make of this finding remains a matter of interpretation. Undeniably, though, this method allows us to see something about a text that before was unknown.[22]

---

[18] Plato, *Phaedrus*, trans. Christopher Rowe (London: Penguin, 2005), p. 63.

[19] Stephen King, *On Writing: A Memoir of the Craft* (London: Hodder, 2012), p. 138.

[20] King, *On Writing*, p. 140.

[21] Also addressed in Ben Blatt, *Nabokov's Favorite Word Is Mauve: What the Numbers Reveal About the Classics, Bestsellers, and Our Own Writing* (New York: Simon & Schuster, 2017).

[22] This result is extracted from work in progress that I am undertaking with Erik Ketzan.

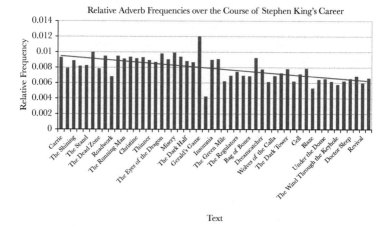

Figure I.1 Relative adverb frequencies over the course of Stephen King's career, excluding temporal adverbs and adverbial phrases using the Stanford PoS tagger english-left3words-distsim model with approximate 3 per cent margin of error. This graph was co-produced with Erik Ketzan.

Did I *need* a computer to produce the result in Figure I.1? I could have sequentially read the novels of Stephen King, marking up the appropriate adverbs and keeping a tally, before plotting these. However, this would probably have taken several months, if not years, of tedious and repetitive reading labour, merely to answer a fundamental empirical question. The computational approach deployed here was not a difference of *type* but a difference of *scale, degree*, and *speed*. It is around these matters of repetition, scale, and speed/time that many digital methods in literary studies orbit.[23]

Indeed, the specific trade-off made in the forms of so-called 'distant reading'—computational methods of examining texts—is between resolution and time. There is a 3 per cent margin of error in my process for tagging parts-of-speech in the above experiment on Stephen King's novels. That is to say that for every 100 words processed, approximately three will be misclassified. In the case of *'Salem's Lot*,

---

[23] For more on this, see Jay Jin, 'Problems of Scale in "Close" and "Distant" Reading', *Philological Quarterly*, 96.1 (2017), 105–29.

to pick on just one example, this means approximately 353 adverbs in my list might not be adverbs. It also means that the system missed some other adverbs that were likewise mislabelled. I lost the resolution and precision that come from actual reading at the expense of having several months more time for other activities and still roughly defining how far off my results might be. That said, there is no guarantee that if I undertook a manual reading exercise and attempted to tag adverbs that I might not also make a comparable number of errors, missing some and incorrectly ascribing others.

In this particular instance of Stephen King's advice, it might be the case that the error margin is too high to draw a sound conclusion. Perhaps the only answer is to read the works 'properly' (although, as above, any such repetitious cataloguing task is also prone to human error). However, many of the problems of scale dealt with by digital literary studies cannot be solved by traditional reading practices. Say, for instance, that one wished to comment on a single year's worth of contemporary fiction and the broad trends within it. But I do not mean award-winning fiction from a single year—I mean *all* fiction. Take the year 2015, for this example. How much would you have to read to be able to say, with absolute certainty, that your statements were accurate across all published fiction in the English language in that year? According to Bowker, almost 220,000 novels were published in English in 2015. Estimating a human lifespan to be approximately 71 years using the World Health Organization's figures, one would have to read ten novels per day, every day from age ten onwards, just to have read all English fiction published in 2015.[24]

Computational methods for the study of literature are not, then, simply an outgrowth of technical capability. Instead, they also respond to specific critiques of canonicity. In a world where it is impossible to read even all the fiction in English published in a single year, the canons to which we devote our time are necessarily limited, but therefore are also biased. We usually delegate to literary prizes and to the internal selection procedures of major publishing houses to filter the

[24] See Erik Fredner, 'How Many Novels Have Been Published in English? (An Attempt)', *Stanford Literary Lab*, 2017 <https://litlab.stanford.edu/how-many-novels-have-been-published-in-english-an-attempt/>; and Eve, *Close Reading With Computers*, introduction.

titles to which we pay attention. This is not a sound basis for examining all literature from any period, though. Under such constraints, 'not reading', as Lisa Marie Rhody puts it, has become 'the dirty open secret of all literary critics'.[25] Between the poles of detailed attention to a limited canon and the void of being unable to read everything sit the digital methods to which the subsequent chapters of this book are dedicated.

*

While the above may have painted a rosy picture of how digital methods might help us with literary empiricism at scale, there are many challenges for our discipline due to digital humanities work. One relates to tool development. Let us say that, instead of King's pronouncements on adverbs above, I had instead taken his advice on similes as the target of my investigation.[26] Here is a reasonable, decomposed question on this subject: 'how frequently does Stephen King use similes compared to a similar corpus of American writers?' However, it turns out that the computational detection and study of simile is a complicated problem with low accuracy rates.[27] Developing the tools that would allow this to work at any scale would take years of software development in cooperation with computer scientists and linguists. Although it might have more general-purpose applications, this development process would likely take longer than reading the material manually; an example of the type of time trade-off that must be considered in any software development.

Another good decomposed question that we might imagine we could answer with computational approaches springs to mind: 'do novels generate similar patterns of affective responses over their plot

---

[25] Lisa Marie Rhody, 'Beyond Darwinian Distance: Situating Distant Reading in a Feminist *Ut Pictura Poesis* Tradition', *PMLA*, 132.3 (2017), 659–67 (p. 659).

[26] King, *On Writing*, pp. 208–9.

[27] Vlad Niculae and Victoria Yaneva, 'Computational Considerations of Comparisons and Similes', in *51st Annual Meeting of the Association for Computational Linguistics Proceedings of the Student Research Workshop* (Sofia, Bulgaria: Association for Computational Linguistics, 2013), pp. 89–95 <http://www.aclweb.org/anthology/P13-3013> [accessed 16 November 2018]; Suzanne Patience Mpouli Njanga Seh, 'Automatic Annotation of Similes in Literary Texts' (unpublished Ph.D., Université Pierre et Marie Curie—Paris VI, 2016).

arcs?' That is, do novels share common plot patterns that create similar emotional ebbs and flows in readers? This is precisely one of the questions that Matt Jockers has been attempting to answer using his *syuzhet* software that tries to map sentiment within literary texts. Again, though, this turns out to be a difficult computational task and one that most literary studies scholars could not even begin to work on.[28] In this respect, there is a labour and domain-knowledge problem for the adoption of digital methods within literary studies.

Yet another problematic element for computational methods in literary studies is the legal availability of the texts themselves.[29] In order to perform computation upon a text, as though it were data, one needs a digital copy of the literary work. This may seem to be a trivial matter in the era of the Amazon Kindle. However, the version needed for most digital methods is a plain-text edition, unencumbered by digital rights management technologies (DRM). In the USA and the UK, stripping the DRM off a protected file is a criminal, not 'just' a civil, offence. This means that one cannot be granted permission to remove the DRM from a digital file, even by the rightsholder, regardless of whether it is technically easy to do so. While many scholars working in digital literary studies seem to ignore this legal situation for the sake of convenience and do not remark upon the sources for their work, this is a difficult ethical and legal position. That said, there are two mitigating factors. First, much digital humanities work takes place upon historical literary material out of copyright (although this still

[28] Matthew L. Jockers, 'A Novel Method for Detecting Plot', 2014 <http://www.matthewjockers.net/2014/06/05/a-novel-method-for-detecting-plot/>; Matthew L. Jockers, 'Requiem for a Low Pass Filter', 2015 <http://www.matthew-jockers.net/2015/04/06/epilogue/>; Annie Swafford, 'Why Syuzhet Doesn't Work and How We Know', *Anglophile in Academia: Annie Swafford's Blog*, 2015 <https://annieswafford.wordpress.com/2015/03/30/why-syuzhet-doesnt-work-and-how-we-know/> [accessed 17 November 2018]; Annie Swafford, 'Continuing the Syuzhet Discussion', *Anglophile in Academia: Annie Swafford's Blog*, 2015 <https://annieswafford.wordpress.com/2015/03/07/continuingsyuzhet/>; Benjamin M. Schmidt, 'Do Digital Humanists Need to Understand Algorithms?', in *Debates in the Digital Humanities 2016*, ed. Matthew K. Gold and Lauren F. Klein (Minneapolis, MN: University of Minnesota Press, 2016), pp. 546–55 <http://dhdebates.gc.cuny.edu/debates/text/99>; Matthew L. Jockers, 'Resurrecting a Low Pass Filter (Well, Kind Of)', 2017 <http://www.matthewjockers.net/2017/01/12/resurrecting/>.

[29] Again, I am grateful to Erik Ketzan for first drawing this to my attention.

requires access to a version unencumbered by DRM, which cannot be presumed). Second, the HathiTrust Research Center—a vast archive of 16.7 million items—has extended access to material that is still in copyright for non-consumptive research.[30] This is a praiseworthy and momentous shift that uses a legal defence under US copyright law and vastly expands access to material that would otherwise be unavailable.

Finally, linked to the genesis of electronic literatures, digital literary studies frequently run aground on the rocky shores of evaluation. Datasets, graphs, interactive timelines, software, and other digital artefacts are often not recognized as valid scholarly outputs within the humanities disciplines. A type of 'design practice' sits at the core of this kind of work, which does not necessarily look like work in literary studies.[31] This essentially leads to a situation in which those who perform digital work are asked to coerce their scholarship into existing, recognized media forms for assessment, hiring, promotion, and tenure.[32] Even the fact that citation styles usually require reference to a *page number* encodes an *assumed media form* within a resource locator. Print media remain firmly enthroned at the heart of such citation practices. To counter this, learned societies have formulated sets of evaluation principles for digital scholarship, although uptake remains slow.[33] At the core of this challenge for digital literary studies, though,

[30] HathiTrust Digital Library, 'HathiTrust Research Center Extends Non-Consumptive Research Tools to Copyrighted Materials: Expanding Research through Fair Use', *Perspectives from HathiTrust*, 2018 <https://www.hathitrust.org/blogs/perspectives-from-hathitrust/hathitrust-research-center-extends-non-consumptive-research-tools> [accessed 17 November 2018].

[31] See Burdick et al.

[32] Sydni Dunn, 'Digital Humanists: If You Want Tenure, Do Double the Work', *Vitae*, 2014 <https://chroniclevitae.com/news/249-digital-humanists-if-you-want-tenure-do-double-the-work> [accessed 21 March 2017].

[33] Bethany Nowviskie, 'Where Credit Is Due: Preconditions for the Evaluation of Collaborative Digital Scholarship', *Profession*, 2011.1 (2011), 169–81 <https://doi.org/10.1632/prof.2011.2011.1.169>; American Historical Association, 'Guidelines for the Professional Evaluation of Digital Scholarship by Historians', *American Historical Association*, 2015 <https://www.historians.org/teaching-and-learning/digital-history-resources/evaluation-of-digital-scholarship-in-history/guidelines-for-the-professional-evaluation-of-digital-scholarship-by-historians> [accessed 24 March 2017]; Hamid R. Jamali, David Nicholas, and Eti Herman, 'Scholarly Reputation in the Digital Age and the Role of Emerging Platforms and Mechanisms', *Research Evaluation*, 25.1 (2016),

lies a far more profound anxiety; an act of soul searching by our discipline. This inward-looking stance asks: is digital literary studies *really* literary studies? Should literary studies scholars produce data, code, and graphs...and should we reward them for doing so? Finally, it seems to ask: is this new model a *threat* to our discipline and its evolved state of practice?

The Digital Humanities and Its Discontents

How can we understand a double logic in which digital literary studies work is at once so powerful as to crowd out the traditional humanists, threatening the discipline with total takeover, while at the same time so poorly understood as to need supplementation by traditional publication? How can conducting digital labour in the humanities be seen by some as a sure-fire path to tenure and funding but, simultaneously, a 'risky thing', as Kathleen Fitzpatrick and Mark Sample put it?[34]

Indeed, as I have already implied, far from everyone is happy with the rise of the digital humanities or digital literary studies. The concurrent ascendancy of digital technologies alongside the political rationality known as neoliberalism has made many deeply suspicious of a digital agenda. Daniel Allington, Sarah Brouillette, and David Golumbia even go so far as to claim that:

> Neoliberal policies and institutions value academic work that produces findings immediately usable by industry and that produces graduates trained for the current requirements of the commercial workplace. [...] By providing a model for humanities teaching and

37–49 <https://doi.org/10.1093/reseval/rvv032>; but see also Samuel Moore et al., 'Excellence R Us: University Research and the Fetishisation of Excellence', *Palgrave Communications*, 3 (2017) <https://doi.org/10.1057/palcomms.2016.105>.

[34] Kathleen Fitzpatrick, 'Do "the Risky Thing" in Digital Humanities', *The Chronicle of Higher Education*, 2011 <http://www.chronicle.com/article/Do-the-Risky-Thing-in/129132/> [accessed 21 March 2017]; Mark Sample, 'Tenure as a Risk-Taking Venture', *Journal of Digital Humanities*, 1.4 (2012) <http://journalofdigitalhumanities. org/1-4/tenure-as-a-risk-taking-venture-by-mark-sample/> [accessed 24 March 2017]; parts of this section appeared previously in Martin Paul Eve, 'Violins in the Subway: Scarcity Correlations, Evaluative Cultures, and Disciplinary Authority in the Digital Humanities', in *Digital Technology and the Practices of Humanities Research*, ed. Jennifer Edmonds (Cambridge: Open Book Publishers, 2019).

research that appears to overcome these perceived limitations, Digital Humanities has played a leading role in the corporatist restructuring of the humanities. [...] What Digital Humanities is *not* about, despite its explicit claims, is the use of digital or quantitative methodologies to answer research questions in the humanities. It is, instead, about the promotion of project-based learning and lab-based research over reading and writing, the rebranding of insecure campus employment as an empowering "alt-ac" career choice, and the redefinition of technical expertise as a form (indeed, the superior form) of humanist knowledge.[35]

Neoliberalism is probably best defined as a mode of political economy that emerged from the 1980s onwards in which politics is disenchanted by economics as the dominant societal logic.[36] Under such logic, economics must form the basis for all state decisions. The state itself merely ensures that the conditions for market exchange are enforced, even while the state itself must work on a market logic—the state under the supervision of the market, as Michel Foucault had it.[37]

Within such a definition, one can begin to see how the digital humanities might appear neoliberal. If neoliberalism is the disenchantment of politics by economics, then digital methods for studying literature appear as the disenchantment of literature by computers. Further, in Allington, Brouillette, and Golumbia's view, the digital humanities' labour structures are the worst aspect. In the privileging of technocratic knowledge, supposedly over and above humanistic epistemologies, they see a replication of wider societal patterns of precarity within the digital humanities. (Although I note that material textual scholarship, for instance, has long had a technocratic interest in, say, the manufacturing processes of books.) It is not my aim here to refute systematically the arguments of Allington, Brouillette, and

---

[35] Allington et al.

[36] William Davies, *The Limits of Neoliberalism: Authority, Sovereignty and the Logic of Competition* (Thousand Oaks, CA: Sage, 2014). See also Wendy Brown, *Undoing the Demos: Neoliberalism's Stealth Revolution* (New York: Zone Books, 2015); Wendy Brown, *In the Ruins of Neoliberalism: The Rise of Antidemocratic Politics in the West*, The Wellek Library Lectures (New York: Columbia University Press, 2019).

[37] Michel Foucault, *The Birth of Biopolitics: Lectures at the Collège de France, 1978–79* (Basingstoke: Palgrave Macmillan, 2008), p. 116.

Golumbia's piece, which moves between specific attacks on the University of Virginia, the Andrew W. Mellon Foundation, and broader statements on labour and neoliberalism, but I will only note that I do find it strange to believe that digital literary studies will produce 'findings immediately usable by industry'. It seems indeed optimistic to think that broad-scale findings about the history of literary genre or gender representation, say, using computational methods, will show themselves to be instantly 'monetizable', to use a current buzz-word.[38]

One of the other criticisms levelled at digital literary studies in this same piece—but echoed elsewhere—is that digital approaches involve 'the displacement of politically progressive humanities scholarship and activism in favor of the manufacture of digital tools and archives'. That is, the claim here is that digital literary studies are apolitical formalism at best and, at worst, immoral in detracting resources from now-conventional modes of political critique in the discipline. One of the most obvious, although distressing, retorts to such a statement is to note that the political effects of literary criticism are often overstated. Certainly, Aime Cesaire, Frantz Fanon, Judith Butler, and many others in the postcolonial and gender studies fields can be said to have had a lasting political legacy. Yet although I do not agree wholeheartedly with her polemical injunction to abandon critique, Rita Felski has a point when she writes that, overall, critique and suspicion in literary studies are 'less heroic and more humdrum and routinized than we might think'.[39] The routinization and normalization of critique in literary studies may have dimmed its power.

That said, it is hard to overstate the influence that critical theory has had upon English departments around the world. This level of disruption to previously formalist departments engendered by literary theoretical paradigms is aptly illustrated in the 'MacCabe Affair' in the UK. In this case, Colin MacCabe was denied tenure at Cambridge University for his support of theoretical approaches—a news story

---

[38] See, for just such an article, Ted Underwood, 'The Life Cycles of Genres', *Journal of Cultural Analytics*, 1.1 (2016) <https://doi.org/10.22148/16.005>.

[39] Rita Felski, *The Limits of Critique* (Chicago, IL: University of Chicago Press, 2015), p. 47.

that, unbelievably, made the front page of the *Guardian* newspaper.[40] Some commentators fear that DH heralds a return to some prior apolitical, formalist stance for these disciplines.

It is also worth noting that this critique of the digital's apoliticality can apply to any other work of formalist-aesthetic literary criticism. Literary criticism has long straddled aesthetic and thematic approaches using political readings. Certainly, the empirical evidence furnished by digital approaches is usually formalist. However, it is what one does with that evidence that matters.[41] As Lisa Gitelman deftly phrases it, following Geoffrey C. Bowker, 'raw data is an oxymoron'.[42] The political import, or otherwise, of digital work rests upon the use one makes of the words on the page, whether filtered through a computer or whether one reads them by eye. As a final note on this, if the critique is that it is the *time* spent on building tools that is here apolitical (or even immoral), then one might say exactly the same of any kind of reading/thinking/note-taking or processual methodology for the study of aesthetics. All types of literary critical work require a level of background labour that contributes towards the endpoint of an argument. When it is digital labour, though, there seems to be an additional level of criticism.

In recent years, however, there has been an explosive growth in the volume of scholarship that connects digital humanities and ethics. For instance, among the most important of these recent works is Ruha Benjamin's *Race After Technology: Abolitionist Tools for the New Jim Code*. In this book, Benjamin argues that racial prejudice is repeatedly inscribed within algorithms under the cloak of objectivity, a phenomenon she calls 'the New Jim Code', riffing on the informal name for the USA's system of segregation.[43] Likewise of significance is

[40] Francis Mulhern, 'The Cambridge Affair', *Marxism Today*, March 1981, pp. 27–8; Marcus Morgan and Patrick Baert, *Conflict in the Academy: A Study in the Sociology of Intellectuals* (London: Palgrave Macmillan, 2015).

[41] See, for instance, Richard Jean So, *Redlining Culture: A Data History of Racial Inequality and Postwar Fiction* (New York: Columbia University Press, 2020) for an example of the use of data-driven approaches for an ethical end.

[42] Lisa Gitelman, ed., *'Raw Data' Is an Oxymoron*, Infrastructures Series (Cambridge, MA: MIT Press, 2013), p. 1.

[43] Ruha Benjamin, *Race After Technology: Abolitionist Tools for the New Jim Code* (Medford, MA: Polity Press, 2019).

Charlton D. McIlwain's *Black Software: The Internet and Racial Justice, from the AfroNet to Black Lives Matter*, which charts the story of a vanguard that 'demonstrates how black people have taken technology not originally designed with our concerns in mind' while, at the same time, showing 'how computing technology was built and developed to keep black America docile and in its place'.[44] Further, Catherine D'Ignazio and Lauren F. Klein's *Data Feminism* is a damning indictment of how gender inequality is inscribed in the cultures of big data that permeate our societies. More than simply diagnosing the problem, though, D'Ignazio and Klein offer a powerful critical framework to redress this imbalance for those working to examine how data are used computationally.[45]

There are further works at the intersection of the digital humanities and ethics that bear closer scrutiny. The first is Roopika Risam's *New Digital Worlds: Postcolonial Digital Humanities in Theory, Praxis, and Pedagogy*; a work that fuses two relevant strands of inquiry. The first is the well-known paradigm of postcolonial studies, in which it is shown that 'the foundations of literary studies and historiography—whether Anglophone, Francophone, Hispanophone, or Lusaphone—are inextricably linked to the rise of European colonialism'.[46] The second is the subject of this book: the digital humanities. The new field of 'postcolonial digital humanities' that Risam posits explores the relationship of digital practice 'to the intersections of race, gender, class, nation, sexuality, ability, and other axes of identity and oppression'. It is a field that 'attends to the politics and theory subtending the creation of scholarship to clear space for new modes of thinking that foreground the particular over the universal and the local over the global in the production of the digital cultural record'.[47]

Perhaps one of the most astute observations of Risam's book lies in her analogy between programming and literature as sharing a communal effort at 'world making'. This may seem far-fetched, but many

[44] Charlton D. McIlwain, *Black Software: The Internet and Racial Justice, from the AfroNet to Black Lives Matter* (New York: Oxford University Press, 2020), p. 7.

[45] Catherine D'Ignazio and Lauren F. Klein, *Data Feminism*, Strong Ideas Series (Cambridge, MA: MIT Press, 2020).

[46] Roopika Risam, *New Digital Worlds: Postcolonial Digital Humanities in Theory, Praxis, and Pedagogy* (Evanston, IL: Northwestern University Press, 2018), p. 25.

[47] Risam, p. 30.

books on the study of programming, such as David West's *Object Thinking*, published by Microsoft, stress that object-oriented programming (OOP) is, at the very least, a form of world *modelling*.[48] For Risam, following Matthew Kirschenbaum, the point is that if 'the coder becomes the world maker, charged with defining the rules and characteristics of the world', then there are both dangers and opportunities in digital approaches. The dangers are that this 'apt description of programming evinces the colonial dynamics of knowledge production' and can end up 'reproducing the hegemonies of the "real" world'. The opportunity that Risam poses is a set of digital worlds that do not fall prey to this 'risk of rehearsal'. Could they, she asks, 'be ones that imagine new forms of resistance through digital knowledge production?'[49]

Risam's work is also very good at undoing the early utopian histories of the internet and cyberculture. As she notes, the initial optimism of scholars such as Frank Biocca, Larry McCaffery, and Michael Benedikt was misplaced. In Risam's words, they saw the internet 'as a space of freedom and creation that exists outside of the iniquities of lived experience'.[50] Yet, as subsequent new media scholars such as Wendy Chun, Anna Everett, and Lisa Nakamura have identified, this democratic space is far less representatively peopled than we might like. The 'putatively democratic space of the internet' has led to the false notion that 'the internet is disembodied and shielded from social inequalities'; a patently untrue assertion that plays out in the replicated racism of, say, artificial intelligence and facial recognition.[51]

---

[48] West. See also Matthew Kirschenbaum, 'Hello Worlds', *The Chronicle of Higher Education*, 23 January 2009 <https://www.chronicle.com/article/Hello-Worlds/5476> [accessed 13 April 2020].

[49] Risam, pp. 33–4.

[50] Risam, p. 36 points to Larry McCaffery, 'Introduction: The Desert of the Real', in *Storming the Reality Studio: A Casebook of Cyberpunk and Postmodern Science Fiction*, ed. Larry McCaffery (Durham, NC: Duke University Press, 1991), pp. 1–16; Frank Biocca, 'Communication Within Virtual Reality: Creating a Space for Research', *Journal of Communication*, 42.4 (1992), 5–22 <https://doi.org/10.1111/j.1460-2466.1992. tb00810.x>; Michael Benedikt, ed., *Cyberspace: First Steps* (Cambridge, MA: MIT Press, 1994).

[51] Risam, p. 36.

'Where', asked Alan Liu in 2012, 'Is Cultural Criticism in the Digital Humanities?'[52] His own critique therein was that 'the digital humanities are noticeably missing in action on the cultural-critical scene', neglecting the reflexive inflection seen in other adjacent fields, such as new media studies. Yet, I would like to venture, if this movement has been slow in coming, projects such as Risam's extend the digital humanities movement outwards into valuable areas of critical discourse—and demonstrate that there have been figures thinking through this area for some time.

A second area where we see an increase in ethical intersections is in digital cultural history. Although not strictly within the purely literary realm, this is also a massively expanding field. In particular, recent work by Marie Hicks has turned to how women formed the core of early computer operators and workers but were erased from these roles as an official computing 'industry' emerged. This, of course, has profound implications for how computing has spread across the globe in general and carries ramifications, I would argue, for how we consider the adoption of digital technologies in the literary studies space.

By way of background, it is worth noting—as does Hicks—that the term 'computer' originally referred to a person. Specifically, it denoted a woman who was employed to undertake calculations. For, 'in the 1940s, computer operation and programming was viewed as women's work—but by the 1960s, as computing gained prominence and influence, men displaced the thousands of women who had been pioneers in a feminized field of endeavor, and the field acquired a distinctly masculine image'.[53]

Hicks's study is perhaps most valuable for the fact that, while it is a study of a technological area of development, its prime object of focus rests on the social conditions that surround the development of computation. That is to say that it is not the development of technology that interests Hicks, but rather how the field replicated social privilege

[52] Alan Liu, 'Where Is Cultural Criticism in the Digital Humanities?', in *Debates in the Digital Humanities*, ed. Matthew K. Gold (Minneapolis, MN: University of Minnesota Press, 2012), pp. 490–509 <https://dhdebates.gc.cuny.edu/read/untitled-88c11800-9446-469b-a3be-3fdb36bfbd1e/section/896742e7-5218-42c5-89b0-0c3c75682a2f> [accessed 14 April 2020].

[53] Marie Hicks, *Programmed Inequality: How Britain Discarded Women Technologists and Lost Its Edge in Computing* (Cambridge, MA: MIT Press, 2018), p. 1.

despite early engagement by women. Indeed, Hicks discerns a regular phase of feminization early in the development of many new technologies: 'a familiar historical pattern seen in everything from textile manufacturing to typewriting'.[54] Yet this did not happen in computing's switch to electro-mechanical components, primarily because education systems privileged male access to computers as playthings of the future and assumed there was a natural interest among boys in computing and its attendant technologies.

Hicks also points, though, to specific national contexts as contributing to the gendered inequality of the computing industry. The British case presents an instance of 'a top-down government initiative to computerize' that came with attendant 'explicit structural discrimination' in, say, the gendered relative pay structures of the British civil service.[55] The modernization of technologies does not—perhaps self-evidently—come with concomitant social advances.

Indirectly, though, sexuality also feeds into the gendering of labour in the British context. The assumption that underpinned much of the British hierarchy of labour value was that a male breadwinner would have to earn enough to support a nuclear family. By contrast, women who worked were assumed not to have the same wage 'requirements' and hence the entire remuneration system was structured to pay women less than their male counterparts. The assumption, in other words, was that all women were heterosexual and would be married—and thereby provided for. In this way, it is impossible to separate assumed sexuality from gender roles in this instance.

Hicks is, of course, far from the only person to have studied the gendered status of labour in the computational environment. Works by Jennifer Light, Jean Jennings Bartik, Nathan Ensmenger, and Janet Abbate, among others, form the background context against which this most recent study is set.[56] We might further consider Margot Lee

---

[54] Hicks, p. 2.   [55] Hicks, p. 3.

[56] Jennifer S. Light, 'When Computers Were Women', *Technology and Culture*, 40.3 (1999), 455–83; Jean Bartik, *Pioneer Programmer: Jean Jennings Bartik and the Computer That Changed the World*, ed. Jon T. Rickman and Kim D. Todd (Kirksville, MO: Truman State University Press, 2013); Nathan Ensmenger, *The Computer Boys Take Over: Computers, Programmers, and the Politics of Technical Expertise*, History of Computing (Cambridge, MA: MIT Press, 2010); Janet Abbate, *Recoding Gender: Women's Changing Participation in Computing*, History of Computing (Cambridge, MA: MIT Press, 2012).

Shetterly, the author of *Hidden Figures: The American Dream and the Untold Story of the Black Women Mathematicians Who Helped Win the Space Race*, now a major Hollywood motion picture.[57]

There is, ultimately though, a nice payback in Hicks's work. The narrative that she charts is about the downfall of the British computing industry, at least in part because of its gendered pay and labour policies. She also gives us pause for thought about the crisis nature of the emergence of computing's gendered labour in the Second World War and the codebreaking facilities at Bletchley Park. As I write in 2021, the world grapples with the COVID-19 coronavirus pandemic—a moment of crisis comparable in its disruption to the two world wars of the previous century. I would be willing to wager that a programme of technological rebuilding of the economy will be key to many government strategies in the aftermath of this catastrophe. Whether we learn the lessons of Hicks's study in replicating socially unequal labour structures in the digital space remains to be seen.

To return to the intersection of these first two conjoined critiques of DH, though—that the digital humanities are neoliberal and that the digital humanities are apolitical—sits a third: that digital literary studies are useless. Timothy Brennan most pointedly articulated this in his *Chronicle of Higher Education* article, 'The Digital Humanities Bust', but it is a common refrain with which almost anyone who has done digital humanities work will be familiar. For Brennan, in digital literary studies, 'some of their interpretations derive from what they knew "in advance" '. This means, in his view, that 'the findings do not need the data and, as a result, are somewhat pointless'.[58]

There are, though, four distinct defences of digital practices that can be raised against such a critique. The first is that digital practices require validation at the micro level in order to scale. I return to this in the final chapter of this book but suffice to say that if you are developing a piece of software that tests certain properties of literary texts, one needs known conclusions with which to begin. Otherwise, you cannot test that the software works as expected before using it on texts

---

[57] Margot Lee Shetterly, *Hidden Figures: The American Dream and the Untold Story of the Black Women Mathematicians Who Helped Win the Space Race* (New York: William Morrow and Company, 2016).

[58] Brennan.

that one has not read. Validating that computer models work to the same conclusions as human readers is the only way of showing that a software model might be useful at scales beyond the human. The second response is that this critique can be levelled at most pieces of literary criticism that perform interpretation. The words were on the page in front of us beforehand, after all. Literary critical knowledge is a type of unearthing of latent content that was always obvious, *after the fact*. This is why literary criticism can hold such power: because it retroactively makes something hidden seem obvious. The third response to this argument is that there is a curious utilitarianism in its premise. Since when did literary studies need to have a 'point'? Since when did we demand of literary critique that it be useful? Indeed, this type of utilitarian insistence that digital literary studies deliver some-thing purposeful, useful, and pointed sits in curious tension with the assertion that the digital humanities are neoliberal. How can digital literary studies win?[59] Produce a useful outcome and one is branded utilitarian and neoliberal. Conduct pointless work and one is told that one is not useful enough.

The fourth, final, and strongest rebuttal to the argument that DH can tell us nothing new is that such an assertion is often simply not true. Digital methods can unearth fresh evidence that can overturn critical consensus. It is in this area of contestation—covered in the final chapter of this book—that digital literary studies often best suc-ceeds; these moments where computational discourse interacts with commonly held literary critical precepts and blows them apart.

There is a final and powerful critique of 'computational literary studies' mounted in 2019 by Nan Z. Da that also cannot be ignored: that many of the findings from quantitative, statistical, and digital approaches to the study of literature are, in fact, wrong and inaccurate.[60] Da spent over two years tracking down data from papers that used digital methods to study literature in order to show that the findings are unreplicable and in some cases drastically misinterpreted.

While the fallout from Da's *Critical Inquiry* article will continue, there are a few points worth noting. The first is that Da holds compu-tational literary studies to a higher standard than conventional literary approaches. As Alan Liu put it, quantitative statements about art are

---

[59] I am grateful to Ted Underwood for this point.   [60] Da.

made all the time in literary criticism, such as 'Wordsworth uses "joy" a lot in important poems like "Tintern Abbey"' and that 'evidence of that sort underlies much of literary studies, going back to close reading'. In other words, for Liu here, Da's criticism of statistical problems in quantitative literary studies is unequally distributed. It picks on the digital, when digital approaches are attempting 'to make it, if not right, [then] better'.[61] This is not, of course, to say that we should not criticize inaccuracies in digital/computational literary studies. It remains important to do so and Da has done a service by pointing to some errors in the secondary literature (although some targets of her critique argue that she has misread them).

The second curious point is that Da's article is extremely critical of the funding that digital approaches reportedly receive. This critique contains elements of a now-common anti-DH polemic: the digital humanities are vastly well funded compared to other areas of the humanities. Yet, the 2019 appropriation of $155,000,000 by the USA's National Endowment for the Humanities contained just 2.97 per cent ($4,600,000) dedicated to digital humanities (and this is not even specifically digital literary studies). Further, this money isn't used to pay for software/infrastructure, as the piece implicitly claims (Da notes that most of the software is free/open source), but for the labour of researchers and developers. Perhaps there is a fair comment to be made on DH's allocation of funding (though it is hardly as large as others make out). But it is disconcerting to see people cheerleading for less money to be put into the study of humanistic objects of inquiry. Perhaps it is not a call for less money to be put into it in general, though, but rather for a reallocation away from digital approaches, as though such funding were a zero-sum game. This, though, plays the very competitive game that we criticize elsewhere, pitting should-be allies against one another, rather than working in concert to ensure a better future for all the humanities.

Finally, there are huge infrastructural implications to Da's piece. In other disciplines, these are already being broached via the rhetorics of

[61] Alan Liu, 'E.g. (Generic Example): "Wordsworth Uses 'joy' a Lot in Important Poems like 'Tintern Abbey'." Evidence of That Sort Underlies Much of Literary Studies, Going Back to Close Reading. Let's Compare the Statistical Validity of _that_ to DH's Attempt to Make It, If Not Right, Better', *@alanyliu*, 2019 <https://twitter.com/alanyliu/status/1106109232661725185> [accessed 17 March 2019].

the reproducibility and replication crises. As Alan Thomas at the University of Chicago Press asked: 'how realistic for authors and publishers' are Da's recommendations of full datawork and replicable software?[62] In the present moment, this is possible. We can lodge most of these artefacts in various preservation-backed repositories with stable identifiers. The question is actually: for how long do we want to be able to replicate a finding? This is a question of usage as opposed to one just of preservation. Certainly, we can make bits and bytes available for a very long time indeed. But how are they interpreted? Usage half-lives of work in the humanities disciplines are long and one might wish to validate some work undertaken, say, six years ago. What guarantee do I have that software written six years ago will still run on the newest operating system? Can you open the files created by your word processor—perhaps the most common tool—from fifteen years ago?

The other challenge is that the term 'data' actually means 'stuff'. Data can range from a tiny CSV representation of a spreadsheet up to terabytes of information. To say to publishers and archivists 'please can I deposit my "data"?', when the spectrum for what that may contain is so wide, is a problem. This is because there is an economic scarcity underlying all digital preservation systems, as the prominent digital preservation expert David S. H. Rosenthal has argued for years. Part of this scarcity consists of pre-selection to militate against all resources being consumed by, say, a single project. Yet blanket calls for all data and software to be available over decadal-plus timespans for replication and repeatability will only be viable while digital literary studies remains a niche, small area. When these data formats and structures are bespoke and customized for specific projects, the problem is even larger. There is an almost directly proportionate relationship between the bespokeness of a digital artefact and the difficulty of preserving it. These are some of the looming challenges for digital literary studies.

---

[62] Alan Thomas, 'Here Are the First of Nan Z. Da's Suggested Guidelines for Peer Review of Computational Literary Studies, from Her Critique of the Field in @CriticalInquiry. How Realistic for Authors and Publishers?', *@alnthomas*, 2019 <https://twitter.com/alnthomas/status/1106616795534934016> [accessed 17 March 2019].

What Has Digital Literary Studies Ever Done for Us?

Despite the naysayers and the challenges, the remainder of this book is dedicated to an exploration of the contributions that digital literary studies have made, continue to make, and look set to make in future. The format for the work is a fusion of original examples—as per the above section on Stephen King—and surveys of innovative work in the field.

The rest of this book proceeds along four different lines that correspond to chapters: authors and writing; space and visualization; place and maps; and distance and history. By way of cartography, I here outline the conceptual route that the rest of this volume will take.

On authors and writing, two central questions posed by literary theory over the past half-century have been: 'what is a literary text?' and 'what is an author?' Indeed, the university discipline of literary studies has never truly known its precise object of study, which is partially why so many diverse practices of scholarship are lodged within English departments. What might it mean for a text, then, to be particularly 'literary'? Do we know? Is there any discernible aspect within language itself that denotes a work as literary? There are ways that we can begin to address these questions through digital approaches.

In this first chapter, I introduce a range of approaches to the measurement and digital quantification of literary style: stylometry or digital stylistics. This begins with a history of stylometric thinking, ranging from approximately 1851 through to contemporary multi-dimensional fingerprinting techniques, such as Burrows's delta method. I then progress to discuss close vs. large-scale literary reading and the problematic terminology of 'distant reading' (namely, that one can use computational techniques to read closely, despite this also being a type of 'distant' reading).

In the second chapter, I turn to space and visualization. For the common link between the section titles of Franco Moretti's well-known book, *Graphs, Maps, and Trees* (2007), is the visuality of his abstract models for literary history. Indeed, graphs, maps, and trees are all structures by which we can downmix complex, multi-dimensional aspects of literature into approximate two-dimensional (or sometimes three-dimensional) space. Much like conventional literary criticism, visualization yields to us new ways to conceive of narrative, reorienting texts through fresh optics and augmenting understanding. Visualization is a form of deformance and interpretation, as Lisa Samuels and Jerome McGann would have it.[63]

The third area of exploration in this book—and its third chapter—pertains to place and maps. The 'spatial turn' in the humanities—exemplified in the work of scholars as far apart as Jo Guldi and Robert Tally Jr—draws our attention to how literary texts structure their senses of place. From J. R. R. Tolkien to W. G. Sebald via the Hundred Acre Wood, literary works have often included maps within their pages. Yet such *topoi* sit distinct and apart from the extra-textual world, even when such places are represented therein. Digital approaches to geographic information systems (GIS) have been among the most commonly deployed technologies to think 'around' these issues of space and place. Whether it be in visualizing the multiple pathways taken by Woolf's characters in *Mrs Dalloway* (1925) or mapping the Lake District of the Romantic poets, attention to literary geography has been extensive in the digital world. It is to these themes that this chapter addresses itself.

The final chapter in this book thinks through notions of distance and history. As above, for many years now, more contemporary fiction has been published every year than a person can read in a lifetime. The implications for literary history here are enormous. Field mastery by a single individual is impossible and the systematizing dreams of the early Russian formalists seem far out of reach. One of the ways in which statistical reading has been billed as useful, though, is in overcoming these human limitations. If we cannot read enough ourselves, perhaps, it is posited, we might delegate this work to the machines. In conclusion, I end this book with a very brief summary of where digital methods might lead us and what their continued presence means for literary studies today.

Perhaps there is one area of work in digital literary studies that, in this book, gets somewhat less of a look-in than it might merit: the production of digital textual editions using the Textual Encoding Initiative's TEI standard. This XML format is widely used to represent digital texts—for instance, in textual editing. At the same time, the TEI consortium has already extensively documented the range of

---

[63] Samuels and McGann.

projects that use this standard: from Inscriptions of Roman Tripolitania to the Darwin Correspondence Project and beyond. In a way, although I do not give much space herein to TEI, this is because a whole book could be (and has been) dedicated to this standard and, still, it would be insufficient to cover all of its ground.[64] Suffice it to say that digital textual editing brings an intense textual focus in the same way as conventional editing; its practices are the very opposite of 'distancing'.

This book cannot do everything. It is impossible not to omit a great deal of valuable work from a survey when writing within the confines of a shorter book and I am certain that many readers will query the selections I have made. I aim nonetheless to give an overview of the scene of contemporary digital literary studies, gesturing towards broad areas for investigation, even while I must inevitably elide many specifics.

[64] For more, I recommend the forthcoming Christopher Ohge, *Inventions of the Text: Editing, Computing, and Publishing Digital Exhibitions of Experience* (Cambridge: Cambridge University Press, 2022).

1

Authors and Writing

How Is an Author?

The pervasive question in poststructuralist literary studies through Foucault and Barthes, in their respective guises, was 'what is an author?' Perhaps we might now playfully reformulate this for present purposes to 'how is an author constructed?' Because it seems that we have conflicting ideas about how authors write and why they appear in various stylistic guises on the page. On the one hand, authors are considered masters of their craft. Much literary analysis unravels the skill of wordsmiths and speculates upon how authorial choices create readerly effects and affects. On the other hand, the legacy of psychoanalysis, felt strongly in the field of literary studies, tells us that language is a slippery thing, surfacing elements buried in the unconscious and over which we do not have complete control. Literary language is at once dexterously controlled and untamedly wild.

Between the rock of linguistic control and the hard place of the unconscious lies the field of stylometry: the measurement of style. Most commonly used to identify authorship, the idea that style may be quantified and measured has a somewhat rocky history and rests on a series of questionable assumptions. For one, a definition of style remains elusive. It combines elements of language, form and order, and congruence with or divergence from the thematics of a text.[1] Style—defined most broadly as how an author writes—changes

[1] For a few instances of work on style, see J. M. Ellis, 'Linguistics, Literature, and the Concept of Style', *WORD*, 26.1 (1970), 65–78 <https://doi.org/10.1080/00437956. 1970.11435581>; Berel Lang, ed., *The Concept of Style* (Ithaca, NY: Cornell University Press, 1987); Edward W. Said, *On Late Style* (London: Bloomsbury, 2006); David James, '"Style Is Morality"? Aesthetics and Politics in the Amis Era', *Textual Practice*, 26.1 (2012), 11–25 <https://doi.org/10.1080/0950236X.2012.638760>.

diachronically over a life and career.[2] Style also changes between genres and the difference between generic spaces can be greater than the difference between authors within a single genre domain.

In terms of its history, stylometry has had some hits and misses. One of the most important breakthroughs occurred in 1964 when Frederick Mosteller and David L. Wallace published their work on the authorship of the pseudonymous *Federalist* papers of 1787–8.[3] (These documents are the letters pushing for the adoption of the proposed Constitution for the United States.) Mosteller and Wallace examine how thirty function words (articles, pronouns, etc.) were distributed through the *Federalist* papers and, using this method, came to the same conclusions around authorship as previous historians. In their case, though, the analysis was based on statistical probabilities and Bayesian analysis. In some ways, this is precisely the kind of 'useless' work decried by Brennan and towards which I gestured in the introduction. It appears to tell us nothing humanistic that we did not already know. By contrast, though, it tells us something new of some significance: this statistical method may have merit.

If Mosteller and Wallace's work was a triumph for stylometric authorship attribution, there have also been, though, a significant set of problematic failures, sometimes with disastrous consequences. In the late twentieth century, several criminal trials relied on stylometric authorship attribution to 'prove' the provenance of documentary evidence.[4] In some ways, this is not surprising. How often do murder

[2] Parts of this chapter are based on work that originally appeared in Eve, *Close Reading With Computers*.

[3] F. Mosteller and D. L. Wallace, *Inference and Disputed Authorship: The Federalist* (Reading, MA: Addison-Wesley, 1964).

[4] See Thomas McCrossen's London appeal in July 1991; the trial of Frank Beck in Leicester in 1992; the Dublin prosecution of Vincent Connell in December 1991; Nicky Kelly's pardon in Ireland in April 1992; the case of Joseph Nelson-Wilson in London in 1992; and the Carl Bridgewater murder trial. David I. Holmes, 'The Evolution of Stylometry in Humanities Scholarship', *Literary and Linguistic Computing*, 13.3 (1998), 111–17 (p. 114); Patrick Juola, 'Authorship Attribution', *Foundations and Trends® in Information Retrieval*, 1.3 (2007), 233–334 (p. 243) <https://doi.org/10.1561/1500000005>; see also Patrick Juola, 'Stylometry and Immigration: A Case Study', *Journal of Law and Policy*, 21.2 (2012), 287–98 for more on real-world applications of stylometry.

mysteries—and, one would presume by inference, real-world court trials—turn on proving the authorship of a letter? The answer, it turns out, is: often.[5]

However, the aforementioned cases relied on a specific method called 'qsum' or 'cusum' ('cumulative sum' of the deviations from the mean), intended to appraise the stability or consistency of a feature of a text.[6] Worryingly, though, the cusum technique was very quickly shown to be flawed, culminating in a live televisual failure of authorship attribution using the method.[7] Nonetheless, some stylometric techniques remain admissible in courts of law.[8]

In the literary domain, as opposed to the historical or legal contexts, stylometry has fared poorly on the public stage. The most notorious case occurred in the early 1990s when the poem 'A Funeral Elegy' was attributed to William Shakespeare by Don Foster, using stylometric techniques.[9] Ever keen on the Authorship Controversy, the media printed Foster's claims on their front pages (the *New York Times*, for instance). Yet traditional Shakespeare scholars were less than persuaded. As Foster would not accept the historicist arguments against his claim, other researchers conducted further stylometric

[5] C. E. Chaski, 'Who's at the Keyboard: Authorship Attribution in Digital Evidence Investigations', *International Journal of Digital Evidence*, 4.1 (2005).

[6] See J. M. Farringdon, *Analyzing for Authorship: A Guide to the Cusum Technique* (Cardiff: University of Wales Press, 1996).

[7] David Canter, 'An Evaluation of "Cusum" Stylistic Analysis of Confessions', *Expert Evidence*, 1.2 (1992), 93–9; R. A. Hardcastle, 'CUSUM: A Credible Method for the Determination of Authorship?', *Science & Justice*, 37.2 (1997), 129–38 <https://doi.org/10.1016/S1355-0306(97)72158-0>; M. L. Hilton, 'An Assessment of Cumulative Sum Charts for Authorship Attribution', *Literary and Linguistic Computing*, 8.2 (1993), 73–80 <https://doi.org/10.1093/llc/8.2.73>; David I. Holmes and Fiona Tweedie, 'Forensic Stylometry: A Review of the Cusum Controversy', *Revue Informatique et Statistique dans les Sciences Humaines*, 31.1–4 (1995), 19–47; Juola, 'Authorship Attribution', pp. 233–4.

[8] C. E. Chaski, 'The Keyboard Dilemma and Forensic Authorship Attribution', *Advances in Digital Forensics*, 3 (2007); G. McMenamin, 'Disputed Authorship in US Law', *International Journal of Speech, Language and the Law*, 11.1 (2004), 73–82.

[9] J. W. Grieve, 'Quantitative Authorship Attribution: A History and an Evaluation of Techniques' (unpublished Masters, Simon Fraser University, 2005) <http://hdl.handle.net/1892/2055>.

analysis. They concluded that John Ford was a much more probable candidate for the poem's authorship.[10]

In some senses, this is, of course, just the way that science and research are supposed to work. A hypothesis was tested and then countered by other researchers. Indeed, as Patrick Juola puts it: 'this cut-and-thrust debate can be regarded as a good (if somewhat bitter) result of the standard scholarly process of criticism'.[11] For many scholars unacquainted with digital literary studies, though, the wild claims and media sensationalism of this episode marked the first and only time they have had any interaction with stylometry. As Elliot and Valenza put it through a baseball metaphor: it does little good to pitch so many hardballs with so few over the plate.[12]

More recent algorithmic developments, such as John Burrows's delta method—coupled with more modest claims—have nonetheless shown some promise in authorship attribution and our understanding of literary style.[13] The delta method is a system that measures how frequently authors use different words. The method allows for cross-textual comparison and, then, groupings of documents that have the same frequency profiles. It has proved a relatively strong technique for ascertaining authorship. However, authorship attribution is itself premised on a set of assumptions about style. The first of these assumptions, that authors possess a 'stylistic naturalism', centres on the notion that writers do not (or *cannot*) consider how our works will be 'read' by computers. As Brennan and Greenstadt note, 'in many historical matters, author-ship has been unintentionally lost to time and it can be assumed that the authors did not have the knowledge or

[10] W. Elliot and R. J. Valenza, 'And Then There Were None: Winnowing the Shakespeare Claimants', *Computers and the Humanities*, 30 (1996), 191–245; W. Elliot and R. J. Valenza, 'The Professor Doth Protest Too Much, Methinks', *Computers and the Humanities*, 32 (1998), 425–90; W. Elliot and R. J. Valenza, 'So Many Hardballs, so Few over the Plate', *Computers and the Humanities*, 36 (2002), 455–60.

[11] Juola, 'Authorship Attribution', p. 245.

[12] Elliot and Valenza, 'So Many Hardballs, so Few over the Plate'.

[13] David Hoover, 'Testing Burrows's Delta', *Literary and Linguistic Computing*, 19.4 (2004), 453–75; S. Stein and S. Argamon, 'A Mathematical Explanation of Burrows' Delta', in *Proceedings of Digital Humanities* 2006 (Paris, France, 2006); S. Argamon, 'Interpreting Burrows's Delta: Geometric and Probabilistic Foundations', *Literary and Linguistic Computing*, 23.2 (2007), 131–47 <https://doi.org/10.1093/llc/fqn003>.

inclination to attempt to hide their linguistic style. However, this may not be the case for modern authors who wish to hide their identity'.[14] Indeed, an author's choice of stylistic devices (rhythm, cadence, word length, repetition) has knock-on effects that are hard to anticipate. Who knows, when they write, for instance, what a rhyme scheme will do to the frequency of one's use of indefinite articles? An author cannot hold every trait of writing in memory while writing. This leads to an idea of what I call stylistic naturalism: the notion that authors have a set of profilable characteristics in their writing over which they can never truly have full control. As Juola puts it, on the one hand 'the assumption of most researchers, then, is that people have a characteristic pattern of language use, a sort of "authorial fingerprint" that can be detected in their writings. [...] On the other hand, there are also good practical reasons to believe that such fingerprints may be very complex, certainly more complex than simple univariate statistics such as average word length or vocabulary size'.[15]

A second and linked flawed assumption of the 'stylistic naturalism' claim in much authorship attribution is the belief that authors behave in the same way when writing their different works. That is, the belief that stylometric profiles do not change even when authors try to modify their writing style. This also assumes consistency in authors' styles throughout their lives, which is a disputed claim.[16]

These ideas around authorial style highlight a core assumption about stylometry: that it can somehow measure the elements of a text of which authors themselves are unaware. As David Holmes writes, at the core of stylometric methods 'lies an assumption that authors have an unconscious aspect to their style, an aspect which cannot consciously be manipulated but which possesses features which are quantifiable and which may be distinctive'.[17]

The final assumption of much stylometry is that *authorship* is the textual feature that can best be studied through quantifying methods.

---

[14] Michael Robert Brennan and Rachel Greenstadt, 'Practical Attacks Against Authorship Recognition Techniques', in *IAAI*, 2009 <http://www.cs.drexel.edu/~mb553/stuff/brennan_iaai09.pdf> [accessed 1 August 2016].

[15] Juola, 'Authorship Attribution', p. 239.

[16] In just the theoretical space, one might consider, for instance, Said.

[17] Holmes, p. 111.

This is tricky even from a publishing studies perspective: how, for instance, are typesetting/text encoding, editorial interventions, copyediting, proofreading, and other labour forms reflected in these measurements? For these are all labour activities that make the effort of authorship collaborative. Indeed, Burrows noted of his own method and the idea of 'authorial fingerprints'—even though the method *does* seem to work very well at identifying authors—that 'we do not yet have either proof or promise' of the 'very existence' of such a phenomenon that constitutes authorship.[18] How an author is constituted backwards from text is complicated by the distributed labour functions of authorship.

Yet, authorship does not have to be considered in binary terms ('was this text written by X?'). Indeed, several recent studies have used stylometric approaches to appraise influence or linguistic similarity between authors where the link has previously been suspected. For instance, James O'Sullivan et al. conducted a set of stylometric analyses on the novels of James Joyce in comparison to those by Flann O'Brien. As they note, O'Brien's *At Swim-Two-Birds* (1939) has long been considered under a Joycean penumbra, with commentators often remarking (sometimes unfavourably) upon the 'long passages in imitation of the Joycean parody', as just one example.[19]

Indeed, O'Sullivan et al. manage convincingly to demonstrate that the gigantism of the 'Cyclops' episode of *Ulysses*—suggested by Neil Corcoran as the central parodic technique of *At Swim-Two-Birds*—is actually most accurately reflected in the 'Oxen of the Sun' and 'Eumaeus' segments of the novel. The method used to demonstrate this is a refinement of Burrows's delta technique, called rolling delta. In a rolling delta method, one slides a moving 'window' across the text, measuring portions of the novel against other texts. The closer the other texts then appear to the X axis, the more stylistically similar they are to that 'window' using the multivariate word comparison/lexical choice comparison approach (see Figure 1.1).

---

[18] John Burrows, '"Delta": A Measure of Stylistic Difference and a Guide to Likely Authorship', *Literary and Linguistic Computing*, 17.3 (2002), 267–87 (p. 268) https://doi.org/10.1093/llc/17.3.267.

[19] Keith Hopper, *Flann O'Brien: A Portrait of the Artist as a Young Post-Modernist* (Cork: Cork University Press, 2009), p. 46.

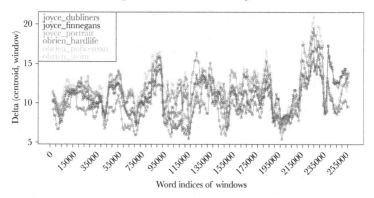

Figure 1.1 James O'Sullivan et al.'s rolling delta analysis of *Ulysses* against other novels by James Joyce and Flann O'Brien. Kindly regenerated at a higher resolution by James O'Sullivan and reproduced under the terms of the Creative Commons Attribution 4.0 License.

There are two important facets of papers such as this. The first is that, as above, this analysis is not about authorship identification. We already know that James Joyce and Flann O'Brien/Brian O'Nolan are not the same author. However, to conduct authorship attribution, one must search for similarities between writers that conform to the above set of assumptions about stylometry. In other words, authorship attribution is concerned with a specific set of similitude measures that can help us to compare authorial features.

Yet it is not the fact that the authors share traits according to a rolling delta method that is most significant here. What is more interesting, as the second facet, is the interpretative spin that O'Sullivan et al. bring to the computational analysis. Rejecting the simple interpretation that these two passages are the ones in which Stephen and Bloom appear together, with Stephen being the prototype for O'Brien's unnamed student character, the authors turn to a 'close reading of the Joycean passages most similar to *At Swim-Two-Birds*'. The conclusion at which they arrive is highly metatextual. It transpires that the most similar portions of these texts pertain to notions of language, mastery, and ownership in the discussion of aesthetics. In O'Sullivan et al.'s reading, O'Brien's narrator 'considers literary tradition not only a reservoir of characters, motifs, and topoi, but also a repository of styles from which writers can and should draw freely'.

However, as their analyses then show, 'O'Brien not only preaches this through his hero, but also effectively puts this into practice'.[20]

It is often surprising to those outside of digital literary studies that researchers should turn to close-reading techniques in tandem with computational methods. After all, the popular story is that computational techniques take us away from texts and into the broad realm of literary history. Yet, as above, this is often not the case. Another good example is Tanya Clement's work on *The Making of Americans* (1925) by Gertrude Stein. Stein's text is well known for its stylistic oddities and, in particular, its use of fractal-like repetition and recursion.[21] It has also been branded 'monumentally tedious'.[22] I can confirm that it is not a great beach read. A typical passage from the novel, for instance, proceeds: 'it was always all right for her when there was not any strong person resisting, for then she was always strong enough to keep on going and then, though mostly, not altogether winning, she came then near enough to winning to give to her her important feeling'.[23]

While some critics have disparaged the reading experience of *The Making of Americans*, Clement's 'distant' approach to the novel has yielded evidence 'that suggests that the text is intricately and purposefully structured', against the seeming arbitrariness of its composition and repetition.[24] The revelation that Clement presents is that chapter nine of *The Making of Americans* 'provides the legend: it is a measurement of relative scale by which we can read the greater map. Understanding how chapter [nine] is structured aids how we can understand the larger text'.[25] Indeed, Clement shows how repetitions

[20] James O'Sullivan et al., 'Measuring Joycean Influences on Flann O'Brien', *Digital Studies/Le Champ Numérique*, 8.1 (2018), 6 <https://doi.org/10.16995/dscn.288>.

[21] Juana T. Guerra de la Torre, 'Fractals in Gertrude Stein's "Word-System": Natural Reality and/or Verbal Reality', *Atlantis*, 17.1/2 (1995), 89–114.

[22] Morton P. Levitt, 'Modernism Bound', *Journal of Modern Literature*, 24.3 (2001), 501–6 (p. 505) <https://doi.org/10.1353/jml.2001.0005>.

[23] Gertrude Stein, *The Making of Americans, Being a History of a Family's Progress* (Project Gutenberg, 2016) <http://gutenberg.net.au/ebooks16/1600671h.html> [accessed 27 November 2018].

[24] Tanya E. Clement, '"A Thing Not Beginning and Not Ending": Using Digital Tools to Distant-Read Gertrude Stein's *The Making of Americans*', *Literary and Linguistic Computing*, 23.3 (2008), 361–81 (p. 363) <https://doi.org/10.1093/llc/fqn020>.

[25] Clement, '"A Thing Not Beginning and Not Ending"', p. 371.

in chapter nine—in which paragraphs consistently begin and end with repetitions, padded by complications—mirror the structure of the text as a whole. For it turns out that *The Making of Americans* is a text of two distinct halves, in which 'the function of the second half of the text is to develop complexities and contradictions that complicate the knowledge produced in the first half of the text by using the same words and sequences introduced there, but using them in variation'.[26] This becomes clear as there is, in Clement's analysis, a 'trend for longer repetitions in the first half of the text with the longest repetition happening exactly in the center of the text'.[27] That is to say that there is a mathematical symmetry to the length of repetitions that cluster precisely around the text's middle and that thematically divide the novel.

While it is difficult to do justice to Clement in summary here, what is most fascinating about her work is that closeness and distance of reading turn out not to be opposed, since the distance can be a depth, not necessarily just a horizontal plane of *longue durée* literary history. As Clement puts it 'accordingly, distant reading has shown us a guide to those relationships that facilitate how to do a closer, combinatory reading. Certainly "only reading" *The Making of Americans*—or reading it in a traditional way—appears to have yielded limited material for scholarly work, but reading the text differently, as an object of pairings or as parts of combinations, ultimately works in contrast to the supposition that the text is only meaningful to the extent that it defeats making meaning'.[28]

Distance and Depth

Despite the above, the model of close reading that distant reading provides is atypical for literary studies.[29] Of course, distant reading persists in pattern recognition and literary interpretation. However, the patterns that can be recognized are often removed from readerly

[26] Clement, ' "A Thing Not Beginning and Not Ending" ', p. 373.

[27] Clement, ' "A Thing Not Beginning and Not Ending" ', pp. 366–7.

[28] Clement, ' "A Thing Not Beginning and Not Ending" ', p. 378.

[29] For more on this, see Katherine Bode, 'The Equivalence of "Close" and "Distant" Reading; Or, Toward a New Object for Data-Rich Literary History', *Modern Language Quarterly*, 78.1 (2017), 77–106 <https://doi.org/10.1215/00267929-3699787>.

perception, which is why we require a computational approach. The formal aesthetics on which computational close reading usually remarks, then, are of mathematical beauty. For, certainly, there is a beauty and aesthetics to mathematical patterns; one need think only of the concept of the golden ratio.[30] How one then interprets those findings, though, is entirely up to the author and reader. It remains perfectly possible to weave a mathematical/patterned interpretation back into mainstream literary-critical approaches.

The more famous use of these pattern-recognition paradigms is to work at a greater scale than the close reading of individual texts. One might consider, here, for instance, Ted Underwood's recent work on approaches to genre, to which I will also return at the close of this volume. For Underwood, 'the real value of quantitative methods could be that they allow scholars to coordinate textual and social approaches to genre', thereby synthesizing a type of close reading with ideas of how genres form and are constituted within socially conditioned spaces.[31]

Specifically, in his article 'The Life Cycle of Genres', Underwood draws attention to the fact that the issue of the historical comparison of genres 'is a pressing one because literary scholars haven't been able to reach much consensus about the life cycles of novelistic genres. The Gothic, for instance, can be treated as a category that lasts for 25 years or for 250'. Certainly, elsewhere, Matthew Jockers has shown how genres within 30-year-or-so windows in the nineteenth century revolve around the same set of linguistic terms. Computational models can identify similar genres of fiction in the nineteenth century based on the clustering of terms within those texts.[32]

Underwood's approach to the study of genre is somewhat different, though. Taking lists of 'detective fiction (or "mystery" or "crime fiction"), science fiction (also defined in a variety of ways), and the Gothic', he compares 'groups of texts associated with different sites of reception and segments of the timeline' to 'ask exactly how stable different categories have been'.

---

[30] Mario Livio, *The Golden Ratio: The Story of Phi, the World's Most Astonishing Number* (New York: Broadway Books, 2003).

[31] Underwood, 'The Life Cycles of Genres'.

[32] Jockers, *Macroanalysis*, pp. 67–81.

Through this approach, Underwood tells a new story of the lifecycle of genres to which I will return later—one that fits neatly with neither of the existing narratives of generational succession (proposed by Franco Moretti) nor gradual consolidation. Underwood sees 'little evidence of the generational waves Moretti's theory would predict. In fact, it's not even the case that books in a chronologically-focused genre (like "the sensation novel, 1860–1880") necessarily resemble each other more closely than books spread out across a long timeline. Detective fiction and science fiction display a textual coherence that is at least as strong as Moretti's shorter-lived genres, and they sustain it over very long periods (160 or perhaps even 200 years). So I think we can set aside the (productive) conjecture that twenty-five-year generational cycles have special importance for the study of genre'.

Conversely, though, Underwood also does not find 'much evidence for the story of gradual consolidation' that he expected. In this piece, Underwood notes that:

> although it is clearly true that the publishing institutions governing genre developed gradually, it appears I was wrong to expect that the textual differences between genres would develop in the same gradual way. In the case of detective fiction, for instance, the textual differences that distinguish twentieth-century stories of detection from other genres can be traced back very clearly as far as "The Murders in the Rue Morgue"—and not much farther. Detective fiction did spread gradually, in the sense that Poe and Vidocq were initially isolated figures, without a supporting cast of imitators, let alone genre-specific magazines and book clubs. But textual patterns don't have to develop as gradually as institutions do. Poe's stories already display many of the same features that distinguish twentieth-century crime fiction from other genres.[33]

While these findings about genre are, on their own, extremely significant—bringing a fresh empirical understanding of how authors work within predefined conventions—there is another feature of this analysis to which I wish here to draw attention: negative or null results.

---

[33] Underwood, 'The Life Cycles of Genres'.

In scientific disciplines, most work proceeds on a hypothesis-driven approach. Before any experiment is conducted, scientists need to formulate ideas of what they think will happen. In particular, in many forms of statistical analysis, one needs what is called a 'null hypothesis'. The null hypothesis is the conjectural statement that, when comparing two groups, there is *no difference* between the studied populations and any perceived difference is due to error, sampling problems, or other cause.

In traditional scientific publishing, a null result is not acceptable. If one does not find anything interesting then why should anyone care? Yet, there has been a move to ensure the publication of negative/null results in recent years.[34] The rationale behind this is that if an experiment *doesn't work*, it is useful for others in the scientific community to know this so that they do not waste their efforts pursuing the same course that has failed elsewhere. The emergence of 'soundness-only' peer review in journals such as *PLOS ONE* is a direct response to this call.[35]

In literary criticism, though, it is paradoxically both very rare and extremely common to have a negative result. Although literary criticism works best when its findings surprise the reader, there is often a strange temporality at work in its argumentation. While literary-critical arguments unfold as a reader reads, within time as they are read, they are not usually documented as method in the same way as a scientific argument. That is: what is usually of interest to those reading literary criticism is not the *process of how* the author arrived at the argument but the *outcome of the argument*. There is also, usually, a transformative element to literary criticism. The idea is that the reader will see a poem, novel, or play in a fresh light after having digested the argument—'extractions of latent content', as Angela Carter put it—from which it is difficult ever again to retreat.[36]

[34] See Martin Paul Eve, *Open Access and the Humanities: Contexts, Controversies and the Future* (Cambridge: Cambridge University Press, 2014), p. 144 <https://doi.org/10.1017/CBO9781316161012>.

[35] For more on *PLOS ONE*, see Martin Paul Eve et al., *Reading Peer Review: PLOS ONE and Institutional Change in Academia* (Cambridge: Cambridge University Press, 2021).

[36] John Haffenden, ed., *Novelists in Interview* (London: Methuen, 1985), p. 80.

Negative results in most literary criticism are, as a result, hard to envisage. What would it mean for a literary critic to write 'I attempted to advance this argument, but it didn't work'? While one could imagine this, it is difficult to believe that many critics would wish to open themselves up to the potential ridicule of the situation. The suspicion might always be that the reason the argument didn't work was that it was either wrongheaded or textually inaccurate, both of which would reflect negatively on the critic.

Conversely, though, the undoing of others' arguments *is* a common occurrence in literary criticism. That is to say that we expect the ongoing dialectic of criticism frequently to criticize the arguments made in earlier work. It is supposed that the results of precedent critical work will be negated, made negative, or null.

How should we understand this double movement whereby literary criticism cannot admit its fallibility in the moment while subsequent works will nonetheless attempt to kill their forebears? It is perhaps because there is a twinned temporality to literary criticism; the time of the argument and the time of discursive negation. These two timescales only allow negative results in the second realm while the first must hold a pretence to its own inviolability and accuracy.

Digital literary studies work differently, though. For instance, the *Journal of Cultural Analytics* specifically invites negative results. Underwood, as above, admits freely that 'it appears [he] was wrong to expect that the textual differences between genres would develop in the same gradual way'. In other words: the hypothesis did not bear out. In some ways, this is a negative result. There was a hypothesis, which was tested, and found to be wanting. However, this is not actually so different to the refutation of others' arguments. For this notion—that genres cross-fertilize into slipstream hybridity—is hardly controversial.[37] Underwood first advanced an argument that seemed plausible and that others have made, then negated it himself.

Not all negative results, however, are equal. As Underwood showed above, sometimes a negative result—that is, one that was different to what one expected—can cause a re-evaluation of one's core

---

[37] Bruce Sterling, 'CATSCAN 5: Slipstream', *SF Eye*, 5, 1989 <http://lib.ru/STERLINGB/catscan05.txt> [accessed 30 November 2018]; Jacques Derrida, 'The Law of Genre', trans. Avital Ronell, *Critical Inquiry*, 7.1 (1980), 55–81.

assumptions about literature. Sometimes, too, they can be banal. This is not to say that there is no worth in the banal; knowing that a particular mathematical or computational approach cannot tell us anything is, itself, useful. This may save others from falling into the same traps or allow them to refine the method in question. Sometimes, though, the initial hypothesis might attract ridicule: how could you think *that*? Thus, asking good questions and having plausible hypotheses at the outset is at least part of the puzzle concerning negative results and digital literary studies.

Finally, on the matters of negative results and failure, this raises the spectre of interdisciplinarity. Digital literary studies projects often necessitate working with computer scientists or statisticians. The difficulty here is that literary studies frequently wish merely to use software to produce literary findings rather than engage in a bidirectional exchange of practice of ideas. As Alexander R. Galloway put it 'ultimately it comes down to this: if you count words in *Moby-Dick*, are you going to learn more about the white whale? I think you probably can—and we have to acknowledge that. But you won't learn anything new about *counting*'.[38]

There are exceptions to this rule. A good instance of a truly interdisciplinary collaboration would be the 'Viral Texts' project at Northeastern, headed by Ryan Cordell on the literary front. In its own words, this project seeks 'to develop theoretical models that will help scholars better understand what qualities—both textual and thematic—helped particular news stories, short fiction, and poetry "go viral" in nineteenth-century newspapers and magazines'. In the case of 'Viral Texts', there were real theoretical challenges in the computational space (as there are also in other areas of Cordell's work).[39] These pertained to the computational detection of text reuse when handling 'dirty data'; that is, poorly scanned documents in which the corrective labour time to create a clean copy is not available. In this

---

[38] Melissa Dinsman and Alexander R. Galloway, 'The Digital in the Humanities: An Interview with Alexander Galloway', *Los Angeles Review of Books* <https://lareviewofbooks.org/article/the-digital-in-the-humanities-an-interview-with-alexander-galloway/> [accessed 19 April 2016].

[39] See also, for instance, Ryan Cordell, '"Q i-Jtb the Raven": Taking Dirty OCR Seriously', *Book History*, 20.1 (2017), 188–225 <https://doi.org/10.1353/bh.2017.0006>.

project's case, this work has led to several publications in the information science discipline.[40]

But let us return from this digression to authorship. Thus far in this chapter I have aimed to show how digital approaches to style can tell us a great theoretical deal about authorship; they can tell us about genre; and they can yield to us new insights on pattern recognition, at either the macro or micro level. Authorship is a core concern for digital literary studies and its users. Given that this is the case, though, it is also now worth considering what happens when computers themselves *write*, if such a proposition even makes sense. If we have first considered how the aesthetic identities of authors are constructed, digitally, let us now turn to how digital authors might be built. How is a computer an author?

Strategies of Self-Consciousness and Context

In her formative work on posthumanism, 'The Cyborg Manifesto', Donna Haraway notes that 'writing is pre-eminently the technology of cyborgs', which breaks down boundaries and always requires techno-organic hybridity.[41] The act of holding a pencil fuses the human with technology. Yet, even before the advent and mass uptake of the word processor, authors and publishers often imagined their erasure at the hands of machines that can write. For instance, as Matthew Kirschenbaum has recently charted, Stephen King famously penned a story—'Word Processor of the Gods' (1983)—in which the 'delete' function of his computer allows him to erase reality; a clear

[40] David A. Smith et al., 'Detecting and Modeling Local Text Reuse', in *IEEE/ACM Joint Conference on Digital Libraries* (presented at the 2014 IEEE/ACM Joint Conference on Digital Libraries (JCDL), London, United Kingdom: IEEE, 2014), pp. 183–92 <https://doi.org/10.1109/JCDL.2014.6970166>.

[41] Donna Haraway, 'A Cyborg Manifesto: Science, Technology, and Socialist-Feminism in the Late Twentieth Century', in Haraway, *Simians, Cyborgs and Women: The Reinvention of Nature* (London: Routledge, 1991), pp. 149–81 (p. 176). Portions of this section come from Martin Paul Eve, 'The Great Automatic Grammatizator: Writing, Labour, Computers', *Critical Quarterly*, 59.3 (2017), 39–54 <https://doi.org/10.1111/criq.12359>.

metaphor for fear of redundancy in the face of the machine's power.[42] William Gibson's self-encrypting (and therefore self-erasing) digital poem, *Agrippa (Book of the Dead)* (1992), also betrays such anxiety of obsolescence in its self-undoing and transfer away from authorial power.

Among the more widely circulated of these fearful prophecies, though, is Roald Dahl's imagined 'Great Automatic Grammatizator', from his 1953 collection, *Someone Like You*—a story that features a machine that quantifies human creativity through the mathematization of language (and that I have already mentioned in this book's introduction). A world away from surrealist conceptions of 'automatic' writing in the early twentieth century, Dahl's machine is a dark device akin to an organ that a human operator 'plays' with the stops set to inject the desired sentiment at any point during the unfolding narrative arc. The most important feature of Dahl's short story, though, is the focus on material textual production and its remuneration. That is, Dahl recognizes that the terror of such a machine is predominantly concerned with the symbolic economics of authors' names as brands; the 'author-function', as Foucault might term it, and not the horror of a machine actually writing.[43] In Dahl's tale, these names are re-minted as coinage within hierarchies of prestige, akin to those recently explored by James F. English and Ted Underwood.[44] Of course, as with all the symbolic economies described by Pierre Bourdieu, these virtualized currencies map onto real economies (if, that is, we can even use the word 'real' to describe an economy). As Dahl's protagonist feels his 'own hand creeping closer and closer to

[42] Stephen King, 'Word Processor of the Gods', in *Skeleton Crew* (London: Hodder, 2012), pp. 327–48; Matthew G. Kirschenbaum, *Track Changes: A Literary History of Word Processing* (Cambridge, MA: The Belknap Press of Harvard University Press, 2016), pp. 77–83.

[43] Michel Foucault, 'What Is an Author?', in *The Essential Works of Michel Foucault, 1954–1984*, 3 vols. (London: Penguin, 2000), II, 205–22.

[44] James F. English, 'Winning the Culture Game: Prizes, Awards, and the Rules of Art', *New Literary History*, 33.1 (2002), 109–35; James F. English, *The Economy of Prestige: Prizes, Awards, and the Circulation of Cultural Value* (Cambridge, MA: Harvard University Press, 2005); Underwood, *Why Literary Periods Mattered*; see also Ted Underwood and Jordan Sellers, 'The Longue Durée of Literary Prestige', *Modern Language Quarterly*, 77.3 (2016), 321–44 <https://doi.org/10.1215/00267929-3570634>.

that golden contract' that will let the machine produce books and other writings on his behalf, he asks for the strength to maintain human creativity in the face of financial ruin, a strength to value an autonomous art over material circumstances, a strength (expressed with Dahl's customary shock hyperbole and echoing my introduction) 'to let our children starve', even while it is ambiguous as to whether the story in the reader's own hands might itself be a product of the Great Automatic Grammatizator.[45]

Scholarly debate around this type of output—and particularly computer-generated poetry—stretches back to the 1970s when it was frequently invoked in discussions around author intentionality.[46] Did it matter, commentators asked, whether a poem was written by a human or a machine in the age of poststructuralist anti-intentionalist readings? It was also clear at this time that applications of humanities computing (the precursor term for 'digital humanities') existed for the study and teaching of poetry.[47] Most importantly, though, 'poetry' written by computers has persistently been found to be *lacking* an author. For instance, P. D. Juhl claims that when we read machine-written poetry 'we are not dealing with anyone's use of the words', although he concedes that the words may 'possibly' be 'the programmer's'.[48] Even the most recent comprehensive surveys of computational poetics continue to note that this authorial deletion lies at the heart of machine-authored poetry: 'contemporary technology radically challenges the creative process of poetry authorship'.[49]

However, what is most significant here is that academic concern about computer-written poetry is far less concerned with artistic merit than the popular imagination might suppose. They are more concerned

[45] Dahl, p. 209.

[46] Monroe C. Beardsley, *The Possibility of Criticism* (Detroit, MI: Wayne State University Press, 1970), pp. 18–19; George Dickie, *Aesthetics: An Introduction* (New York: Pegasus, 1971); P. D. Juhl, 'Do Computer Poems Show That an Author's Intention Is Irrelevant to the Meaning of a Literary Work?', *Critical Inquiry*, 5.3 (1979), 481–7.

[47] James V. Catano, 'Poetry and Computers: Experimenting with the Communal Text', *Computers and the Humanities*, 13.4 (1979), 269–75 (p. 269).

[48] Juhl, p. 481.

[49] David Jhave Johnston, *Aesthetic Animism: Digital Poetry's Ontological Implications* (Cambridge, MA: MIT Press, 2016), p. 125 <http://www.jstor.org/stable/j.ctt1cd-0mcs> [accessed 14 April 2017].

with labour, expertise, prestige, and control. For 'it is important', writes David Johnston, 'that poets (and not technologists/linguists) interrogate what the practice of poetry is in a big data/cloud world', a re-inscription of the poet as a valid and distinct labour specialist at the heart of such an enterprise but framed in terms of sentiment and taste.[50] Certainly, there is a prevalent sense that what is lost to the machine is art-for-art's sake, the 'creative urge'. Yet markets and business saturate Dahl's story; it is all about the labour and remuneration of writing and publishing. Despite the predictable nature of Dahl's own brand of shock-twist short story, 'The Great Automatic Grammatizator' instead aims its ire at formulaic genre fiction that is decried as the output of older writers who have 'run out of ideas' but who comprise 'seventy per cent' of the work accepted by publishers.[51] In turn, this feels akin to John W. Aldridge's formulation of an 'assembly-line fiction'; for Dahl's protagonist, Adolph Knipe, is surely a swipe at Alfred Knopf, the publisher of *Someone Like You* but who would also later drop Dahl in 1981.[52]

That the target here is not truly computational writing but instead labour and publishing economics does not mean that there is nothing to say about the conjunction of publisher markets and machine prose to which the story draws attention. Instead, the fundamental crux that we continue to elide in the space of electronic literature and machine writing is the locus of different labour functions that underwrite their production, reception, circulation, and preservation. For the digital space is often imagined as infinitely abundant. The ability to copy any extant artefact at a near-infinitesimal cost leads the digital imagination to perceive of labour limitations as a technical rather than a social problem. In fact, digital abundance rests upon scarce material labour and requires additional forms of technical expertise to develop and maintain electronic infrastructures. An underlying material economy restricts the ability to harness abundant digital potentialities. In this way, the digital space provides us with a new commodity fetishism, in which we focus upon our technical relationships with the digital

---

[50] Johnston, p. 125.   [51] Dahl, p. 209.

[52] John W. Aldridge, *Talents and Technicians: Literary Chic and the New Assembly-Line Fiction* (New York: Scribner's, 1992); see also Robert Gottlieb, *Avid Reader: A Life* (New York: Farrar, Straus and Giroux, 2016).

prostheses with which we all now write, instead of our labour relationships between people that underwrite such technologies.

What I am interested in addressing here, then, is a question that comes out of the work of Jerome McGann in his writing on the information age.[53] Suppose a work of computer-generated literature is a social text or event. What forms of labour are invested in the technological toolchains that contribute to its creation but often lie unrecognized by our contemporary authorship systems? As McGann asks: 'where is information technology driving literary and cultural studies?'[54] Pushing this question to its limit is to ask what labour underpins such textual socialization when, in the current age of books in the making, we believe that computers can write.

The Work of Computational Writing

What does it mean to say that computers can write? What are the human labour forms that underpin such authorship? The metaphor of 'writing' certainly runs throughout computational terminology. From processor registers through random access memory to solid state and hard drives, forms of computer storage are 'read' and 'written' via minute physical magnetic manipulations and reflections.[55] Computational media are deemed read- or write-protected in some instances. Yet this metaphor is not the type of writing of which we speak when we claim that computational writing is on the rise.

Most authors are now used to writing *with* computers. The process of fabricating the material codex has been digitally intermediated for many years now.[56] Even those contemporary authors—Don DeLillos and Jennifer Egans—who cling to typewriters and pens and paper will

---

[53] See Jerome McGann, *A Critique of Modern Textual Criticism* (Charlottesville, VA: University of Virginia Press, 1983).

[54] Jerome McGann, 'From Text to Work: Digital Tools and the Emergence of the Social Text', *Text*, 16 (2006), 49–62 (p. 50).

[55] For the best work on this, see Matthew G. Kirschenbaum, *Mechanisms: New Media and the Forensic Imagination* (Cambridge, MA: MIT Press, 2008).

[56] Hayles, *How We Think*, p. 6.

have their words re-wrought into various digital forms by others in an often-gendered division of labour.[57]

Yet what we talk about when we talk about computational writing is the production of text that appears as though it was generated directly and unmediatedly by humans even while this is not the case. That is, the precise selection of sequential words was decided neither by an individual person nor by that individual working in conjunction with an editor or co-authors. The roots of such a system go back a long way and at least as far as 1845 when John Clark demonstrated his 'Eureka machine' that was designed automatically to generate Latin verses.[58] As with so-called 'artificial intelligence', the benchmark of success is the exact mimicry, or even out-performance, of human characteristics of intelligence or writing. This is why some of the most well-known historical natural-language generative systems have been interactive chatbots.[59] Among the famous examples here are ELIZA—a bot from the 1960s that attempted to imitate a Rogerian psychotherapist by echoing back the user's own reformulated questions—and SHRDLU, a system that had a rudimentary understanding of natural language combined with a memory system. Other early systems included TALE-SPIN, which generated Aesopian fables, AUTHOR, MINSTREL, UNIVERSE, and GRANDMOTHER.[60]

This is to say that ideas of artificial intelligence and computational writing are saturated with anthropocentric thought. To succeed, attempts at producing artificial intelligence and computational writing must strive to transcend a mechanistic logic through a type of incomprehensibility. A 'free will' or vitalism should animate the

---

[57] Camilla Nelson, '#ThanksforTyping: The Women behind Famous Male Writers', *The Conversation*, 2017 <http://theconversation.com/thanksfortyping-the-women-behind-famous-male-writers-75770> [accessed 15 April 2017]; see also Sara Louise Muhr and Alf Rehn, 'On Gendered Technologies and Cyborg Writing', *Gender, Work & Organization*, 22.2 (2015), 129–38 <https://doi.org/10.1111/gwao.12057>.

[58] Jason David Hall, 'Popular Prosody: Spectacle and the Politics of Victorian Versification', *Nineteenth-Century Literature*, 62.2 (2007), 222–49 (p. 227) <https://doi.org/10.1525/ncl.2007.62.2.222>.

[59] See Simone Natale, *Deceitful Media: Artificial Intelligence and Social Life after the Turing Test* (Oxford: Oxford University Press, 2021).

[60] Leah Henrickson, *Reading Computer-Generated Texts* (Cambridge: Cambridge University Press, 2021), pp. 11–14 <https://doi.org/10.1017/9781108906463>.

computational process and produce work that is indistinguishable (by humans) from those created by a human imagination. But the success or failure of computer writing sits on a spectrum of evaluation. Computers can write badly (as can people) or they can strive to pass Turing tests (and people can even fail such tests). Nonetheless, in both cases, the computer is 'writing'. It could even be the case that a computer could pass a Turing test *by* writing badly. After all, many people write badly.

This in-built quest for computerized human mimicry can be seen in many works of contemporary electronic literature, such as Johannes Heldén and Håkan Jonson's *Evolution* (2014). *Evolution*, the winner of the inaugural N. Katherine Hayles Prize, is described by its creators as 'a Java-based AI application that emulates the writing and compositions of poet and artist Johannes Heldén. The application analyzes a database with all published text- and soundwork by the artist and generates a continuously evolving poem that simulates Heldén's style: in vocabulary, the spacing in-between words, syntax, sound'. The artwork, we are told, has 'the ultimate goal of passing "The Imitation Game Test" as proposed by Alan Turing in 1951' and its release 'will mark the end of Johannes Heldén writing poetry books. He has, in a sense, been replaced'.[61] Thus, the final biological aspiration of this computational work is integral to its titular Darwinian resonance and it also follows the narrative of authors being replaced by machines. We are left in no doubt that *Evolution* seeks to be the fittest and to out-survive its human progenitors.

Evolution also aspires to a type of print bookishness, a material textuality in a digital space. For while *Evolution* is not called a 'book' by its creators (it is referred to as an 'application' and an 'online artwork-in-progress'), it has been assigned an ISBN and further appears in an extremely limited print form.[62] The web page itself on which the software is displayed is styled in the guise of a codex that even incorporates a page-staining effect (or a de-generation: see Figure 1.2).

By way of compositional analysis, *Evolution*'s codebase consists of two components: a front-facing HTML and JavaScript library that

---

[61] Johannes Heldén and Håkan Jonson, 'Evolution', 2014 <http://www.textevolution.net/> [accessed 15 April 2016].

[62] Johannes Heldén and Håkan Jonson, *Evolution* (OEI editör, 2014).

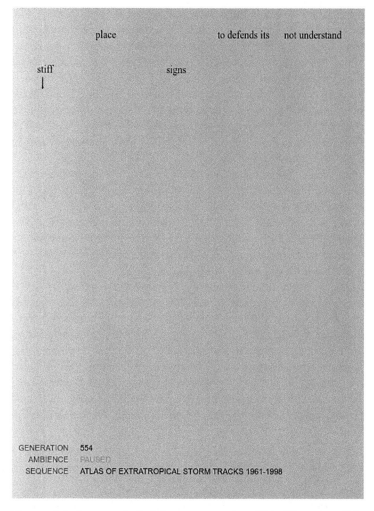

Figure 1.2 A run of *Evolution* at generation 554. Note the slight discolouration/page-staining and crease effect that runs from left to right across the page in a gradated fashion. By permission of the author. This image is not covered by the terms of the Creative Commons License of this publication. For permission to reuse, please contact the rights holder.

controls the playback and a back-end server-based component. The front end fetches a set of formatting and music playback instructions from the server. The server returns information about 100 'generations' at a time and is accessed by the JavaScript client at locations on the Amazon Elastic Compute Cloud. Each set of generations is grouped under a string of text that serves as a 'sequence' identifier for random seed data, ranging from 'cups of coffee per episode of twin peaks' through to 'atlas of extratropical storm tracks (1961–1998)'. A generation itself is composed of a set of instructions encoded in a JSON data format: for example, '{"word":"night","age":2577, "index":9,"delta":false}'.[63] These instructions are created by a server-side application that deploys an evolutionary algorithmic strategy for stochastic text selection—another reason for the piece's name—based on the work of Andrei Markov and Ingo Rechenberg and selected by 'a semi-deterministic random seed [...] derived from atmospheric data, visual imagery, space observations and popular culture'.[64] Or, at least, that is what the authors claim.

Evolution is, in some ways, just the latest version of a form that overlaps with concrete poetry and that Bronač Ferran, following Haroldo de Campos, has dubbed 'typoetical', emanating from the print-publisher networks of Hansjörg Mayer, Max Bense, and Dieter Roth among others over the past six decades.[65] (The term 'evolution' also appears in the 'Pilot Plan for Concrete Poetry', defining the mode as the 'product of a critical evolution of forms', surely an inspiration for *Evolution*.[66]) This form incorporates iterative process, overlay, and spatial layout, strongly resonating with various algorithmic Oulipo techniques.

---

[63] JSON is the JavaScript Object Notation format. It encodes pairs of values in a key:value dictionary. For instance {"Firstname": "Martin"} is the way that JSON would store the value Martin under the key Firstname.

[64] Heldén and Jonson, *Evolution*, pt. appendix 10. Stochastic processes (that is, random events) are simulated in computational environments using one-time seed values, usually derived from a combination of the current time and various mathematical representations of hardware.

[65] See Bronač Ferran, *The Smell of Ink and Soil: The Story of (Edition) Hansjörg Mayer* (Cologne: Walther Koenig, 2017).

[66] Augusto de Campos, Decio Pignatari, and Harold de Campos, 'Pilot Plan for Concrete Poetry', in *Concrete Poetry: A World View*, ed. Mary Ellen Solt (Bloomington, IN: Indiana University Press, 1968), pp. 71–2 (p. 71).

This model has also been called 'kinetic poetry' by Christopher Funkhouser, a mode in which 'images can be a mélange of fragments of words complemented or replaced by imagistic forms'.[67]

Let us be clear, though: *Evolution* will not pass a Turing test any time soon. In fact, *Evolution* is not even going to pass itself off as a substitute for Heldén's own poetry. While it may be true that its computational processes result in an *ur*-version of Heldén's poetics, this *ur*-text lacks the specificity and coherence of his earlier work, as in the 2013 *Terraforming*. For even radical poetry is rarely stochastic. *Evolution* represents, then, an abstraction of the mathematics of language, but its techniques do not countenance linguistic sense in the way that Heldén does when he writes. *Evolution* may yield a syntactically rich but semantically empty mathematical average of Heldén's poetry, his layout, and his musical or poetic essence. However, it also points, I argue, to a set of infrastructures and labours that are its own conditions of possibility.

Before turning back to this core of my argument, I want to move to a second example at the forefront of human language emulation: character-based recurrent neural networks (RNNs). RNNs are software simulations of biological neurons, in which many small processing units are passed the output from other 'neurons', all of which have a memory of input that they have processed before and which they use to modify their output. In short, the machine adapts by passing output from its different processing units as input back into itself. Character-based RNNs take text as input and build a statistical matrix of the most likely next character in any sequence. Unlike teaching a human to read or write, this approach does not focus on words but rather on single characters and their statistical likelihood of occurring in any sequence run. Also, unlike teaching a human, character-based RNNs that are not run on high-performance computing hardware have only a limited number of neurons, somewhat more akin to the capacity of a nematode worm than a person.

[67] Christopher Funkhouser, 'Digital Poetry', in *A Companion to Digital Literary Studies*, ed. Ray Siemens and Susan Schreibman, Blackwell Companions to Literature and Culture (New York: Wiley-Blackwell, 2013), pp. 318–35 (p. 322).

How well can a worm write when it is taught to predict characters?[68] Over a 24-hour period, I trained a torch-RNN model using the entire corpus (until 2016) of the literary studies journal *Textual Practice* and then sampled 5,000-character chunks from its saved checkpoints.[69] The machine learned to produce text that certainly feels emblematic of the journal and that might unnerve others in its uncanny proximity to Alan Sokal's 1996 *faux*-pomo prose ('*faux*-mo', perhaps?).[70] It told me that 'the series of temporal inventions of the object is intelligible only afterwards' but that 'in the early twentieth century, these recognitions are contingent'. In one of its more poetic moments, the network claimed that 'the world was right to have to introduce its choice: that meaning was a palimpsestuous scholarship, the literary moment'.

Without any knowledge of the English language, the network also became proficient at generating bibliographic and footnote items, including 'Slavoj Žižek, *Live Fiction*, trans. Rushdie and Jean-Luc Nancy (London: Bohestock Press, 1994)'; 'John Spottisley, "The Privatized Climax". (1929), p. 4, emphasis in original'; and the instruction to 'see David Pillar, *New Bibliography*, ed. Donald Davis (London: Lawrence & Wishart, 1979)'. The network learned the capitalization structure of English proper nouns, the formatting of references, common names, publishers and date structures, and the likely labour functions of editors and translators. While he is often improbable, my colleague Žižek is, of course, real, although Spottisley's master work has no true author so far as I can determine. This was all achieved simply through probabilistic modelling of the character sequences already present within *Textual Practice*, using fewer processing units than those inside the neural system of a nematode.

Of course, even when it accidentally distils nuggets of truth, the network has no motivation towards communication and no

---

[68] For a more detailed performance exploration, see Cedric De Boom et al., 'Efficiency Evaluation of Character-Level RNN Training Schedules', *ArXiv*, 1605.02486, 2016 <http://arxiv.org/abs/1605.02486> [accessed 17 April 2017].

[69] For this process, I used Justin Johnson, *torn-rnn*, 2016 <https://github.com/jcjohnson/torch-rnn> [accessed 17 April 2017].

[70] See Alan Sokal, *Beyond the Hoax: Science, Philosophy and Culture* (Oxford: Oxford University Press, 2009).

epistemological goal except to achieve ever-more perfection in its stylistic mimicry of the articles in *Textual Practice*. (Of course, one could also ask whether any computing system can be said to have 'motivation'.) As it noted in one of my samplings, in a remark that could apply well to itself, 'I shall find our intellectual values, by rewriting their very ties'. For the machine is one of pure textual practice; even while it knows to include footnotes, its references are dead ends and subversions of traditional academic epistemologies.[71] They 'provide the fraud of the epistemological practices of knowledge'; another generation of the network. Taken together with the *faux* aesthetics of *Evolution*, these two models of linguistic aping contain within them contradictory logics of artificial intelligence that continually point to social labour. 'The problem', as the network aptly phrased it, 'is that the poem is a construction of the self as a strategy of self-consciousness and context'. As Leah Henrickson has put it, communicating with meaning 'requires awareness of the self, and of the self in relation to surrounding circumstances. NLG systems cannot (yet) be said to possess such awareness, but many have *appeared* to'.[72]

The RNN that I trained in 2016 was an extremely basic example of technology that has since escalated to a frightening level. Since then, the size of the language models produced by large corporations such as Google, including BERT, GPT-2, T-NLG, GPT-3, and Switch-C, has spiralled out of control. In just a few short years, the models' size went from BERT's 16GB up to Switch-C's enormous 745GB, with an increase in parameter size from $3.4\mathrm{E}{+}08$ to $1.57\mathrm{E}{+}12$.[73] Even if those numbers mean very little to you in absolute terms, they can be summarized with ease: language models are growing at an exponential rate. This, in turn, means that the ability of such models to generate plausible imitations of human language is increasing dramatically.

---

[71] See Anthony Grafton, *The Footnote: A Curious History* (Cambridge, MA: Harvard University Press, 1999).

[72] Henrickson, p. 15.

[73] Emily M. Bender and others, 'On the Dangers of Stochastic Parrots: Can Language Models Be Too Big? 🦜', in *Proceedings of the* 2021 *ACM Conference on Fairness, Accountability, and Transparency* (presented at the FAccT '21: 2021 ACM Conference on Fairness, Accountability, and Transparency, Virtual Event Canada: ACM, 2021), pp. 610–23 (p. 2) <https://doi.org/10.1145/3442188.3445922>.

The ethics of such language models are complicated for several reasons. First, they require an enormous amount of energy (and associated carbon output) to train. It has been claimed that 'training a single BERT base model [...] was estimated to require as much energy as a trans-American flight'.[74] Second, the training data do not necessarily represent an entirely representative cross-section of the population. Indeed, as the relatively well-known article, 'On the Dangers of Stochastic Parrots: Can Language Models Be Too Big? 🦜', notes, large language models exclude many voices from marginalized identities and replicate biases against such figures that are present in the underlying dataset.[75] That is to say that if the underlying source on which these language models are trained contains racial slurs and biases against different groups (i.e. is racist), the resultant language model will learn those traits. Such models lead to a situation in which 'the mix of human biases and seemingly coherent language heightens the potential for automation bias, deliberate misuse, and amplification of a hegemonic worldview'.[76]

This ethical problem of racism in computational models extends far beyond these language models as natural language generating curiosities. These models are, in fact, now embedded in our everyday routines at major search engines. Yet despite the enormous gains in the past two decades in information retrieval, it is a mistake to believe that we now have an objective and neutral way to discover material amid the massive decentralized network of the World Wide Web. Instead, as Safiya Umoja Noble shows, algorithmic bias is just as prone to replicate extant, damaging social trends as any previous cataloguing system—and natural language models are part of this problem. However, as Noble also demonstrates, the dangers in the digital realm are perhaps greater because authority can be spread between multiple (sometimes malicious) actors. There is also an unfounded belief that, somehow, this delegation constitutes an immutably acceptable and neutral objectivity with which we cannot interfere.

---

[74] Bender et al., p. 3.

[75] Although, for a critique of this, see Yoav Goldberg, 'A Criticism of Stochastic Parrots', 2021 <https://gist.github.com/yoavg/9fc9be2f98b47c189a513573d902fb27> [accessed 31 March 2021].

[76] Bender et al., p. 7.

Indeed, in a particularly striking chapter of her *Algorithms of Oppression: How Search Engines Reinforce Racism*, Noble points to how racialized search terms such as 'black girls' and 'white girls' return pornographic results and wholesome stock images, respectively.[77] This problematic situation also extends to 'professional' vs. 'unprofessional' hairstyles returning extremely racialized results.[78]

How is this possible? Google and other search engines use a system of link weighting that essentially assigns value and keywords to a site based on which other sites link to it using that term. This means that, with enough resources, one can effectively manipulate Google results in a practice known as Googlewashing or Google Bombing.[79] There are various controls in place to ensure that such malicious manipulation is difficult: established sites that, themselves, have a higher rating are given more of a 'vote' in determining whether another site will rate highly for a particular keyword. Google argues that, using such an algorithm, its search results 'organically' mirror the structure of the web that it seeks to crawl. In Google's view, it seems, discoverability should be technologically premised on holding a mere mirror to what others have determined is important on their terms.

Such a stance is deeply troubling. It is even more so when one examines Noble's statistics from a 2012 Pew study on search engine use. For example, 59 per cent of Americans report using a search engine every day and 83 per cent of search engine users use Google. Even more worryingly, though, 73 per cent of search engine users believe that 'most or all the information they find as they use search engines is accurate and trustworthy'. Further, of the daily users, 66 per cent said that 'search engines are a fair and unbiased source of information'.[80] This all paints an alarming picture where most people use a search engine daily, believing the information they find to be a fair and unbiased set of results. At the same time, Google argues that

[77] Safiya Umoja Noble, *Algorithms of Oppression: How Search Engines Reinforce Racism* (New York: New York University Press, 2018), pp. 64–109.

[78] Noble, p. 83.

[79] Tom Zeller, Jr, 'A New Campaign Tactic: Manipulating Google Data', *The New York Times*, 26 October 2006, section U.S. <https://www.nytimes.com/2006/10/26/us/politics/26googlebomb.html> [accessed 14 April 2020].

[80] Noble, pp. 53–4.

its results are indeed fair and unbiased in one sense: that they reflect the web. But this does not mean that the results returned are fair and unbiased in another: they can be racist, sexist, homophobic, ableist, and discriminatory along many other axes.

Search engines have argued for years that they should not 'interfere' with the 'organic' rankings that their (synthetic) algorithms produced. It is also worth noting that this problem is not confined wholly to search engines in the digital age. Our existing library cataloguing systems are often premised on decisions that reflect the personal and political biases of those who designed them. Take for instance the recent protests at Dartmouth College about the US Library of Congress classification of 'illegal aliens', as opposed to say, 'undocumented immigrants'.[81] Such language mirrors the legal systems of the time and reflects this upon the individuals catalogued as such for a protracted period into the future.[82]

Indeed, library catalogue entries require anti-racist intervention if they are to classify people.[83] Noble argues that the same is true of search engines, which 'might want, at minimum, to do something like a "disclaimer" and, at maximum, to produce a permanent "technical fix" to the proliferation of racist or sexist content'.[84] After all, companies such as Google have vast levels of revenue and profit that they could turn towards a solution to this problem. However, they do not. As a result, for Noble, the question is whether 'search engines such as Google should be regulated over the values they assign to racial, gendered, and sexual identities, as evidenced by the types of results that are retrieved'.[85]

Ultimately, Noble's study is valuable for highlighting that the social, not the technical, must be critically addressed if we are to rectify the

[81] Noble, p. 134; Lisa Peet, 'Library of Congress Drops Illegal Alien Subject Heading, Provokes Backlash Legislation', *Library Journal*, 2016 <https://www.library-journal.com?detailStory=library-of-congress-drops-illegal-alien-subject-heading-provokes-backlash-legislation> [accessed 15 April 2020].

[82] Hope A. Olson, 'Mapping Beyond Dewey's Boundaries: Constructing Classificatory Space for Marginalized Knowledge Domains', *Library Trends*, 47.2 (1998), 233–54.

[83] Sanford Berman, *Prejudices and Antipathies: A Tract on the LC Subject Heads Concerning People* (Jefferson, NC: McFarland and Co., 2014).

[84] Noble, p. 155.   [85] Noble, p. 158.

finding aids through which material is located in the digital era—of massive relevance for digital literary studies. 'An app', she writes, 'will not save us'.[86] The same is true of digital humanities practices in literary studies. Without critical and reflexive thought, these methods are doomed as any other to appropriation and triviality. However, the point I have been making throughout this book is that there are plenty of people who *have already been* working in such a mode of critical digital humanities. It is not as though a brand of technocrat simply arose and attempted to appropriate the humanities' and literary studies' objects of study (if these were even well defined in the first place). Humanities computing and its eventual successor term, digital humanities, have long had critical thought at their core as they study digital objects or use digital methods to study objects that may even be not.

To return to the natural language generators that sparked this ethical reflection, though: GPT-3 is, nonetheless, alarmingly good. Its outputs are virtually indistinguishable from high-quality human-authored text. Yet, at the same time, as Robert Dale notes, its 'outputs may lack semantic coherence, resulting in text that is gibberish and increasingly nonsensical as the output grows longer'; they 'embody all the biases that might be found in its training data' and these outputs 'may correspond to assertions that are not consonant with the truth'.[87] The implications of such an achievement are, nonetheless, extensive. Although GPT-3 is not yet able to do this, were a computer able to produce extended and plausible responses to stimulus prompts, how soon would it be before, say, the essay form was no longer a suitable mode of assessment in school and other educational environments?[88] How long will it be before the art of writing is so computationally assisted that it becomes a lost skill for people themselves? And does that even matter? 'GPT-3 anxiety', writes Carlos Montemayor, 'is based on the possibility that what separates us from other species and what we think of as the pinnacle of human intelligence, namely our

[86] Noble, p. 165.

[87] Robert Dale, 'GPT-3: What's It Good For?', *Natural Language Engineering*, 27.1 (2021), 113–18 <https://doi.org/10.1017/S1351324920000601>.

[88] Katherine Elkins and Jon Chun, 'Can GPT-3 Pass a Writer's Turing Test?', *Journal of Cultural Analytics*, 2020, 17212 <https://doi.org/10.22148/001c.17212>.

linguistic capacities, could in principle be found in machines, which we consider to be inferior to animals'.[89]

Textual Practice as Social Undertaking

Digital literary aesthetics assume the presence of human readers encountering works of literature. We could also imagine, though, creative outputs designed solely *for* other computational systems, much like in the intermediate feedback stage of directed cycle neural networks. That said, the existence of digital artworks presupposes, as Alan Liu put it, 'a scene of encounters'.[90] Indeed, the dynamic temporal inventions of the machine are intelligible only afterwards to a human reader. Yet where is the line in textual creation between the machine as tool and the machine as author? For 'computers have long been employed', notes Leah Henrickson, 'as tools for creating textual artefacts'.[91]

As of 2021 we have already witnessed the rise of computer-generated business and sports journalism.[92] The formalized, highly generic prose style of this work lends itself to repetitious statistical natural language generation. (There is in itself an article to be written about the evolution of the term 'natural language generator' as opposed to 'artificial neural network' and the ongoing erosion of this artificial/natural binary.) Small-scale studies have even demonstrated that human audiences cannot discriminate between this machine-written prose and articles written by people.[93] In this case statistical

[89] Carlos Montemayor, 'Language and Intelligence', *Daily Nous*, 2020 <https://dailynous.com/2020/07/30/philosophers-gpt-3/> [accessed 31 March 2021].

[90] Alan Liu, 'Imagining the New Media Encounter', in *A Companion to Digital Literary Studies*, ed. Ray Siemens and Susan Schreibman, Blackwell Companions to Literature and Culture (New York: Wiley-Blackwell, 2013), pp. 3–26 (p. 3).

[91] Henrickson, p. 42.

[92] Tim Adams, 'And the Pulitzer Goes To... a Computer', *The Guardian*, 28 June 2015, section Technology <https://www.theguardian.com/technology/2015/jun/28/computer-writing-journalism-artificial-intelligence> [accessed 15 April 2017].

[93] Christer Clerwall, 'Enter the Robot Journalist: Users' Perceptions of Automated Content', *Journalism Practice*, 8.5 (2014), 519–31 <https://doi.org/10.1080/17512786.2014.883116>.

reporting on the stock market and soccer games can be automatically churned out for mass consumption.

Admittedly, something is alarming in such a trend; it feels connected to a decentring of the human in written language production. Yet companies such as 'Narrative Science'—corporate specialists in this field—claim that their job lies in 'humanizing data like never before, with technology that interprets your data', and that 'then transforms it into Intelligent Narratives at unprecedented speed and scale'. That is, the organization paradoxically seeks to humanize through a chiastic mode of mechanization. Their software also, clearly, requires human calibration and operation.

The profusion of the concept of 'narrative' beyond the walls of academic literary criticism—and as nothing less than an apparent 'science'—is alarming. It undoubtedly cedes what literary critics and journalists, among other groups, have known for many years: that narrative possesses a power worthy of study. In its corporate excess and buzz-speak, this movement also gestures towards the large-scale population-manipulation through narrative that is a feature of most contemporary news media and that undoubtedly played a role in the ascent of democratically elected neo-authoritarians around 2016.[94] At the same time, though, in its utilitarian mobilization through companies such as Narrative Science, there are other worrying aspects to this growth of computational narrative. These anxieties can be grouped under two headings: first, as a means of eradicating or re-situating authorial labour through mechanization; and second, in its dividing naturalization of a realm of scientific data, that apparently sit apart from narrative (as though scientific hermeneutics were not, themselves, an interpretation and narrativization), opposed to a 'humanized', narrative version of those data.

However, on this second point, we might also ask what the difference is between such a piece of guided 'helper' software and the existing systems of word processing that are in broad circulation. Is the use of an automated spellchecker a machine writing? It certainly changes

---

[94] For more on this, see John Holmwood, 'Open Access, "Publicity", and Democratic Knowledge', in *Reassembling Scholarly Communications: Histories, Infrastructures, and Global Politics of Open Access*, ed. Martin Paul Eve and Jonathan Gray (Cambridge, MA: MIT Press, 2020), pp. 181–91.

the word that an author may have typed. What about a thesaurus that suggests wholly different words? Grammatical checking that alters sentence structure? My word processor, LibreOffice Writer, even provides automatic completions for words based on the characters that I begin to type, conditioning future possibilities through suggestion. As William Winder has put it, 'formatters, spell checkers, thesauri, grammar checkers, and personal printers support our writing almost silently'.[95] 'Almost'. For Winder, the question comes down to whether computers are 'typists or writers' in our use of such prostheses.[96] Or, put otherwise: is the Great Automatic Grammatizator different by type or degree from other forms of writing aid? In Henrickson's view, certainly some 'NLG systems may be regarded as fitting comfortably within the lineage of writing tools'. However, as she notes, in 'other systems, particularly those wherein the embodied figure is obscured, the distinction between tool and agent is not so clear'.[97] While publishing has, for many decades, been dependent on computational technologies, we can certainly find, as Donna Haraway put it many years ago, that 'our machines are disturbingly lively, and we ourselves frighteningly inert'.[98]

Evolution implies, by its very title and mission statement, that its efforts are in competition with human writers and are on the same plane.[99] As a survival of the fittest comes into play, the piece proclaims, the human author will stop writing poetry and the machine will take over; a process of unnatural selection or 'uncreative writing', to quote Kenneth Goldsmith.[100] Likewise, injecting structural flow components into the decision-making portions of RNNs would allow argumentative progression, overcoming many of the claimed objections about

[95] William Winder, 'Writing Machines', in *A Companion to Digital Literary Studies*, ed. Ray Siemens and Susan Schreibman, Blackwell Companions to Literature and Culture (New York: Wiley-Blackwell, 2013), pp. 492–516 (p. 492).

[96] Winder, p. 493.　　　　[97] Henrickson, pp. 49–50.

[98] R. Lyle Skains, *Digital Authorship: Publishing in the Attention Economy* (Cambridge: Cambridge University Press, 2019), pp. 17–18; Haraway, p. 152.

[99] In a similar way that, as I have argued elsewhere, authors and critics compete for cultural authority. Martin Paul Eve, *Literature Against Criticism: University English and Contemporary Fiction in Conflict* (Cambridge: Open Book Publishers, 2016).

[100] Kenneth Goldsmith, *Uncreative Writing* (New York: Columbia University Press, 2011).

computational mastery of narrative form. Yet, by their respective modelling on the works of Heldén and by their directed cyclical structures for training, these models of language and aesthetics are inherently conservative. Of course, even in human writing there is an interplay between the individual talent (a progressive randomness and invention) and traditions (a conservatism and fallback to a model of existing work). It is also frequently argued that there is nothing new under the sun and that all writing is a working through of a grand set of master narratives, an almost Kabbalistic approach to permuting the name of God. This inward-looking approach to language generation by people is, further, clearly reflected in my neural network's accidental pronouncement that the poem is a construction of the self as a strategy of self-consciousness and context. The self that it uses, in this case, is an aggregate of human selves. Whether or not it has such a self-consciousness, though, is a different matter. However, the absolute history of computer writing rests upon this human writing and labour. Were the human race to die out but the machines to keep on writing, they would continue to produce ever-more conservative texts, training themselves upon their own regurgitated outputs with only semi-deterministic random seeds to aid progress and foster change.

Of course, were the human race to die out and the machines to continue writing, this would be a remarkable occurrence. This is because of the vast infrastructures that underpin our technologies and the substantial volumes of labour necessary for their perpetuation. *Evolution* gestures towards this challenge of digital preservation in a post-human (in the sense of 'after human') era. Its 'pages' are stained as though the digital fabric has been damaged by light exposure, thereby calling attention to the enormous global technologies of preservation that we have constructed to retain print: libraries.[101] However, because this aspect sits within a digital framework, it also calls attention to digital preservation matters.

Digital preservation is a good space within which to examine such issues of labour since it is dogged by a series of challenges that are, at core, all social rather than technical. Given infinite resources it would be possible to preserve most digital artefacts produced today. However,

[101] For more on this, see Kathleen Fitzpatrick, *Planned Obsolescence: Publishing, Technology, and the Future of the Academy* (New York: New York University Press, 2011).

we are not given infinite resources. There is a scarcity of remuneration available within our systems of economic exchange that itself causes a cascade of other problems. For instance, if we cannot preserve everything because we have insufficient resources, how do we decide where to invest our preservation efforts, given that our abilities to forecast value fare extremely poorly under experimental conditions?[102] This is exemplary of the core difficulty of scarcity against abundance in the digital space. The ability to copy infinitely leads to the belief that virtual environments are ripe for proliferation, be that in file formats or volume of material. Yet without underlying remuneration for human labour, there is a problem in the long-term retention and ability to access or execute arbitrary binary data.

Works such as *Evolution* gesture towards this problem. On the one hand, *Evolution* is an artwork about proliferation, as is the natural language generation of the RNN. Both programs promise ever-evolving sets of textual permutations, offering an abundance of inscription. On the other hand, both programs also rest upon vast quantities of computer scientific research. Moreover, they both require infrastructures of material production to manufacture silicon chips, run power facilities, educate their operators, debug their software, and so on. *Evolution*'s infrastructure even requires Amazon's hosting facilities for its server components. That is, it relies upon what is both the greatest 'virtualizer' but also the most miraculous materializer that the world has seen in recent years. With the click of a virtual button at Amazon, it seems, objects appear in the mailbox. Yet we also know that Amazon works only by drawing upon vast reservoirs of poorly paid warehouse staff and by pricing its artefacts as cheaply as possible to achieve market domination even while not turning a profit for many years. In other words, a material scarcity underpins such infrastructures. This dichotomy is also apparent in the structure of *Evolution*. For the work's algorithms run not on text alone but on text and whitespace, on abundance and scarcity.[103]

---

[102] See Moore et al.

[103] For more on this, see Martin Paul Eve, 'Scarcity and Abundance', in *The Bloomsbury Handbook of Electronic Literature*, ed. Joseph Tabbi (London: Bloomsbury, 2017), pp. 385–98.

Indeed, *Evolution* samples not only the words of the poet that it is meant to replace, but also the blanks. Like music, which always includes *silence* with sound, *Evolution* continually points towards the importance of emptiness. In fact, the blankness and space—that is, of course, not truly blank, but actually a falsely stained 'page', thereby drawing attention to its own quasi-absence—that sit behind the text are metaphorically indicative of the very problem that I am attempting to draw out. Even while the space of computational writing is seen as one of proliferation ('computers can write!') it remains bound to a scarcity—a blankness in recognition—of labour forms that underwrite its possibilities. The print volume of *Evolution* pushes this even further, oscillating between black background and white foreground for computer code against 'human' exegesis with a white background and black text (the data component of *Evolution*'s print book is presented with a white background and black foreground). Even this binary reduction to a black-and-white print format contains within it the seeds of a material critique: that print economics can determine, shape, and limit the contrasts of form that are available to poets, be they computational or human.

That we continue to refer to computer poetry and literature as lacking an author seems, therefore, somewhat strange. Many labour forms were as integral to its creation as the above-listed labours will be to its preservation. Yet at what point between the spellchecker and the RNN does the author disappear? The question cannot be boiled down to a percentage of the labour involved; it is conceivable that a text could be written in which the spellchecker was used to correct every single term—or even a digital thesaurus was used to replace every word—but still we would not give a byline to the authors of those software. There are also historical precedents for this division between the labour of manufacturing the tool instead of the output. Thoreau, certainly, did not fully credit his own family's pencil-making industry in the authorship of *Walden*. Yet the pencil is an 'advanced technology' of cyborg writing.[104]

Academic publishing has also encountered the dilemma of representing labour, even while efforts continue to use computers to mine

---

[104] See Dennis E. Baron, *A Better Pencil: Readers, Writers, and the Digital Revolution* (Oxford: Oxford University Press, 2009), p. 34.

papers at high volume ('distant-reading', to which I will turn more in the final chapter).[105] High-energy physics experiments such as those conducted at the Large Hadron Collider or the Laser Interferometer Gravitational-Wave Observatory require diverse types of labour forms in order to conduct their work. However, since academic systems of hiring, promotion, and tenure are geared towards authorship of research outputs as their primary measure, we arrive at the somewhat curious state of papers with over 5,000 authors, as in the case of the recent Higgs Boson experiment, credited to G. Aad et al. (where listing the 'et al.' consumes 24 pages of the article's 33-page total).[106]

What is further remarkable about the increasing accomplishments of computational writing prostheses is that their success at imitating human writing leads to an imagination of a post-anthropocentric era. There is a temporality of 'afterwardness' inherent in computational natural language processing and generation. That is, in achieving mimesis of human writing—remember, a measure of intelligence formed only by anthropocentric reference to the human—computational writing asks us to imagine a world in which there are no more humans undertaking such labour. Such thinking only emerges, though, in the imagined substitution of the human with human-like automata. This imagined 'afterwards' is both a post-anthropocentric world for writers and a world in which a writing machine legitimated by human-like characteristics is inscribed at the centre. It is concurrently an imagined world in which we have no benchmark of contemporary writing success but one that is nonetheless dominated by machines that meet that nostalgic target.

What, then, of the Great Automatic Grammatizator? Have our hands already crept to the other side of the desk, seeking to avoid the starvation of our children? Can you identify which portions of this chapter should be attributed to me and which portions to the artificial neural network and, hence, to the software authors in some mediated

---

[105] Martin Paul Eve, 'Reading Scholarship Digitally', in *Reassembling Scholarly Communications: Histories, Infrastructures, and Global Politics of Open Access*, ed. Martin Paul Eve and Jonathan Gray (Cambridge, MA: MIT Press, 2020), pp. 277–84.

[106] G. Aad et al., 'Combined Measurement of the Higgs Boson Mass in p p Collisions at s = 7 and 8 TeV with the ATLAS and CMS Experiments', *Physical Review Letters*, 114.19 (2015) <https://doi.org/10.1103/PhysRevLett.114.191803>.

sense? The words from the network do not all appear in quotation marks. Or should we instead be more concerned that we seem unwilling to represent the vast quantities of human labour that have already been invested in creating our technological writing prostheses? Ever more frequently, vast volumes of computational labour—programming, infrastructure, and communications labours—underpin our social textual production. As we do not credit them now, I would like to ask what meagre credit our authorial inputs can expect once the literary market has fallen under Knipe's malign influence?

*

In this chapter, I have addressed how computational approaches to literary study have grappled with authorship, authorial theory, style and its measurement, and the challenging circumstances for future work on the role of writers in the age of natural-language generation. I have also tried to emphasize a core tenet of this book throughout this chapter, though. Namely, digital practices are not those that produce seemingly objective data that could replace narrative and argument. Instead, interpretation and hermeneutics remain central.

However, a notable feature that some readers may already have noticed is that this chapter has featured visualizations, diagrams, and figures. It is probably fair to say that these feature more frequently in digital humanities work than in 'traditional' literary theory. The subject of why this is and what such diagrammatic constructs add to our understanding of literature are the topics to which the next chapter is devoted.

2

Space and Visualization

Literary criticism is, in many ways, the art of telling stories about stories. Using textual evidence, convincing critics weave alternative narratives around texts that re-contextualize them forever, making it impossible to re-read a work in the same way again. Thus, criticism is a performance of a new narrative and a deformation of the original, now-reshaped text. Literary criticism routinely undertakes, then, what Lisa Samuels and Jerome McGann call 'deformance'.[1]

Philosophy and literary criticism have also turned to non-textual media in their quests for deforming explication. Wittgenstein, for instance, is famed for his use of images alongside text, deployed to undermine so-called 'common sense' principles by 'speaking' across two different registers simultaneously.[2] Indeed, Wittgenstein uses images in such a way as to call into question their alleged perspicacity. 'You only need to look at the figure to see', he begins, only to undermine this by saying that he 'only need to look at the figure to see'... something different. Visualization and figures, despite their surface obviousness, betray complex and subjectively rooted interpretative processes. Pictures are alternative, supplementary, or even contradictory narratives that sit in difficult parataxis with the thousand words they paint. As David Staley has noted, visualizations can be used for 'the organization of meaningful information in two- or

[1] Samuels and McGann.

[2] For just one example, see Ludwig Wittgenstein, *Remarks on the Foundations of Mathematics*, 3rd edn. (Oxford: Blackwell, 1978), p. 52.

three-dimensional spatial form intended to further a systematic inquiry' or treated as a 'supplement or illustration' to the text.[3]

Most frequently, images are used for expository purposes. Robert Darnton, for instance, famously illustrated the communications circuit of publishing in his landmark 1982 essay 'What Is the History of Books?'[4] Indeed, this particular diagram has become so well known that as of 2020 there is even a 'Robot Darnton' Twitter bot that regularly produces parody versions of the image.[5] Another notable example would be Kurt Vonnegut's rejected Master's thesis at the University of Chicago, which charted the outline shapes of novelistic plots using graphs.[6] As just another demonstration, several works have attempted to plot the structures of James Joyce's *Finnegans Wake* and *Ulysses*.[7]

Images, then, have a long pedigree in literary studies, even when the majority of an argument remains centred on text. Yet, these illustrations are usually different to the diagrams found in works that bill themselves as 'digital humanities' projects.[8] The difference, of course, between much—although not all—literary criticism and DH is the quantification in the latter. Specifically, there are many visualizations in digital literary studies because humans are poor at comprehending multi-dimensional feature-sets in anything except two and three dimensions, to which our perceptions are limited. We are not good, as a species, at pattern recognition—as William Gibson might

[3] David J. Staley, *Computers, Visualization, and History: How New Technology Will Transform Our Understanding of the Past*, History, Humanities, and New Technology (Armonk, NY: Sharpe, 2003), p. 9.

[4] Robert Darnton, 'What Is the History of Books?', *Daedalus*, 111.3 (1982), 65–83 (p. 68).

[5] See, for instance, Robot Darnton, 'Book Historians Should Consider the Role of Airline Pilots in the Book Trade', *@RobotDarnton*, 2018 <https://twitter.com/RobotDarnton/status/1072470428755607552> [accessed 11 December 2018].

[6] Kurt Vonnegut, *Palm Sunday: An Autobiographical Collage* (New York: Random House Publishing Group, 2009), p. 288.

[7] For just one well-known instance, see László Moholy-Nagy, *Vision in Motion* (Chicago, IL: P. Theobald, 1947), pp. 345–50.

[8] Even if, as Erik Champion has recently claimed, DH remains 'visualization light'. Erik Malcolm Champion, 'Digital Humanities Is Text Heavy, Visualization Light, and Simulation Poor', *Digital Scholarship in the Humanities*, 32.suppl_1 (2017), i25–32 <https://doi.org/10.1093/llc/fqw053>.

have it—at scale. Graphs, maps, and trees—the three titular elements of Franco Moretti's work on the subject—are each ways of spatializing numerical data (be they time-series information, geospatial data, or lineages) in order to render them comprehensible or legible, even while such representations are also necessarily a 'condensed or reduced representation'.[9] As such, 'visualization now becomes a means', write Evelyn Ruppert, John Law, and Mike Savave, 'of showing how "excessive" information can be reduced to a form in which it can be meaningfully, if partially, rendered for interpretation'.[10] As Johanna Drucker puts it, in the fact that they must select what and decide how to present these data, 'most information visualizations are acts of interpretation masquerading as presentation'.[11]

In this chapter, I turn to the importance of visualization but also to its challenges. In their reductive mapping of complex phenomena onto flattened plains or isomorphic grids, visualizations can present themselves as unassailable, as though their very presence demonstrated the facts. Graphs can appear as self-evident 'raw data'. Yet, as we know, 'raw data' do not exist. Following the remarks in Chapter 1 on negative results, this chapter tackles ideas of replication, data, and verification of the claims made by digital and quantitative scholarship.

The Treachery of Images

In literary studies, the age-old divide between formalism and thematics, between knowledge and sensibility, as Seth Lerer has it, continues to carve a rift in various critical practices.[12] What is the relationship, as the adage goes, between words and things? How do we understand how language clusters around concepts, conjuring mental images and

[9] Bernhard Rieder and Theo Röhle, 'Digital Methods: Five Challenges', in *Understanding Digital Humanities*, ed. David M. Berry (Basingstoke: Palgrave Macmillan, 2012), pp. 67–84 (p. 73) <https://doi.org/10.1057/9780230371934_4>.

[10] Evelyn Ruppert, John Law, and Mike Savage, 'Reassembling Social Science Methods: The Challenge of Digital Devices', *Theory, Culture & Society*, 30.4 (2013), 22–46 (p. 36) <https://doi.org/10.1177/0263276413484941>.

[11] Johanna Drucker, *Graphesis: Visual Forms of Knowledge Production* (Cambridge, MA: Harvard University Press, 2014), p. 10.

[12] Seth Lerer, *Tradition: A Feeling for the Literary Past*, The Literary Agenda (Oxford: Oxford University Press, 2016), p. 14.

societal situations for a reader? Well, there are ways in which computational visualization can help us to understand such phenomena.

One individual who has explored this more thoroughly than most is David McClure, now based at the MIT Media Lab and previously the Technical Director of the Stanford Literary Lab. In an experiment on Tolstoy's *War and Peace* (1869), McClure notes that he was interested in how words distribute inside texts. While some words are 'spaced evenly throughout the document, and their distribution doesn't say much about the overall structure of the text', others 'have a really strong semantic focus—they occur unevenly, and they tend to hang together with other words that orbit around a shared topic'.[13] This seems, notes McClure, particularly so of novels that have binary section thematics, such as *War and Peace*: 'if you open to a random page and see words like "Natasha," "Sonya," "mother," "love," or "tender," it's a pretty good bet that you're in a peace-y section. But if you see words like "Napoleon," "war," "military," "general," or "order," it's probably a war section'.

McClure explains in his work that this type of clustering—where words tend to gravitate around a specific point—can be captured in a kernel density estimate metric. Essentially, this is where one measures the frequency with which a term occurs along an x-axis representing a novel's chronological progression. As one moves through the pages of a novel, one measures the frequency with which a term occurs. The 'kernel density estimate' part—as opposed to a simple histogram of frequencies—shows how frequencies grow and decay around a specific point, rather than being an absolute measure.[14] McClure gives the example of how the term 'horse' is distributed in *War and Peace*, shown in Figure 2.1. One can then correlate various kernel density graphs to show whether the co-occurrence was significant, as postulated above and shown in Figures 2.2 and 2.3.

---

[13] David McClure, '(Mental) Maps of Texts', *David McClure*, 2014 <http://dclure.org/essays/mental-maps-of-texts/> [accessed 22 December 2018].

[14] Histogram representations are problematic because the selection of bin size (the width of the bars) can arbitrarily and perniciously affect the interpretation of the results, whereas kernel density bandwidth can give a much clearer outcome, although the choice of kernel also matters.

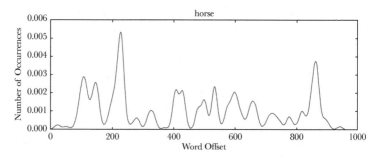

Figure 2.1 Kernel density estimate of 'horse' in *War and Peace*. Image by David McClure (2014) and released under a Creative Commons Attribution License.

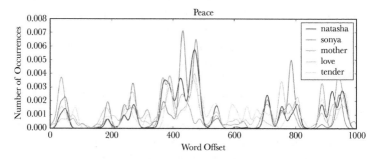

Figure 2.2 Comparative kernel density estimate of 'Natasha', 'Sonya', 'mother', 'love', and 'tender' in *War and Peace*. Image by David McClure (2014) and released under a Creative Commons Attribution License.

While these graphs are a practical and aesthetically pleasing way of mapping collocations of terms across unfolding novel time, McClure has a more interesting structural-textual map that we can produce from these data. From a kernel density estimate, it is possible, McClure notes, to use a range of distance-measuring algorithms to cluster the terms.[15] This means that 'for any given word, you can compute its similarity score with *every other word* in the text, and then sort the results

[15] For a good list of methods, to which McClure also points, see Sung-Hyuk Cha, 'Comprehensive Survey on Distance/Similarity Measures between Probability Density

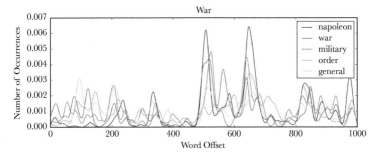

Figure 2.3 Comparative kernel density estimate of 'Napoleon', 'war', 'military', 'order', and 'general' in *War and Peace*. Image by David McClure (2014) and released under a Creative Commons Attribution License.

in descending order to create a kind of "more-like-this" list'.[16] Table 2.1, for instance, shows this function mapped against the term 'Natasha' in the novel.

The best result of this type of distance mapping, though, according to McClure, is that 'it makes it possible to traverse the internal topic structure of the document, instead of just sliding back and forth on the linear axis of words'. This plotting is a type of deformance that, for McClure, '*de-linearizes* the text', which brings the representation 'closer to the form it takes when it's staged in the mind of a reader', shown as a visualized network in Figure 2.4.

What is perhaps most significant about this image is the way that the algorithm manages to cluster portions of the narrative together in terms that make sense for the plot, based on linguistic similitude. As McClure notes, 'war to the left, peace to the right, and history on top', although the precise orientation of one element to another here is not meaningful; it is the clustering that matters. Of course, at present we are in the dangerous digital humanities territory of 'so what?' It is clear to most readers that *War and Peace* is subdivided into portions representing war, sections handling peace, and a meta-historical strand.

Functions', *International Journal of Mathematical Models and Methods in Applied Sciences*, 4.1 (2007), 300–7.

[16] McClure.

Table 2.1 Comparative distance measures against the kernel density estimate of 'Natasha' in *War and Peace*. Data by David McClure (2014) and released under a Creative Commons Attribution License.

Term	Density Similarity Score
Natasha (root)	1.0
Sonya	0.70886263341693823
Countess	0.69992603393549424
Mother	0.69396076158543107
Love	0.69394361206264776
Tender	0.69022062349028213
Family	0.63830887117531232
Marry	0.63600169904982695
Secret	0.6352113995040839
Happy	0.63179263139217623
Girl	0.62577947223072128
Flushed	0.61694787819224595
Rapturous	0.61229277139972438
Sad	0.6121299034400407
Happened	0.60853750169005538
Invited	0.60431370654414285
Parents	0.60292426299430668
Jumped	0.59803596295531403
Realized	0.59801227498210729
Lady	0.596816756054939

First, to reiterate, one of the most important functions that such visualization fulfils is to create a bridge between the formalistic and the thematic. This is about the relationship between language and the things that it represents in a text. Yet, in these computational visualizations, the intra-actions between different lexemes are mapped to create a thematic overview of the text. From the formal parataxis of terminologies, we can see the structural-thematic outline of the novel and how linguistic clustering works to create coherent thematic groupings. This is what I have called a kind of new 'computational formalism'.[17]

---

[17] Eve, *Close Reading With Computers*.

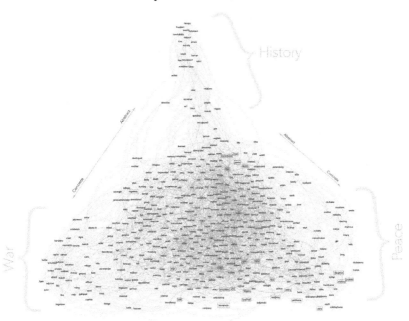

Figure 2.4 Network visualization of kernel density estimates of all terms in *War and Peace*. Image by David McClure (2014) and released under a Creative Commons Attribution License.

Where this method gets more interesting, though, is when it turns up a surprise. In his *War and Peace* diagram, McClure draws to our attention that 'Napoleon' and 'Bonaparte' are some distance from one another, indicating that the terms occur in different contexts. ' "Napoleon" ', McClure notes, 'sits along the top left shoulder of the triangle, along the gradient between "battle" and "history," in the middle of a section related to military strategy and tactics ("military," "plan," "campaign," "men," "group"). Whereas "Bonaparte" is way down at the bottom of the triangle, almost exactly in the middle of the gradient running between war and peace, just shy of a cluster of words related to the aristocratic salon ("Anna," "Pavlovna," "sitting," "laughing") and right next to "company"'.

What is going on here? In McClure's reading, this hinges on the way that different groups in the novel refer to the individual: 'the two names enact different roles in the text—"Napoleon" is the man himself, winning battles and participating in the abstract notion of history, and "Bonaparte" is the Russian imagination of the man, a name whispered at parties in Moscow and St. Petersburg'. Again, of course, it would have been possible for a discerning close reader of the novel to have figured this out without the visualization. The advantage of the graphical depiction is the speed of location and how it becomes possible quickly to spot outlying terms through its deformance of the novel. This approach does not negate the need to know the text or interpret why the linguistic terms appear in the way they do. As before, many imagine that digital approaches wish somehow to destroy actual reading. This could not be further from the truth.

McClure goes on, in his demonstration, to show how, linguistically, *The Odyssey* clusters into home and away; how Thoreau's *Walden* is split between nature and civilization; how linguistic markers of heaven and hell can be grouped in the *Divine Comedy*; among many other facets. McClure does note, though, a flaw in his visualizations: 'the big weakness with this, of course, is that it doesn't work nearly as well with texts that don't naturally split up into these kinds of cleanly-defined sections'. For instance, Whitman's *Leaves of Grass* is 'more scrambled, less differentiated, less obviously "accurate" than the tidy triangle of *War and Peace* or the cosmological pillar of the *Divine Comedy*'.

However, this is not always the case. In order to test McClure's deformance techniques elsewhere, I produced a similar map of Thomas Pynchon's 1973 novel, *Gravity's Rainbow*. For those unfamiliar with this text, it is an epic—or encyclopaedic, to borrow Edward Mendelson's coinage—novel set during the last years of the Second World War with a highly fragmented narrative voice and a cast of over four hundred characters.[18] The plot (in so far as there is one) revolves around the hunt for a mysterious black V-2 rocket/device. But this is, to quote the famous adage, akin to saying that *Ulysses* is a novel about two men in Dublin. It hardly captures the richness and diversity of a book that features a Dodo hunt, a psychic octopus, lengthy debates on the relative merits of Rossini and Beethoven, and almost every kind of sexual paraphilia that one could imagine

---

[18] Edward Mendelson, 'Encyclopedic Narrative: From Dante to Pynchon', *MLN*, 91.6 (1976), 1267–75; see also David Letzler, *The Cruft of Fiction: Mega-Novels and the Science of Paying Attention*, Frontiers of Narrative (Lincoln, NE: University of Nebraska Press, 2017).

(and several that one wishes one could not).[19] *Gravity's Rainbow* is an ultra-dense, interconnected, sprawling mess of a novel. It is not a cleanly separated text.

In other words, one would expect *Gravity's Rainbow*, using the kernel density visualization technique, to fare poorly. For the most part, this expectation is fulfilled. The bulk of the linguistic terms in *Gravity's Rainbow* are meshed together in tight and indecipherable webs, as seen in Figure 2.5.

Yet, amid this car crash of a visualization, there are some interesting interpretative points. The first is to note the outlying term 'Byron' at the extreme left of this graphic. In *Gravity's Rainbow*, this refers to the episode chronicling the immortal light-bulb dubbed 'Byron' who defies the Phoebus cartel's scheming towards planned obsolescence, a section that drew the critical notice of Harold Bloom.[20] Indeed, this is one of several surreal narrative moments in the novel that digress from the reality of the Second World War into fantasy that nonetheless serves as political allegory.

For a novel with a broad range of cultural references, it is strange that the only mention of the Romantic poet, Lord Byron, is through this narrative (the light-bulb Byron is a romantic dreamer of revolution). Despite this novel containing episodes where various artforms are debated by characters there is no comparable scene for poetry. This is curious as the early Pynchon, at age twenty-two, divided his writing into a set of five phases, the third of which was a 'romantic' phase with specific reference to imitations of Lord Byron.[21] While it is hard to know how seriously to take these reflexive statements from the young Pynchon, the fact that the Byron episode is linguistically isolated is significant, as it appears to represent one of the few co-occurrent occasions in the novel of lexical and thematic segregation.

---

[19] Although it is worth noting that, on a daily basis, the British tabloid press manages to produce material that by now far surpasses some of the obscenity that landed this novel in such trouble at the time of its publication. See, for example, Barney Samuels, 'I Voted Leave ... But Now I've Got 10,000 SEX ARSES Stuck at Calais!', *Daily Sport*, 2 January 2021.

[20] Harold Bloom, 'Introduction', in *Thomas Pynchon* (Broomall, PA: Chelsea House Publishers, 2003), pp. 1–11.

[21] Steven Weisenburger, 'Thomas Pynchon at Twenty-Two: A Recovered Autobiographical Sketch', *American Literature*, 62.4 (1990), 692–7 (p. 696).

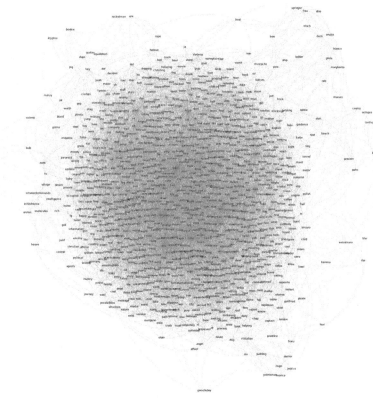

Figure 2.5 Kernel density estimation plot of Thomas Pynchon's *Gravity's Rainbow*. Author's own.

A few other similarly significant moments in the novel are also visible in the above visualization. These are: the orgiastic scene aboard the Anubis ship;[22] the fisherman's-wife-esque staging of the abduction of Katja by the psychic octopus, Grigori;[23] Tchitcherine and the

---

[22] Christopher Ames, 'Power and the Obscene Word: Discourses of Extremity in Thomas Pynchon's "Gravity's Rainbow"', *Contemporary Literature*, 31.2 (1990), 191–207.

[23] Antonio Marquez, 'The Cinematic Imagination in Thomas Pynchon's *Gravity's Rainbow*', *Rocky Mountain Review of Language and Literature*, 33.4 (1979), 165–79; David Cowart, 'Pynchon, Genealogy, History: *Against the Day*', *Modern Philology*, 109.3 (2012), 385–407 <https://doi.org/10.1086/663688>.

Schwarzkommando;[24] the Herero back-story;[25] Brigadier Pudding's night-time feast;[26] Der Springer;[27] Rocketman's Potsdam Pickup;[28] Roger and Jessica's romance; among several others.[29] Each of these episodes exhibits some degree of parity between its linguistic disconnectedness and its thematic isolation. Perhaps what is most notable about this correlation is that, as my above citation notes show, each of these episodes has received significant independent critical attention in the extensive secondary literature on the novel.

This seems to indicate the possibility that critics may be drawn to those moments in novels—or, at least, in *Gravity's Rainbow*—that concurrently isolate themselves linguistically *and* thematically. Perhaps this is unremarkable: critics are drawn to exceptional scenes and language in texts. In this diagram, the episodes pushed to the diagram's edges are distinctive, isolated moments. It is my educated guess, or hypothesis, that literary critics are more frequently drawn to write about identifiable segments of text that exhibit the linguistic-thematic isolation that can be highlighted by kernel density estimation clustering. (Perhaps aside from the beginning and ends of text, which we already know receive more literary critical attention than other areas of novels).[30]

---

[24] Brian McHale, 'Modernist Reading, Post-Modern Text: The Case of *Gravity's Rainbow*', *Poetics Today*, 1.1/2 (1979), 85–110.

[25] Steven Weisenburger, 'The End of History? Thomas Pynchon and the Uses of the Past', *Twentieth Century Literature*, 25.1 (1979), 54–72.

[26] Paul Fussell, *The Great War and Modern Memory* (New York: Oxford University Press, 2000).

[27] N. Katherine Hayles, 'Caught in the Web: Cosmology and the Point of (No) Return in Pynchon's *Gravity's Rainbow*', in *The Cosmic Web: Scientific Field Models and Literary Strategies in the Twentieth Century*, Scientific Field Models and Literary Strategies in the Twentieth Century (Ithaca, NY: Cornell University Press, 1984), pp. 168–98 <http://www.jstor.org/stable/10.7591/j.ctt207g6gx.10> [accessed 6 April 2021].

[28] Martin Paul Eve, *Pynchon and Philosophy: Wittgenstein, Foucault and Adorno* (Basingstoke: Palgrave Macmillan, 2014), p. 62.

[29] Leo Bersani, 'Pynchon, Paranoia, and Literature', *Representations*, 25 (1989), 99–118.

[30] Giuliana Adamo, 'Twentieth-Century Recent Theories on Beginnings and Endings of Novels', *Annali d'Italianistica*, 18 (2000), 49–76; Giuliana Adamo, 'Beginnings and Endings in Novels', *New Readings*, 1.1 (2011) <http://ojs.cf.ac.uk/index.php/newreadings/article/view/62> [accessed 30 January 2020].

Such a pattern is visible in Figure 2.5. These episodes, all of which have featured extensively in the secondary literature, are prominent. There are some false positives (instances that appear isolated but not that widely remarked upon). The clearest of these to me is the minor character Gwenhidy, who here sticks out a mile but is not really that extensively covered in the secondary literature. There are also some false negatives: 'paranoia' has been extensively analysed in the secondary literature on Pynchon, but it is not here a distinctly isolated term. What I wonder is this, though: does this have potential predictive power? If I examined other encyclopaedic novels, could such exploratory methods like this direct us to the most probable sources of critical attention?

This may be of interest, although it is also feasible that we will be misled by visualization. Performing the same analysis on *Moby-Dick* yields us some peripheral entities that have been the subject of much critical investment. For instance, the character Fedallah has been of note to scholars since the 1950s and is a peripheral edge node.[31] Likewise, there is a whole peripheral cluster on Queequeg, the subject of much critical discourse. Even 'whale' and 'Ahab' are relatively peripheral nodes under a Force Atlas algorithm, perhaps surprisingly. But these findings are tarnished by the fact that I already know the structure of this novel and, to some extent, its secondary critical literature. Other words like 'oars' and 'perch' are equally peripheral, but they hardly appear as central points in the secondary literature, except in the context of Melville's, sometimes parodic, seafaring lexicon.[32] There is a temptation to 'cherry pick' the peripheral nodes that I *know* to be important when we work retrospectively in this fashion. On the one hand, visualizations such as this can sometimes help us understand texts, their flows and interconnections, and how episodes relate to one another. On the other hand, they can also mislead us into thinking that we can see things that simply are not there in the text.

---

[31] Dorothee Grdseloff, 'A Note on the Origin of Fedallah in *Moby-Dick*', *American Literature*, 27.3 (1955), 396–403.

[32] C. Merton Babcock, 'Herman Melville's Whaling Vocabulary', *American Speech*, 29.3 (1954), 161–74 <https://doi.org/10.2307/454235>.

Turning the Tables

As a result of its ongoing professionalization, literary studies has developed its poles of theory, interpretation, and archival modes, among many others and with multiple sub-groupings, often along periodizing lines.[33] These categories are, of course, hardly mutually exclusive. Approaches to the archive, for example, require theorization, but archival findings can alter interpretation.

Digital approaches to literary studies are usually imagined to fall at the drier end of this spectrum; fact-finding interrogations of texts to produce new empirical, quantified data. As Andrew Elfenbein puts it, 'when the humanities have less money and fewer students than ever before, engaging empirical work looks like going over to the enemy'.[34] As I have begun to show already, though, the reality is far more complex than this. One area where this is plain to see can be found in the computational visualization of version variance using tabulation.

While many studies of version variance sit in the earlier periodizations of literary studies, contemporary fiction has its own crisis of uniformity. Sometimes this has been due to an earlier self-published edition coming under acquisitioned editorial control, as was the case with Andy Weir's bestselling novel, *The Martian* (2011).[35] Often, due to a positivist belief in the progress of book production techniques, these differences in contemporary fiction go unremarked upon for long periods, although there is certainly some work on this topic.[36] This is part of the phenomenon noted by Esther Allen, who believes that

---

[33] For more on this, see Underwood, *Why Literary Periods Mattered*.

[34] Andrew Elfenbein, *The Gist of Reading* (Stanford, CA: Stanford University Press, 2018), p. 11.

[35] Erik Ketzan and Christian Schöch, 'What Changed When Andy Weir's *The Martian* Got Edited?' (presented at the Digital Humanities 2017, Montreal, 2017) <https://dh2017.adho.org/abstracts/317/317.pdf> [accessed 8 October 2017].

[36] For just a few examples, see Luc Herman and John M. Krafft, 'Fast Learner: The Typescript of Pynchon's *V.* at the Harry Ransom Center in Austin', *Texas Studies in Literature and Language*, 49.1 (2007), 1–20 <https://doi.org/10.1353/tsl.2007.0005>; Alan Galey, 'The Enkindling Reciter: E-Books in the Bibliographical Imagination', *Book History*, 15.1 (2012), 210–47 <https://doi.org/10.1353/bh.2012.0008>; Albert Rolls, 'The Two *V*s of Thomas Pynchon, or From Lippincott to Jonathan Cape and Beyond', *Orbit: Writing Around Pynchon*, 1.1 (2012) <https://doi.org/10.7766/orbit.v1.1.33>; John Roache, '"The Realer, More Enduring and Sentimental Part of Him": David

works of contemporary fiction remain for quite some time 'unfixed by scholarship', uncommented upon while the time lag of academic work catches up.[37] Bob Eaglestone has noted, also, in a prominent *Textual Practice* article, that the 'contemporary history of the book' is distinctly under-studied by scholars of contemporary literature.[38] On a similar theme, albeit with anticipation of retrospection, Matthew G. Kirschenbaum has called for a greater engagement with what he termed the 'future history of the book' at his Mellon-sponsored Books. Files event in 2018.[39]

Yet consider, for instance, the first published work by the Pulitzer Prize-winning author, Jennifer Egan.[40] Egan, an increasingly important contemporary writer who came to public notice for her experimental 2010 work, *A Visit from the Goon Squad*, has received a steadily growing volume of academic and interview attention in recent years.[41]

Foster Wallace's Personal Library and Marginalia', *Orbit: A Journal of American Literature*, 5.1 (2017) <https://doi.org/10.16995/orbit.142>.

[37] Esther Allen, 'Footnotes *sans Frontières*: Translation and Textual Scholarship', in *Perspectives on Literature and Translation: Creation, Circulation, Reception*, ed. Brian Nelson and Brigid Maher, Routledge Advances in Translation Studies, 5 (New York: Routledge, 2013), pp. 210–20 (p. 217).

[38] Robert Eaglestone, 'Contemporary Fiction in the Academy: Towards a Manifesto', *Textual Practice*, 27.7 (2013), 1089–1101 (p. 1096) <https://doi.org/10.1080/0950236X.2013.840113>.

[39] Matthew G. Kirschenbaum, 'Closing Remarks', in *Books.Files* (The Morgan Library, New York, 2018). See also Matthew G. Kirschenbaum, 'Books.Files: Preservation of Digital Assets in the Contemporary Publishing Industry', 2020 <https://doi.org/10.13016/1i33-pl0y>.

[40] This section is derived from Martin Paul Eve, 'Textual Scholarship and Contemporary Literary Studies: Jennifer Egan's Editorial Processes and the Archival Edition of *Emerald City*', *Lit: Literature Interpretation Theory*, 31.1 (2020), 25–41 <https://doi.org/10.1080/10436928.2020.1709713>, here reproduced under a Creative Commons Attribution License.

[41] For a selection, see Charlie Reilly, 'An Interview with Jennifer Egan', *Contemporary Literature*, 50.3 (2009), 439–60 <https://doi.org/10.1353/cli.0.0074>; Adam Kelly, 'Beginning with Postmodernism', *Twentieth Century Literature*, 57.3/4 (2011), 391–422; Danel Olson, 'Renovation Is Hell, and Other Gothic Truths Deep Inside Jennifer Egan's *The Keep*', in 21*st-Century Gothic: Great Gothic Novels since* 2000, ed. Danel Olson (Lanham, MD: Scarecrow Press, 2011), pp. 327–41; Wolfgang Funk, 'Found Objects: Narrative (as) Reconstruction in Jennifer Egan's *A Visit from the Goon Squad*', in *The Aesthetics of Authenticity: Medial Constructions of the Real*, ed. Wolfgang Funk, Florian Groß, and Irmtraud Huber (Bielefeld: Transcript Verlag, 2012), pp. 41–61; Alan Kirby,

It is, therefore, of interest that the 'prior UK edition' of her first short-story collection, *Emerald City*, is, in Egan's own words, 'missing material and full of mistakes and hopefully consigned to oblivion by now'.[42] I found that this earlier edition contains short-story material that has never appeared elsewhere and is unknown in the scholarly literature. The original version of the collection is nearly impossible to buy at the time of writing. However, it is available for consultation in national deposit libraries in the UK, such as the British Library (with classmark Nov.1993/1643).

Indeed, as seen in Table 2.2, the two versions of Egan's first book have drastically different tables of contents, despite sharing a title. In addition to Egan's aforementioned lamentations about missing material, the most visible difference between the two texts is the presence of the short story 'After the Revolution' in *Emerald A*; a work that appears

---

'Digimodern Textual Endlessness', *American Book Review*, 34.4 (2013), 12 <https://doi.org/10.1353/abr.2013.0056>; Danica van de Velde, '"Every Song Ends": Musical Pauses, Gendered Nostalgia, and Loss in Jennifer Egan's *A Visit from the Goon Squad*', in *Write in Tune: Contemporary Music in Fiction*, ed. Erich Hertz and Jeffrey Roessner (New York: Bloomsbury, 2014), pp. 125–35; David Cowart, 'Thirteen Ways of Looking: Jennifer Egan's *A Visit from the Goon Squad*', *Critique: Studies in Contemporary Fiction*, 56.3 (2015), 241–54 <https://doi.org/10.1080/00111619.2014.905448>; Martin Paul Eve, '"Structural Dissatisfaction": Academics on Safari in the Novels of Jennifer Egan', *Open Library of Humanities*, 1.1 (2015) <https://doi.org/10.16995/olh.29>; Wolfgang Funk, *The Literature of Reconstruction: Authentic Fiction in the New Millennium* (London: Bloomsbury Academic, 2015); Johanna Hartmann, 'Paratextualized Forms of Fictional Self-Narration: Footnotes, Headnotes and Endnotes in Jennifer Egan's *A Visit from the Goon Squad*', in *Symbolism* 15, ed. Rüdiger Ahrens and Klaus Stierstorfer (Berlin: De Gruyter, 2015), pp. 101–20 <https://doi.org/10.1515/9783110449075-007>; Amelia Precup, 'The Posthuman Body in Jennifer Egan's "Black Box"', *American, British, and Canadian Studies*, 25.1 (2015), 171–86; Roger Bellin, 'Techno-Anxiety and the Middlebrow: Science-Fictionalization in the Fictional Mainstream of the Early Twenty-First Century', in *The Poetics of Genre in the Contemporary Novel*, ed. Tim Lanzendörfer (Lanham, MD: Lexington Books, 2016), pp. 115–25; Jørgen Bruhn, 'Between Punk and PowerPoint: Authenticity Versus Medialities in Jennifer Egan's *A Visit from the Goon Squad*', in *The Intermediality of Narrative Literature* (London: Palgrave Macmillan, 2016), pp. 103–21 <https://doi.org/10.1057/978-1-137-57841-9_6>; Dinnen; Alexander Moran, 'The Genrefication of Contemporary American Fiction', *Textual Practice*, 33.2 (2019), 229–44 <https://doi.org/10.1080/0950236X.2018.1509272>; Melissa J. Strong, 'Found Time: *Kairos* in *A Visit from the Goon Squad*', *Critique: Studies in Contemporary Fiction*, 59.4 (2018), 471–80 <https://doi.org/10.1080/00111619.2018.1427544>.

[42] Jennifer Egan, personal correspondence with the author, 21 August 2017.

Table 2.2 The tables of contents of the two versions of *Emerald City* with paginations. Author's own.

Chapter Number	*Emerald A* [page range]	*Emerald B* [page range]
1	The Stylist [1–16]	Why China? [1–25]
2	Sacred Heart [17–32]	Sacred Heart [26–39]
3	Passing the Hat [33–45]	Emerald City [40–54]
4	Letter to Josephine [45–66]	The Stylist [55–68]
5	One Piece [67–84]	One Piece [69–84]
6	Spanish Winter [85–100]	The Watch Trick [85–99]
7	The Watch–Trick [101–118]	Passing the Hat [100–110]
8	Puerto Vallarta [119–136]	Puerto Vallarta [111–127]
9	After the Revolution [137–152]	Spanish Winter [128–140]
10	Emerald City [153–169]	Letter to Josephine [141–159]
11		Sisters of the Moon [160–170]

nowhere else in Egan's published oeuvre. However, this story forms, extremely loosely, the background to 'Why China?' that would appear in the subsequent collection (*Emerald B*). The table of contents here is also substantially reordered, with Egan's favourite/strongest stories appearing as bookends to the work in *Emerald B*. Curiously, however, 'Sacred Heart', the story for which Egan won the initial book contract, is not placed at the forefront of either edition.

How to understand these edits? One of the most important aspects to note about the different editions of *Emerald City* is that the initial 'bad' publication of *Emerald A* was housed in the United Kingdom, meaning that many of the changes to the text from US serialization could be expected to accommodate British English. *Emerald B* would then have to adjust this back to US English for worldwide publication, or so I assumed. Thus, while chronologically we can see that the texts progress from serialization (~1990 in US English) → *Emerald A* (1993 in British English) → *Emerald B* (1996 in US English), there is no straightforward chain of authority here within the above logic, since *Emerald B* would need to undo many of the localization changes in *Emerald A*. Certainly, at the very least we would expect the stemma to run in parallel, with *Emerald B* more closely representing the original serialization in terms of American and British English. One of the first questions that I wanted to answer was: what was Egan's editorial sequence in the construction of the final collection, *Emerald B*?

It transpires that the non-linearity of revision in Egan's early short stories is convoluted. Consider the opening lines of 'The Stylist', first published in *The New Yorker* in 1989, shown in Table 2.3.[43]

While we might expect to see *Emerald A* adopting a change to the sentence and then *Emerald B* either rejecting or accepting that variance, we rather see a nonlinear path from serialized to *A* to *B*. Instead, *Emerald A* and *B* adopt the text of *The New Yorker*'s version, but *Emerald B* introduces an entirely different word: 'duties' instead of 'dunes'. Certainly, the word choice in serialized and *A* ('dunes') makes more sense, and we might posit that this is some kind of optical character recognition error (i.e. that in terms of the publication process, a publisher scanned a typewritten version from 1989, ran this through a defective automatic text processor, and that this error in the process was never corrected). Further, the crossbar of the t could link to the 'i' in 'duties' that could confuse a digital system into perceiving an 'n' instead of 'ti'. Without recourse to the serialized version or to the *Emerald A* text, however, this term might be assumed to be a photographic reference. Perhaps it could also be a reference to the work of modelling; that is, that the characters have to return to their 'duties', even though the setup for the sandy environment of the story is then less clear here.

Importantly, though, of the thirty-three textual variations between the editions of the 'The Stylist', it is notable that not once does *Emerald B* completely adopt wholesale a modification to *The New Yorker* version introduced by *Emerald A*.[44] Certainly, *Emerald A* and *Emerald B* both draw on the serialized version. However, this seems likely to imply that, despite the 1993 edition appearing before *Emerald B*, when Egan returned to the collection in 1995 she went *back to the source* at *The New*

---

[43] Jennifer Egan, 'The Stylist [The New Yorker]', *The New Yorker*, 13 March 1989, 32–7.

[44] For the full version of the changes, see Martin Paul Eve, 'Data Appendices for "Textual Scholarship and Contemporary Literary Studies: Jennifer Egan's Editorial Processes and the Archival Edition of *Emerald City*"', 2019 <https://doi.org/10.5281/zenodo.3253829>.

Table 2.3 The opening to 'The Stylist' in different editions. Author's own.

Serial Page	Serial Text	Emerald A Page	Emerald A Text	Emerald B Page	Emerald B Text
32	When they finally reached the dunes, Jann, the photographer, opens a silver umbrella.	3	When they finally reached the dunes, Jann, the photographer, opens a silver umbrella.	55	When they finally reach the duties, Jann, the photographer opens a silver umbrella.

Yorker. That said, as there is the overlapping change in the lines 'fragile as a newly risen moon' → 'fragile as a birdcage' → 'delicate as a birdcage', there is *some connection* between *Emerald A* and *Emerald B*. Egan seems to have re-implemented some of the same changes that she made in *Emerald A* from the serialization, even though the source of *Emerald B* also draws directly on the original serial publications.

These descriptions, in textual and tabular form (the latter visualized stylings of database-like approaches), can help us understand the changes made to texts, even when they are under copyright and when the potential to produce a critical edition does not exist. Yet, it remains difficult to *understand* what these changes look like across the scope of a novel, even though the section above on Jennifer Egan suggests that version variance in contemporary fiction is more common than usually imagined.

As another example of this problem, consider, for example, the opening of David Mitchell's 2001 novel *number9dream*. The first sentence of this novel is 'we are both busy people, so let's cut the small talk'. Except, as Ali Rahmjoo drew to my attention, in the US edition, it is not. Instead, the reader is given: 'it is a simple matter'.[45]

Indeed, *number9dream* is spread as a distributed media form between editions that differ significantly from one another. Given the numerological significance of the title and the critical material that has played on this, the doubling effect of this newly discovered version variance has serious interpretative consequences for what Rose Harris-Birtill has called Mitchell's 'macroverse'.[46] Far from consisting of nine parts, the rewritings and changes total seventeen distinct chapters, with only part nine (which is blank) being identical between the two texts.

How, though, can we see what this looks like at scale? We could use the long-evolved style of the critical edition to build painstakingly a new version that documents such changes. However, as I have hinted, this is difficult when texts are in copyright. Visual 'diff' tools that highlight

[45] David Mitchell, *Number9dream* (London: Sceptre, 2001); David Mitchell, *Number9dream* (New York: Random House, 2010).

[46] Rose Harris-Birtill, *David Mitchell's Post-Secular World: Buddhism, Belief and the Urgency of Compassion*, New Horizons in Contemporary Writing (London: Bloomsbury, 2018); Peter Childs and James Green, 'The Novels in Nine Parts', in *David Mitchell: Critical Essays*, ed. Sarah Dillon (Canterbury: Gylphi, 2011), pp. 25–47.

changes between texts are not good at demonstrating substantial textual variation, as shown in Figure 2.6. Textual summaries of differences are also difficult to read and tend to become bogged down in detail, losing the potential clarity that is the purpose of visualization.

This is why *Cloud Atlas*—another of David Mitchell's novels—presents a much better opportunity for a visualization that allows us to understand the textual editing process. The re-writes to this novel (of which there are many) primarily occur within one chapter that consists of interview questions and answers. Thus, it is possible to number each question and answer and correlate them for a 'functional equivalence'. Of course, one could also do this for paragraphs in prose fiction, lines in poetic verse, and so on.

By way of background: *Cloud Atlas*—a multiple-award-winning bestseller—was 'orphaned' while at its US publishing house because the editor in charge changed jobs. During this changeover period, the UK edition went to press, before a new US editor came on board. The new US editor asked for significant changes that were never incorporated back into the UK version. This has resulted in two very different versions of the novel entering general circulation alongside translations deriving from different editions, visualized in Figure 2.7. As above, though, most of the changes occur in the section 'An Orison of Sonmi~451', an interview with a death-penalty convict in a standard question-answer format.[47]

This case of *Cloud Atlas* presented a tidy exemplar within which I could explore how visualization might allow us to understand the reordering of this novel. Certainly, I still needed to detail much of the change and its interpretative consequences using textual argument. However, once functional units were correlated in the texts, it was possible to create a visualization showing how the text had been moved around, cut, edited, and so forth. This can be seen in Figure 2.8.

This type of diagram is called a Sankey diagram and this variant was created using a modified version of *d3.js* that I authored, called

[47] For more, see Martin Paul Eve, '"You Have to Keep Track of Your Changes": The Version Variants and Publishing History of David Mitchell's *Cloud Atlas*', *Open Library of Humanities*, 2.2 (2016), 1–34 <https://doi.org/10.16995/olh.82>; Eve, *Close Reading With Computers*.

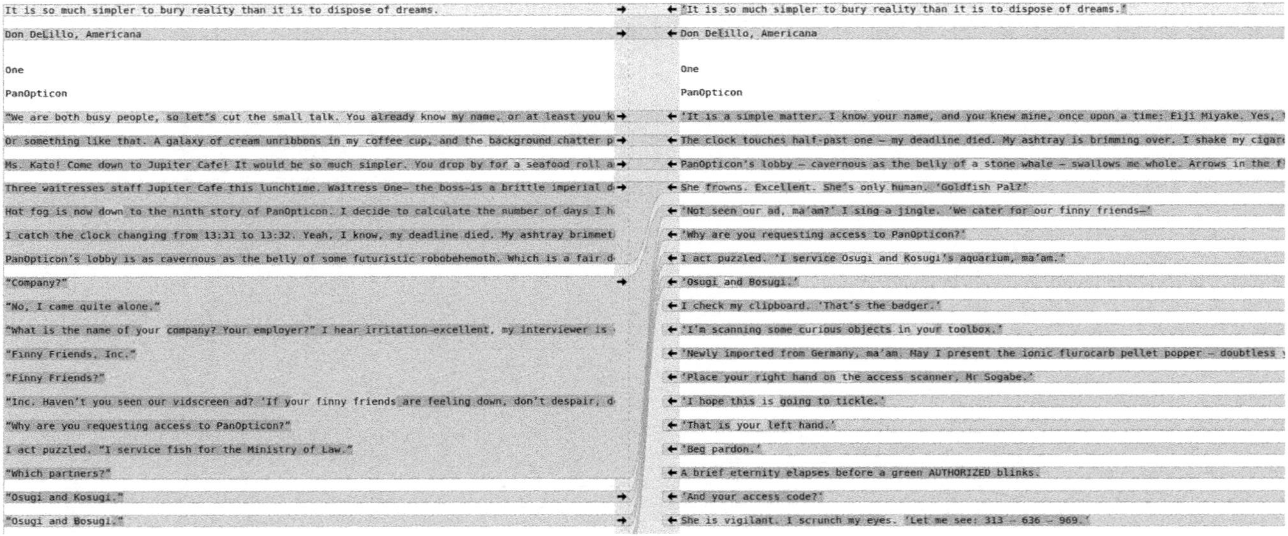

Figure 2.6 Visualizing the differences between the opening of David Mitchell's *number9dream*. Author's own.

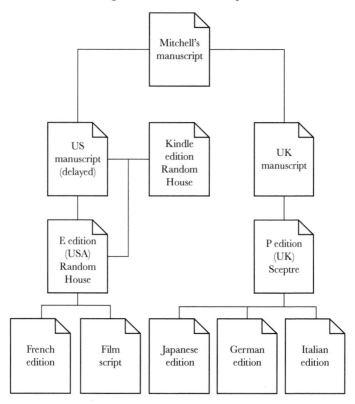

Figure 2.7 The versions of *Cloud Atlas*. Author's own.

SankeyTextualVariant.[48] Such charts traditionally indicate flows, from left to right, to show how one pathway can lead to another. However, in this instance, as with most textual editing projects, the chart is not meant to state that the version on the left is authoritative in any way.

Indeed, in this chart, what we see from top to bottom is a progression through the question and answers of the Sonmi section of *Cloud Atlas*. The column on the left represents the UK Sceptre edition, while

[48] Martin Paul Eve, 'SankeyTextualVariant', *GitHub*, 2015 <https://github.com/MartinPaulEve/SankeyTextualVariant> [accessed 20 December 2015].

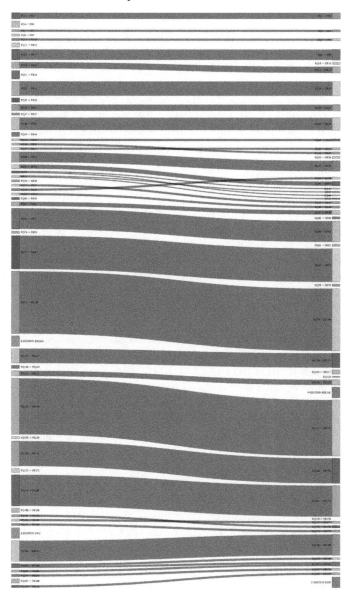

Figure 2.8 The differences between the variants of *Cloud Atlas*. Author's own.

that on the right is the US Random House version.[49] Joined lines between the editions represent contiguous blocks of consistent, shared material. In this instance, this does not necessarily mean that the writing is identical between the portions that have been correlated; it means that they perform the same function within the novel. As just one example, at one point in the UK edition, we are given: 'how did you respond?' In the USA, though, the text reads: 'how did you respond to such blasphemous hubris?' These two pieces of text do the same thing in terms of narrative progression and so are here marked as functionally equivalent. Admittedly, there is room for interpretative contention here. Where there is whitespace between the editions, this represents instances where there is no correlative block in one or other of the texts; that is, something happens in one version of the novel that is not present in the other.

Perhaps the most interesting parts of this diagram are where the lines cross. For, in four instances, the order of questions within the narrative is reversed across editions. Calling the UK version 'P' and the US version 'E', it becomes clear that P46 and P47 (equivalent to E31 and E32) are reversed, P191 and P192 (equivalent to E176 and E177) are switched, P58 moves to E40, and P55 is split into E43–44. These pertain respectively to whether Yoona discussed her escape plan with Sonmi (P36/P47 and E32/E31), and the video evidence of 'xultation' (P191/P192 and E177/E176). P58, however, moves up to E40 and concerns the memory capacity of fabricants (the clone-like servant class/species to which Sonmi belongs). The final switch concerns the split of P55 into E43–44, which discusses Sonmi's comet birthmark. These are the points where the *syuzhet* of the story is changed; that is, the order in which events are unveiled to the reader is different between the versions of the text.

Why does such reordering matter? As the concept of *belles lettres* gave way in the early twentieth century to the formalist New Criticism pioneered by I. A. Richards, the notion of close reading became central to the disciplines of English. In his 1924 *The Principles of Literary Criticism*, Richards noted his belief that 'unpredictable and miraculous

---

[49] David Mitchell, *Cloud Atlas* (London: Sceptre, 2004); David Mitchell, *Cloud Atlas* (New York: Random House, 2004).

differences' might be rendered 'in the total responses' to a text from 'slight changes in the arrangement of stimuli'.[50] This, of course, then justifies comment on the order in which matters are presented in literature. Given Richards's fascination with empiricist experiments around reading practices—exemplified in his later *Practical Criticism*—to have variant texts, branded as the same novel, but with an altered *syuzhet*, seems the ultimate test case for Richards's principle.[51]

Unfortunately, I am unsure that there are 'miraculous' differences at work in this particular instance. Indeed, even though these version variants were unknown before I began my work documenting the changes, worldwide audiences had happily been discussing *Cloud Atlas* together, believing that their discussions were about the same novel when they were not. Perhaps such amateur readers were simply not attentive enough for Richards's close methods. As another hypothesis, it could be that Richards's model is, in reality, merely only a 'fantasy of what would happen [...] if a reader had an infinite working memory capacity', as Andrew Elfenbein puts it.[52] This certainly tells us something about how a general readership engages with fiction. What it does not tell us is how we might expect readers to feel as a result of this literary reordering.

Further, while understanding textual variance remains an important activity, visualization has its limits for this purpose. Tabulation is one way of visualizing difference—as I showed above with Egan's works—but the more sophisticated reordering diagrams I have presented are wanting at the microscopic textual level. Simply too much resolution is lost in the flattening to visualization and it seems that extant methods for marking up critical editions are probably a better way to proceed, despite the steep learning curve involved in understanding such annotations (which are also, themselves, a type of visualization).

[50] I. A. Richards, *The Principles of Literary Criticism*, 2nd edn. (London: Routledge, 1926), p. 158.

[51] Ivor Armstrong Richards, *Practical Criticism: A Study of Literary Judgment* (London: Transaction Publishers, 2008).

[52] Elfenbein, p. 86.

Digital Concrete

For the final section in this chapter on visual forms within digital literary studies, I will turn to a specific, strange instance where we can study virtualized artefacts that have a visualized quality, even while the methods that I use to read them will be more conventional. In this final section, I examine a type of digital visual 'poetry', created from textual forms.

Indeed, for many decades and well into the twenty-first century, several online communities have produced digital documents that emulate and meld two distinct aesthetic forebears: the Bulletin Board Systems of the mid-1980s and the trans-continental concrete poetry movement. The community to which I am referring in particular here is illicit and relatively unknown. Known as the 'warez scene', this is the highest-tier of people who pirate software, music, films, and almost any other media format that one might choose to imagine. A highly complex network of individuals and groups make up this invitation-only online subculture. However, for this final section, what is most interesting about this underground community of pirates is the aesthetic works of ASCII art that are disseminated alongside every item of pirated content.[53]

These files—called NFOs (for iNFO)—contain details of the pirate release, how to install the software, notes on the 'cracking' process in the cases of software (a 'crack' is a modification to a piece of copy-protected software to remove its digital rights management protections), shout outs to other release groups (in both positive and negative terms), and other general information about the release. NFOs are information communication tools. Most significantly, though, these groups encode *visual-textual artwork* inside these NFO files, even though they are 'plain' text.[54] This form of plain-text decoration is called 'ASCII (American Standard Code for Information Interchange) art'. It is based on using textual character codes to create a visual effect.

---

[53] Much of this section is derived from the forthcoming Martin Paul Eve, *Warez: The Infrastructure and Aesthetics of Piracy* (New York: punctum books, 2022) [accessed 10 April 2021].

[54] Although, of course, as Dennis Tenen reminds us, the term 'plain text' hides a plethora of dangerous assumptions. Dennis Tenen, *Plain Text: The Poetics of Computation* (Stanford, CA: Stanford University Press, 2017).

ASCII is an underlying standard that converts a binary numerical representation into universal character representations (in much the same way as children might devise a simple code in which A = 1, B = 2 etc.).

When viewed in a standard text viewer, NFO files can appear very messy. Figure 2.9 shows one of these files from around the year 2000. As is clear, the file is composed of a number of several characters not used in the English language. These include 'Ü', 'Ý', 'Þ' and many others.

What may not be immediately clear here is that if one switches the font to an appropriate monospaced terminal style, these characters are transformed into blocks, as shown in Figure 2.10.

While the (possibly deliberate) spelling errors in this document ('ment') might dissuade some of the literary merits of such artefacts, the significant point here is very different. Indeed, following the aforementioned work of Bronač Ferran, to whom this section is deeply indebted, I believe that these digital documents can best be located within a broad history of visual/spatial concrete poetry that exhibits

```
ÚÍÄÍÄÍÄÍÄÍÄÍÄÍÄÍÄÍÄÍÄÍÄÍÄÍ¿          ÚÍÄÍÄÍÄÍÄÍÄÍÄÍÄÍÄÍÄÍÄÍÄÍÄÍ¿
º    -.=.Z.L.A.i.S.O.=.-   ÄÄÍÄÍÄÍÄÍÄÍÄŽ   -.=.Z.L.A.M.P.3.=.-   º
ÀÍÄÍÄÍÄÍÄÍÄÍÄÍÄÍÄÍÄÍÄÍÄÍÄÍÙ          ÀÍÄÍÄÍÄÍÄÍÄÍÄÍÄÍÄÍÄÍÄÍÄÍÄÍÙ

ÜÜßÛÛÛÛ²Ûßß      ²²Ý         ÜÜ ß      ß
 ÛÛßÛÛÛ      ß Ü       ÛÛÛÛÛÛß    ÜÜ     ßÜ     ÜÜ            ÛÛÜÜ    ÛÜß
 PÛÛÛÛÛÝ    ÛÛÛÛÝÜÜ      ßß ßÛÛÛÛÛßÛÛÛÛÛÛÛÛÛÛÛÜßÛÛÛÛÛÛÛÛÛÜ ÛÛÛß PÛÛÛÛ²   Þ
 ÛÛÛÛÛ²Ü²ßß    ßß²²ÛÛÛ      PÛÜ²ÛÛÛÛÛÛÛÛ²ÛÛÛÛÛÛÛÛÛÛÛÛÛÛÝ ÛÛÛ²ßÛÛÛÝß
 ÛÛÛÛÛÛÝ  Ü °Ý PÛÛÛÛÛ²      ÛÛÛÛ²ÛÛß   ßÛÛÛßÛÛß ßÜ ÛÛÛÛÛÛÛ     ÛßßÛÛÛÛ
 Þ²ÛÛßßÜ Ûß   ÛÛÝ   ²ÛÛÛÛÝ ßÛÛÛÛÛÛÛ      PÛÛÛÛÝ   PßÛÛÛÛÛÝ  ÛPÛÛÛÛÛ
 PÛÛÛÛÛP²     ÛÛÝ   ßÛÛÛÛ²Ý PÛÛÛÛ²Ý     Ü ÛÛÛÛÛ     ß²ÛÛÛÛÝ PÝPÛÛÛÛÛÝ
 ÛPÛÛÛÛ²      ÛÛÝ   PÛÛÛÛ²Ý ²ÛÛÛßÛ     ÛßÛÛ    ßÛÛÛßÛÛÛ²    ßÛÛÛßÛÛÛ
 PÝ ²ÛÛÛÛÛÝ    ÛÛÝ   ÛÛÛÛÛßß PÛ²²ÛÛÛ      ²ßÛ      ÛÛÛ²²ÛÝ Û  ÛÛßßÛÛÛ     Û
 ÛÛ PÛÛÛÛÛÝ    ÛÛÝ   ÛÛÛÛÛÛÛ  PÛÛÛÛÛÛ              ÛÛÛÛÛÛÝ  ßßPÛÛÛÛÛßÛÜß
 PÛÝPÛÛÛÛÛÝ     ÛÛÝ   ²ÛÛßÛÛÛ PÛÛÛÛÛÛ             PÛÛÛÛÛÛÛÛÛÛÛ ÛPÛÛÛÛ ÛÝ
²Û° ßÛÛÛÛßßßÛÛÛ °²ÛÛÛÛÛ° Û²²²Ûß²² PÛÛÛÛÛÛÝ °²ÛÛÛÛÛÛÛÛÛÛ² PÛÛÛÛÛÛ ÛÛÛ  ²²ÛßÛÛPß ÛÛ²Ý
   ßßßÛÛÛ     ÛÛÝ   ÛÛÛÛÛÛÛÛÛ  ²ÛÛÛÛÛÝ              PÛÛÛÛÛ²    PÛÛÛÛÛ²
hetero ²ÛÛÛ ßÛ  ÛÛÝ   PÛ²²²ÛÝ  ÛÛÛÛÛÛßß             PÛÛÛÛÛ²   ÛÛ²ÛÛÛÛ²
úsacú PÛÛÛÝPÝPÝ ÛÛÝ   Ûß°ßÛÛß  ÛÛÛÛÛÛÛ              PÛÛÛÛÛÝ   ÛP²ÛÛÛÛÝ
   PÛÛÛ°P²P     ÛÛÝ   ²²ÛÛÛß   PÛ²ÛÛÛÛÝ            ÛÛÛÛÛ²ÛÝ PÝPÛÛÛÛÛÛ
      ²ÛÛÛ Û    ÛÛÝ  PÛ²ÛÛÛ²Û  ÛÛÛÛß ÛÛÛÛÛ Û   ÛÛÛßßÛÛ ßÛÛÝ PÝÛÛÛÛÛÛÛ
    ÛßÛÛÛÛßÝ    ²ÝÛ   ÛÛÛÛÛÛÛßßßÛÛÛ²ÛÛÛ²²ßß     ÛÛß      ßßÛÛ²Û ÛÛÛÛÛÛ²ÛÛÝ
    PÝ ßßPÛÛÛ Û Û ÛÛÛÛßßÛÛÛ   ÛÛßß ÛßÛÛÛ Û   Þ  ÛÛ    ÛÛÛÛ ßßÛ P²ÛßÛÛÛ ÛÛ
    ßÛÛ    ßÛß ÛÝ                  þ                  ßÛÛÛßß      ßÛ
        ßß þ    °²Ý         BeatMasters International 2000           Û
```

Figure 2.9 BeatMasters International (BMI) NFO from the year 2000 with ASCII art by hetero/sac. This image is not covered by the terms of the Creative Commons License of this publication.

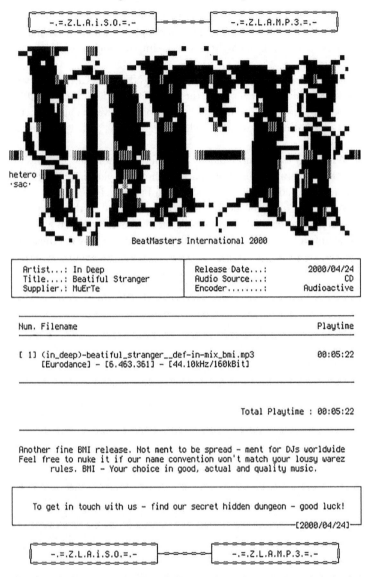

```
  -.=.Z.L.A.i.S.O.=.-    |----|    -.=.Z.L.A.M.P.3.=.-
```

hetero
·sac·

                    BeatMasters International 2000

```
Artist...: In Deep              Release Date...:    2000/04/24
Title....: Beatiful Stranger    Audio Source...:           CD
Supplier.: MuErTe               Encoder........:    Audioactive
```

```
Num. Filename                                       Playtime


[ 1] (in_deep)-beatiful_stranger__def-in-mix_bmi.mp3    00:05:22
     [Eurodance] - [6.463.361] - [44.10kHz/160kBit]



                                      Total Playtime : 00:05:22
```

```
Another fine BMI release. Not ment to be spread - ment for DJs worldwide
Feel free to nuke it if our name convention won't match your lousy warez
         rules. BMI - Your choice in good, actual and quality music.
```

```
   To get in touch with us - find our secret hidden dungeon - good luck!
                                                      -[2000/04/24]-
```

```
  -.=.Z.L.A.i.S.O.=.-    |======|    -.=.Z.L.A.M.P.3.=.-
```

Figure 2.10 The same BMI NFO file transformed into its intended viewing format. ASCII art by hetero/sac. This image is not covered by the terms of the Creative Commons License of this publication.

both constructivist and de(con)structivist tendencies.[55] They can also be considered a type of computational textual visualization, that we can study.

The history of concrete poetry—a form of writing in which the visual elements play a key poetic role—is difficult to explain concisely. The terms of engagement are contested, and the debate's terrain is international, spanning West Germany to Brazil from the 1950s onwards.[56] Concrete poetic form has a complex relationship to modernism and particularly Ezra Pound, from whose work the *noigandres* journal and loosely affiliated group (the authors of the 'Pilot Plan for Concrete Poetry') took their name.[57] Key properties of concrete poetry include a focus on typography, spatial layout and positioning as poetic qualities, and some idea of movement and kinesis; a 'critical evolution of forms' as the Pilot Plan has it.

Core to much concrete poetry are the ideas of economy and sparsity. Hansjörg Mayer's *oil*, for instance, resolutely sticks to its deconstructing, minimalist use of three letters, repetitiously placed within its invisible grid. At the same time, though, there is a concurrent constructivist counter-tendency at work. This often takes the form of the aforementioned repetition and overprinting (in which typographical elements are overlaid atop one another in the printing process). Hence we see reduction and overload side by side.

---

[55] This section is entirely indebted to Ferran's doctoral thesis, which I am supervising. All credit for anything here should be attributed to her while any errors are mine alone.

[56] Some of the better known background sources that have handled this include Mary Ellen Solt, *Concrete Poetry: A World View* (Bloomington, IN: Indiana University Press, 1970); Stephen Bann, *Concrete Poetry: An International Anthology* (London: London Magazine Editions, 1967); Stephen Bann, ed., *The Tradition of Constructivism: Documents of Contemporary Art* (London: Thames and Hudson, 1974); Johanna Drucker, *The Visible World: Experimental Typography and Modern Art, 1909–1923* (Chicago, IL: University of Chicago Press, 1994); Johanna Drucker, *Figuring the Word: Essays on Books, Writing, and Visual Poetics* (New York: Granary Books, 1998); Drucker, *Graphesis*; Marjorie Perloff, *The Poetics of Indeterminacy: Rimbaud to Cage* (Princeton, NJ: Princeton University Press, 1981); Marjorie Perloff, *Radical Artifice: Writing Poetry in the Age of Media* (Chicago, IL: University of Chicago Press, 1991); Marjorie Perloff, *Unoriginal Genius: Poetry by Other Means in the New Century* (Chicago, IL: University of Chicago Press, 2010).

[57] de Campos et al.

Such a model for poetry thereby yields a double temporality, in which the building and the breakdown are simultaneously present. Ideas of construction and deconstruction are prompted into temporal translation on the page of the concrete poem. Even the final logical endpoint of overloaded constructivism—say, overprinting to the extent that the page is totally black once more—leads to a form of destruction. When translated into temporal terms by a reader, this dialectical formulation is how the concrete poem includes a notion of motion within its otherwise (and, in reality) static environment.

The NFO file shown in Figures 2.9 and 2.10 possesses some of the qualities of this temporal movement, across the multiple display forms in which it can be accessed. Indeed, as well as possessing the spatial framing layout seen in much concrete poetry that prompts the afore-mentioned dialectic, where alphanumerical typographical elements are laid out in a particular form on the page for aesthetic effect, these digital artefacts are versioned and mutable in their display. The reader can access the form in its textual, or graphical/visualized modes, demonstrating the principle of kinesis attributed to much concrete poetry, but in a very different way. The form can move between text-uality and visualization. For while Mayer and others were interested in typographical control (for example, the sustained use of the Futura typeface, which Ferran notes was perceived to be a highly 'neutral' font), the movement of NFOs comes from reader control over display technologies. The text moves from its constructivist phase, where ASCII characters are visible in their alphanumeric forms, into a breakdown of those characters into solid blocks as the 'correct' monospacing font is applied. There is, in this movement, at once a distinct loss of detail—we no longer know what the underlying *linguistic* or *symbolic* representation of the character might be, even though it has not changed in its underlying digital representation—but also a further construction as the 'image' form of the document becomes visible.

In many ways, this is the type of metaphorical slippage that Dennis Tenen has charted and to which I will later return.[58] It is a model in which the digital-metaphorical form presented to the end user is only frictionally associated with the physicality and materiality of the

[58] Tenen, pp. 23–54.

operation. The example that Tenen gives is the 'delete' operation on a computer system. One might assume that pressing 'delete' within one's operating system would lead to the removal of the relevant file's contents from the hard drive. This is not actually the case, though. In many contemporary journaling file systems, files are stored in at least two, and sometimes three, separate locations. The first, the metadata inode, contains a pointer to the second storage location, called the indirect block. The second storage location (the indirect block) contains two numbers that point to two further locations on the disk: a start block and an end block for the file in question. (In some file systems, the inode directly contains the indirect block information; hence, sometimes there are two stages and sometimes three.) The file is then actually written on disk to the space between these location numbers. That is to say: there is a pointer on the disk that directs the operating system to the actual physical sectors on the storage device where the file's contents lie.

When one deletes a file, the file contents itself are not usually removed from the disk. Instead, the inode is unlinked. That is, the *metadata* for the file is removed, but the actual contents remain on the storage and the space where the file is stored is made available for the storage of other files. This means that, in specific circumstances, it is possible (although difficult) to recover deleted files. Over time, of course, the file's location will be overwritten with new file data, linked to different inodes. Files will, themselves, also be distributed between inodes at different on-disk locations for different fragments of their data.

The point here, though, is that the metaphor of deletion—often signified by a skeuomorphic trash can in the iconography of desktop operating systems—rarely performs an analogous 'trashing' of the underlying data. It is more akin to saying that one will empty one's bookshelf by crossing out the books one does not want from a list of books but that one will actually remove the books only at a later date when one has a new book to add. Certainly, such metaphorical slippage is *useful* to an end user. But few users are aware of the implications masked by such metaphorical terminology; one's files remain on the disk, even after one has deleted them.

The NFO is subject to an analogous metaphorical representation between its layers in which different font overlays transform typographic blocks into visual analogies of the underlying characters. Because the format takes advantage of particular typographic features that rely on the selection of specific fonts and with highly particular domain-knowledge requirements, elements of the process of metaphorization become more visible as we shift between the graphic and typographic modes. Once one knows that certain accented characters in the Unicode format are (mis)represented as solid blocks when one switches the font to a monospaced terminal layout, the perspectival/meta-phorical trickery of the mediating layers is rendered transparent. Of course, for some readers, this will remain opaque; they just will not understand why the file can appear in two different forms and the metaphor will continue to function. (Which is not to say that meta-phor does not function even when we *know* it is metaphor, it is just that a critical ability to appraise metaphor depends on recognition of substitutability.)

There is, further though, a history of computational colonialism at work in this double-layered process that can be read out of the NFO files. For the characters that translate into ASCII art blocks when used in an appropriate font are all drawn from the non-English alphabet. Just as search engines have premised their models on the cultural assumption of the transcendental white subject and the history of computing has worked to erase women from its record, here we see a geographic and linguistic bias, to which I also turned earlier.[59] The acutely accented 'u' ('ú'), for instance, is a glyph used in Czech, Faroese, Portuguese, Spanish, and Vietnamese, among others. It does not occur in English, though. For this reason, this character appears in the Latin-1 Supplement of the Unicode specification.

This translation of certain non-English characters to blocks is just part of how a longer computational linguistic colonialism has emerged in the development of contemporary writing. Another instance of this can be seen in the response to the Unicode implementation of the Ho language. In 2007, Harrison and Anderson noted in a letter to the Unicode consortium that:

> The current Unicode proposal (authored by Michael Everson, dated 1999-01-29) is incomplete in its current form and notably requires

[59] Noble; Hicks.

consultation and fact-checking with the user community. While it is crucial that the Ho orthography be included in Unicode, this can only be done in close consultation with Ho scholars at every step of the process. As a practical and ethical matter, we urge the Unicode consortium to accept only proposals that emerge from or are formulated in close consultation with native speaker communities. To do otherwise is to espouse a kind of linguistic colonialism that will only widen the digital divide.[60]

Indeed, one of the basic premises seen in the Unicode specification is that English-language Latinate characters are the first to appear in the table, while other linguistic systems are relegated to much higher assignations. Sometimes, as Sharjeel Imam points out, these 'other' languages are spread across many different blocks rather than in the more concentrated forms of the Latin alphabet.[61] 'Internationalization' here means a spread outwards from a centred English to other 'peripheral' cultures, demonstrating a strong Anglocentrism. As Don Osborn puts it, for example, 'apart from Arabic, the development of the use of African languages in computing and the internet has been relatively slow for a number of linguistic, educational, policy and technical reasons' while 'a particular problem for a number of languages written with modified letters or diacritic characters—or entire alphabets—beyond the basic Latin alphabet (the 26 letters used in English) or the ASCII character set (that alphabet plus basic symbols) has been the way in which computer systems and software handle these'.[62] As 'an industrial standard controlled by the industry', in Domenico

[60] K. David Harrison and Gregory Anderson, 'Review of Proposal for Encoding Warang Chiti (Ho Orthography) in Unicode', 22 April 2007 <https://www.unicode.org/L2/L2007/07137-warang-chiti-review.pdf>.

[61] Sharjeel Imam, 'Digital Colonialism: 1. All Latin Alphabets and Symbols Are Denoted in Unicode by the Range of 0 to 500 in One Single Block. But Urdu-Arabic Alphabets Are Scattered in Five Different Blocks Ranging 1500 to around 64000', *@_imaams*, 2017 <https://twitter.com/_imaams/status/934109280285765632> [accessed 4 April 2019].

[62] Don Osborn, *African Languages in a Digital Age: Challenges and Opportunities for Indigenous Language Computing* (Cape Town: HSRC Press, 2010), pp. 59–60.

Fiormonte's words, we should be sceptical around 'claims about the neutrality or impartiality' of Unicode.[63]

The doubled nature of the layering here at once both highlights and masks this history. Those from countries using Latinate alphabets who open the text file while using a font that does not support the standard terminal block depiction will encounter characters from Cyrillic alphabets, as just one example, and may be perplexed about why their screen is full of unfamiliar accented characters. After all, the artwork is not clear, as Figure 2.9 shows, without the correct font being used. In this instance, a more savvy user will understand that the problem lies in the intermediating font's lack of support for the extended character set.

To explain this a little further: the font's depiction of the underlying ASCII character is contingent upon an economy of choice. For each character displayed, the font must provide a corresponding glyph that the operating system can render. That is, the designer must craft an 'a', a 'b', a 'c', but also a 'ú'. Given that there are thousands upon thousands of characters that each need a glyph, often font designers may restrict themselves to a subset of the total Unicode specification, selecting only the glyphs that they feel will be commonly used. They may then substitute all other glyphs with a different display character, such as a solid block. Needless to say, Latinate alphabets, as the first contiguous block of the Unicode specification, are far more rarely 'blocked out'. Thus, priority is placed upon these characters while the disregard for glyphs that are specific to non-Anglophone cultures continues.

In another sense, though, this intermediation of font design masks this relegation. If a user goes straight into the '*correct*' font, they will be unaware that below the surface of the smooth blocks lurks this colonial history and the economy of choice in font design. Indeed, it will be completely opaque that the character is anything other than the design block as which it appears. In other words, the exploitation of marginalized font glyphs apparent in the crafting of NFO files is at once one that hides and highlights colonial histories of computing culture, even when this is not apparent to those working within the subcultures producing such artefacts.

[63] Domenico Fiormonte, 'Towards a Cultural Critique of the Digital Humanities', *Historical Social Research/Historische Sozialforschung*, 37.3 (141) (2012), 59–76 (p. 64).

There is a further level of intermediation here that can act to mask these historical systems. Namely, designers of NFO files often work with software that assists them in their designs. A designer would rarely craft the NFO file entirely by hand. Instead, pieces of software will attempt to match a set of undefined/unspecified non-Latinate font glyphs to the pixel shades within an image. Under this creation model, there is an even greater obfuscation of the underlying histories because even the designer is unlikely to be aware that the shadings that s/he is producing result from undefined glyphs within the font set, let alone aware of the specific glyphs that are being blocked.

Yet there is another challenge here. The NFO, as its abbreviated name implies, is *not* a poem, although it is an artefact that contains a textual aesthetic ('literary') and visualized component as a core part of its existence. It is instead primarily the vessel for the dissemination of information about material that is being circulated in contravention of civil copyright law (and perhaps even criminal copyright conspiracy laws). Thus, as Jacques Rancière put it, the 'ideal effect' of a work that entwines art and politics (or, I would argue, information) 'is always the object of a negotiation between opposites, between the readability of the message that threatens to destroy the sensible form of art and the radical uncanniness that threatens to destroy all political meaning'.[64] The NFO is a documentary object, often poorly written with crude slurs made on other groups ('lousy warez rules' is about as mild as it will get).[65] At the same time, the artefacts have an aesthetic quality to them due to the ASCII art frames. These are enmeshed within a complex play of symbolic and material capital that Alan Liu has framed as 'cool'.

To understand the ways that the laws of cool play out requires a little more background social context.[66] Certainly, James F. English

---

[64] Jacques Rancière, *The Politics of Aesthetics: The Distribution of the Sensible*, trans. Gabriel Rockhill (London: Bloomsbury, 2018), p. 59.

[65] It is often surprising to outsiders to learn that the high-level, secretive warez scene has a strict and highly codified set of internal rules and regulations. There are even teams of individuals who enforce this at the site and broader levels. These individuals belong to a class called 'nukers' and scene-wide automatic enforcement is often carried out by NukeNets, which might, say, mark a film release as 'bad' if it contains skips across many sites at the same time.

[66] Alan Liu, *The Laws of Cool: Knowledge Work and the Culture of Information* (Chicago, IL: University of Chicago Press, 2004).

has traced how the cultural prestige of prize culture works among the big literary prize-winning novels of our day.[67] Ted Underwood has, likewise, examined the phenomena that lead to literary status and prestige over a long period.[68] Yet what is in it for 'hetero "sac"', the originator of this NFO file's design? Certainly, this work is not going to be entered into any high-brow poetry or design competitions (and it wouldn't win anyway if it did).

Yet the author has taken considerable time and effort to craft the logo, understand how it will appear across multiple systems, and produce the template within which the release group can insert its documenting information. Why? Following Pierre Bourdieu's models of symbolic capital, the simple answer is that there is a type of exchange from cultural cachet into a material reward.

Release groups work on a system of access to 'topsites' (FTP [File Transfer Protocol] servers with vast reservoirs of bandwidth and disk space for storing and distributing pirated media), where they promise a kind of exclusivity for their releases. For instance, BMI is likely to have held slots on sites in different geographical regions—the UK, the USA, Europe, and Asia—where they are given, for example, five accounts with unlimited download privileges. In exchange, BMI would give all of their sites first access rights to the material that they pirate, simultaneously releasing the material across these venues. The better the group is at what it does—say, in terms of volume of high-quality illicit releases—the more user slots, storage, and bandwidth it can demand from the sites to which it is affiliated. 'hetero "sac"' will likely have a leech slot on one such site as a reward for designing the NFO. This material reward provides quality-controlled access to reservoirs of pirate artefacts well ahead of any peer-to-peer or other filesharing system.

But the simple answer—that there is a material reward—is also wrong or overly simple. For those who hold such leech slots often have them across multiple sites and almost all releases end up on all sites within a few second of release (that is: the exclusivity of affiliation to groups is a matter of minutes' or seconds' difference in whether a site has access to such material). Hence, although the terminology of

[67] English, *The Economy of Prestige Prizes*.

[68] Underwood, *Distant Horizons*, pp. 68–110.

subcultures is hotly contested, it strikes me that there is a prestige economy of a subculture at work here that does not translate back into determinate and precisely commensurable material reward.[69] That is to say: the levels of prestige of design work and the groups for which a designer works will determine the quality of the sites to which s/he is given access. But this quality is not really to do with access to pirated material. It is, instead, more about the 'cool' of the site; boasting rights of access and eliteness of status here are seen as far more important than actually downloading the material that is released.

In this last section on visualization, I have offered an insight into a rarely studied illegal digital subculture that produces a type of visualized typographic aesthetic artefact within a system of symbolic and material reward. In so doing, I have reversed the paradigm seen throughout much of this book where I document practices of studying more conventional works of literary art using digital methods. Instead, here, I have examined a digital artwork using more conventional literary and cultural methods—a type of crossover between digital literary studies and new media methodologies that forms part of the contemporary digital scene. The 'visualization' here is different from the graphs, maps, and trees of much DH. It is, instead, a textual focus on visualized digital artefacts.

From here, we now move to a more specific type of visualization with which computer approaches to literary studies have been involved: maps and cartography. While there is nothing specifically computational about literary map-making—maps were made long before computers—contemporary Geographical Information Systems (GIS) have opened these possibilities to ever-more scholars working in literary studies. Yet, the relationship between maps, places, and fictional realms is complex and convoluted. It is to such wayfaring that the next chapter turns.

---

[69] For a few of the key texts in this area, see Dick Hebdige, *Subculture: The Meaning of Style* (London: Routledge, 1979); Sarah Thornton, *Club Cultures: Music, Media and Subcultural Capital* (Cambridge: Polity Press, 1995); David Muggleton and Rupert Weinzierl, eds., *The Post-Subcultures Reader* (Oxford: Berg, 2003); Geoff Stahl, 'Tastefully Renovating Subcultural Theory: Making Space for a New Model', in *The Post-Subcultures Reader*, ed. Muggleton and Weinzierl, pp. 27–40.

3

Maps and Place

Shortly into Herman Melville's epic, *Moby-Dick*, the narrator remarks that 'it is not down on any map; true places never are', thereby making a sceptical claim about cartography's attempts to represent truth within an Enlightenment tradition.[1] The narrator also implies that resistance to cartography is itself possessed of a truth function. Maps, it seems, only add a layer of falsehood. Reality, it is implicitly claimed, will always elude the reductive processes of mapping (exactly as, in the previous chapter, texts always exceed their visualizations). Further, though, this statement is situated within a work of fiction, where the places, spaces, and maps all bear some connection to an extra-diegetic reality but are not themselves equal to that externality. The true places of Melville's fiction both appear and do not appear on maps. Melville's fiction is, itself, a type of cartographic *representation* of a reality that does not truly exist but that may capture somehow the truth of reality better than a real-world map.

Long subordinated to philosophical discourses about time, such as Bakhtin's chronotope, ideas of place and space have recently resurged in literary criticism as part of a so-called 'spatial turn'.[2] This model of literary analysis, known as geocriticism after the work of Bertrand Westphal and Robert T. Tally, is one that 'explores, seeks, surveys, digs

[1] Herman Melville, *Moby-Dick: An Authoritative Text, Contexts, Criticism*, ed. Hershel Parker, A Norton Critical Edition, 3rd edn. (New York: W. W. Norton, 2018), p. 54.

[2] M. M. Bakhtin, 'Forms of Time and of the Chronotope in the Novel', in *The Dialogic Imagination: Four Essays*, ed. Michael Holquist, trans. Caryl Emerson and Michael Holquist (Austin, TX: University of Texas Press, 2006), pp. 84–258; Bertrand Westphal, 'Foreword', in *Geocritical Explorations: Space, Place, and Mapping in Literary and Cultural Studies*, ed. Robert T. Tally (New York: Palgrave Macmillan, 2011), pp. xi–xv (p. xi); Sten Pultz Moslund, 'The Presencing of Place in Literature: Toward an Embodied Topopetic Mode of Reading', in *Geocritical Explorations*, ed. Tally, pp. 29–43 (p. 29).

into, reads, and writes a place'.[3] A 'geocritic would', Tally imagined, 'read these maps' of literary cartography, 'drawing particular attention to the spatial practices involved in literature'—akin to that termed the 'cartographic trope' by David Cosgrove a decade earlier.[4]

Yet maps have always also occupied a difficult space in literary thought. In his *Graphs, Maps, Trees*, Franco Moretti polemically notes that 'there is a very simple question about literary maps: what exactly do they *do*? [...] Do maps *add* anything, to our knowledge of literature?'[5] In Moretti's case, such a provocation is used as a straw man to be knocked down. Indeed, Moretti has famously written an entire book on how geographical space informs the literary imagination. This is a world in which 'geography is not an inert container, is not a box where cultural history "happens", but an active force, that pervades the literary field and shapes it in depth'.[6] However, many scholars have nonetheless critiqued the 'problematically positivist, and non-intellectual, practice of using GIS [geographic Information Systems] to map out quantitative data'.[7] 'So naturalized', writes Johanna Drucker, 'are the Google maps and bar charts generated from spread sheets that they pass', often, 'as unquestioned representations of "what is"'.[8] By contrast, others have been far more enthusiastic about how such digital systems could help us visualize and interpret geographical research.[9]

---

[3] Robert T. Tally, 'On Geocriticism', in *Geocritical Explorations*, ed. Tally, pp. 1–9 (p. 2).

[4] Tally, p. 1; Denis E. Cosgrove, ed., *Mappings* (London: Reaktion Books, 1999), p. 3.

[5] Moretti, *Graphs, Maps, Trees*, p. 35.

[6] Franco Moretti, *Atlas of the European Novel: 1800–1900* (London: Verso, 1998), p. 3.

[7] David Cooper and Ian N. Gregory, 'Mapping the English Lake District: A Literary GIS', *Transactions of the Institute of British Geographers*, 36.1 (2011), 89–108 (p. 89).

[8] Johanna Drucker, 'Humanities Approaches to Graphical Display', *Digital Humanities Quarterly*, 5.1 (2011) <http://www.digitalhumanities.org/dhq/vol/5/1/000091/000091.html>.

[9] S. Openshaw, 'A View on the GIS Crisis in Geography, or, Using GIS to Put Humpty-Dumpty Back Together Again', *Environment and Planning A: Economy and Space*, 23.5 (1991), 621–8 <https://doi.org/10.1068/a230621>; S. Openshaw, 'The Truth about Ground Truth', *Transactions in GIS*, 2.1 (1997), 7–24 <https://doi.org/10.1111/j.1467-9671.1997.tb00002.x>; Laura L. Paterson and Ian N. Gregory, 'Geographical Information Systems and Textual Sources', in *Representations of Poverty and Place* (Cham: Springer International Publishing, 2019), pp. 41–60 <https://doi.org/10.1007/978-3-319-93503-4_3>.

In order to understand maps, space, and place in literature, one needs to have some grounding—if you will forgive the pun—in these terminological definitions, many of which have been derived from social scientific disciplines.[10] For instance, ideas of 'place' can be split into 'phenomenological, poststructuralist, identitarian, and environmental' variants.[11] Phenomenological approaches to space, for instance—pioneered by Gaston Bachelard[12]—emphasize how subjective embeddedness in space contributes to its construction. How do domestic arrangements precede and prefigure how we experience the space of the house, for example? The poststructuralist mode takes this even further, emphasizing what Eric Prieto calls 'the indirectness of so much of our knowledge of the world' and the semiotics of spatial representation: how signs of space are read and, in turn, reshape how we read those spaces.[13] Identitarian or activist approaches to space consider how various constructions of identity—feminisms, for example—interact with ideas of space. Which spaces are open or exclusionary to those who fall under various identity types? And finally, environmental versions of spatial thinking note how identity subjectivities are situated within broader paradigms of planetary or interplanetary ecological settings and do not/cannot exist apart from such considerations.

If these ideas of space are complicated, then things are even more involved when we come to literary place. What does it mean to set a novel, for example, in London or New York? These cities, in real life, have distinct topological features and characteristics that, when referenced, are identifiable to literary audiences. But the place that is referenced in a work of fiction is *not* the actual place (whatever 'actual' is taken here to mean). Characteristics and geographies of places are imported but can be altered, warped, re-constituted, and bent to the literary ambition of the work. Peter Ackroyd's London of *Hawksmoor* (1985) is both London and not. Further, places are rooted within times

---

[10] Eric Prieto, 'Geocriticism, Geopoetics, Geophilosophy, and Beyond', in *Geocritical Explorations*, ed. Tally (New York: Palgrave Macmillan, 2011), pp. 13–27 (p. 13).

[11] Much of this background is derived from Prieto.

[12] Gaston Bachelard and Maria Jolas, *The Poetics of Space* (Boston: Beacon Press, 1994).

[13] Prieto, p. 17.

and are temporally mutable. We somehow understand Shakespeare's Venice both as the actual Venice of the 1590s and a fictionalized, off-reality version of the hydropolis. We know that Calvino's Venice of *Invisible Cities* (1972 [1974 in English]) is a Venice of a different time to Antonio and Shylock's. Yet these are also Venices of *no time* and *no place* as they are not purporting to represent with determinate truth, as might history, the places and spaces of Venice within definitive, actually occurring timeframes.[14]

Due to the rise and prevalence of geographic information systems (GIS), digital humanities practices have often become involved in ideas of mapping with respect to literary and historical texts. The above theoretical considerations are but a few of the issues with which such projects must grapple. Indeed, questions of fictional sense-making here come to the fore. Does it *make sense* to plot the location of Ackroyd's fictional Little St Hugh within a real-world version of London, keyed to the purported time of the novel's setting? What is the merit of mapping the fictional walking routes of *Mrs Dalloway* (1925) or plotting the Lake District of the Romantic poets?

Further, do such practices simply contribute further to the idea of the neoliberal digital humanities? Certainly, for Bruno Latour, maps bring with them a homogenizing, flattening, and potentially deadening capacity under a watchful and synthesizing eye: 'the main quality of the new space [of mapping] is not to be "objective" as a naïve definition of realism often claims, but rather to have optical consistency'.[15]

One must also consider, as do Cooper and Gregory, that ideas of literary cartography can be split into two categories: 'writerly mapping, which refers to the ways in which an author explicitly explores the relationship between cartography and textuality; and readerly mapping, which denotes the ways in which an individual literary GIS may recalibrate this relationship between textual and cartographical representations of geographical space through the reading process'.[16]

---

[14] For more on Venice, see Rodney James Giblett, *Cities and Wetlands: The Return of the Repressed in Nature and Culture*, Environmental Cultures Series (London: Bloomsbury Academic, 2016), p. 86.

[15] Bruno Latour, 'Visualisation and Cognition: Drawing Things Together', *Knowledge and Society: Studies in the Sociology of Culture and Present*, 6 (1986), 1–33 (p. 10).

[16] Cooper and Gregory, p. 91.

That is to say that considerations of space, place, and maps in literary studies vary according to the perspective from which one views them.

It has often been presumed, by those outside digital literary studies, that digital mapping approaches are naive and do not consider such philosophical questions. But the answer to the questions above—'what is the merit in mapping the fictional walking routes of *Mrs Dalloway*?', for instance—are complex but well understood by those who work with digital mapping technologies. Put simply: digital mapping approaches allow for deeper understandings of the chronologies in and interpersonal characterisations of literary texts. However, let us turn in more detail to some of the projects that have used such techniques.

Body Language

Despite longstanding literary-critical aversions to studying intentionality, originating in the New Critical idiom and culminating with Foucault's and Barthes's respective claims for the 'death of the author', mapping techniques can provide us with insight into creative processes.[17] This can work bidirectionally. For it is not just the case that knowing that Wordsworth wrote *Lines Composed a Few Miles above Tintern Abbey, on Revisiting the Banks of the Wye during a Tour, July 13, 1798* when he was a few miles above Tintern Abbey on the thirteenth of July in 1798 tells us something about the compositional process. Instead, in a New Historicist fashion, we can also read the environment out of the text, of 'steep and lofty cliffs' and 'hedge-rows'.[18]

---

[17] Roland Barthes, 'The Death of the Author', in *Image, Music, Text*, trans. Stephen Heath (London: Fontana Press, 1987), pp. 142–8; Sean Burke, *The Death and Return of the Author: Criticism and Subjectivity in Barthes, Foucault and Derrida* (Edinburgh: Edinburgh University Press, 2008); Foucault, 'What Is an Author?'; Jonathan Culler, 'The Closeness of Close Reading', *ADE Bulletin*, 149 (2010), 20–5 <https://doi.org/10.1632/ade.149.20>; Barbara Herrnstein Smith, 'What Was "Close Reading"? A Century of Method in Literary Studies', *The Minnesota Review*, 87 (2016), 57–75 <https://doi.org/10.1215/00265667-3630844>; Jane Gallop, 'The Historicization of Literary Studies and the Fate of Close Reading', *Profession* (2007), 181–6 <https://doi.org/10.1632/prof.2007.2007.1.181>.

[18] See for instance Stephen Greenblatt, *Renaissance Self-Fashioning: From More to Shakespeare* (Chicago, IL: University of Chicago Press, 2005); Howard Felperin,

One such project on this relationship between place and Romantic poetry is Matthew Sangster's *Romantic London*. As Sangster describes it, *Romantic London* is 'a research project exploring life and culture in London around the turn of the nineteenth century using Richard Horwood's pioneering *PLAN of the Cities of LONDON and WESTMINSTER the Borough of SOUTHWARK, and PARTS adjoining Shewing every HOUSE* (published between 1792 and 1799)'.[19] The project, however, also overlays several other documents atop historical maps of London:

- *Harris's List of Covent-Garden Ladies: or, Man of Pleasure's Kalender, For the YEAR, 1788. Containing the Histories and some curious Anecdotes of the most celebrated Ladies now on the Town, and also many of their Keepers* (1788);
- *Fores's New Guide for Foreigners, containing the most complete and accurate description of the Cities of LONDON and WESTMINSTER, and their Environs, That has yet been offered to the Public...* (1789);
- John Thomas Smith's *Antiquities of London* (1791–1800);
- Thomas Malton's *A Picturesque Tour Through the Cities of London and Westminster, illustrated with the most interesting Views, accurately delineated, and executed in Aquatinta* (1792–1801);
- Richard Phillips's *Modern London* (1804);
- Rudolph Ackermann's *Microcosm of London* (1808–10);
- John B. Papworth's *Select Views of London; with Historical and Descriptive Sketches of Some of the Most Interesting of its Public Buildings* (1816);
- Pierce Egan's *Life in London: Or, The Day and Night Scenes of Jerry Hawthorne, Esq. and his Elegant Friend Corinthian Tom, accompanied by Bob Logic, the Oxonian, in Their Rambles and Sprees Through the Metropolis* (1921);
- The London locations of Wordsworth's 'Residence in London' from *The Prelude* (from the 1850 text rather than the 1805 version).

'Making It "Neo": The New Historicism and Renaissance Literature', *Textual Practice*, 1.3 (1987), 262–77 <https://doi.org/10.1080/09502368708582017>; Jürgen Pieters, '"I Was Never a New Historicist": Catherine Belsey's "History at the Level of the Signifier"', *Textual Practice*, 24.6 (2010), 1033–44 <https://doi.org/10.1080/09502 36X.2010.521671>.

[19] Matthew Sangster, 'Romantic London', 2017 <http://www.romanticlondon.org/> [accessed 24 February 2020].

These documents can, to oversimplify, be decomposed into the categories of sociological, pictorial, and literary overlays. Each source is also contextualized within the project. For example, *Harris's List*—a 'guide' appraising sex workers in the Covent Garden area—is described as 'lewd and frequently misogynistic, romanticising prostitution while largely silencing the women involved'. The maps become particularly interesting, though, when they are brought into conjunction with one another and overlayed with the last of these: Wordsworth's *The Prelude*.

The Prelude was Wordsworth's lifelong project that was supposed to act as a precursor to his never-completed philosophical work, *The Recluse*. It is a long, book-length poem addressed to his friend Samuel Taylor Coleridge. The poem takes, as its subject, the poet's own life and mentally transformative relationship to nature, while explicitly aiming to supersede John Milton in terms of its epic form.[20] Wordsworth revised and expanded *The Prelude* throughout his life, but there are generally four recognized versions: 'Was It For This', a short poem of 1798, the two-part *Prelude* of 1799, the thirteen-book *Prelude* of 1805, and the fourteen-book version from 1850. Book Seven of *The Prelude*s of 1805 and 1850 is concerned with Wordsworth's stay in London. It is the latter of these that Sangster plots.

Critics have already noted the importance of space to Book Seven.[21] In particular, Book Seven is of interest for its critical focus on the crude spectacle of the urban space: the 'painted bloom' and 'false tints' of the city that designate the prostitute in Wordsworth's text.[22] Yet, curiously in light of the ambivalent appraisal of the city—the 'perceptual confusion' that Raymond Williams notes—many of the spots charted by Wordsworth's 'Residence in London' are far from the prostitution centres of *Harris's List*.[23] This may imply that Wordsworth's views of London were skewed away from the city's seedier core,

---

[20] For more on this, see Jonathan Wordsworth, 'Introduction', in William Wordsworth, *The Prelude: The Four Texts (*1798, 1799, 1805, 1850*)*, Penguin Classics (London: Penguin Books, 1995), pp. xxv–xlvii.

[21] François Hugo, 'The City and the Country: Books VII and VIII of Wordsworth's "The Prelude"', *Theoria: A Journal of Social and Political Theory*, 69 (1987), 1–14.

[22] Wordsworth, *The Prelude*, bk. 1805 vii.373, 1850 345.

[23] Raymond Williams, *The Country and the City* (New York: Oxford University Press, 1975), p. 151.

despite the zest with which he describes the city (and which often surprises first-time readers). However, several areas mentioned in the poem are coincident with figures in *Harris's List*. In particular, Drury Lane Theatre is a focal epicentre for salacious goings-on, rivalled only by the Union Street and Kings Street areas.

Of his visit to the Drury Lane Theatre, Wordsworth writes in the 1850 *Prelude*:

> Yet was the theatre my dear delight;
> The very gilding, lamps and painted scrolls,
> And all the mean upholstery of the place,
> Wanted not animation, when the tide
> Of pleasure ebbed but to return as fast
> With the ever-shifting figures of the scene,
> Solemn or gay: whether some beauteous dame,
> Advanced in radiance through a deep recess
> Of thick entangled forest, like the moon
> Opening the clouds; or sovereign king, announced
> With flourishing trumpet, came in full-blown state
> Of the world's greatness, winding round with train
> Of courtiers, banners, and a length of guards;
> Or captive led in abject weeds, and jingling
> His slender manacles; or romping girl,
> Bounced, leapt, and pawed the air; or mumbling sire,
> A scare-crow pattern of old age dressed up
> In all the tatters of infirmity
> All loosely put together, hobbled in,
> Stumping upon a cane with which he smites,
> From time to time, the solid boards, and makes them
> Prate somewhat loudly of the whereabout
> Of one so overloaded with his years.
> [...]
> The matter that detains us now may seem
> To many, neither dignified enough
> [...]
> For though I was most passionately moved
> And yielded to all changes of the scene
> With an obsequious promptness, yet the storm
> Passed not beyond the suburbs of the mind;
> Save when realities of act and mien,
> The incarnation of the spirits that move

> In harmony amid the Poet's world,
> Rose to ideal grandeur, or called forth
> By power of contrast, made me recognise,
> As at a glance, the things which I had shaped,
> And yet not shaped, had seen and scarcely seen,
> When, having closed the mighty Shakespeare's page,
> I mused, and thought, and felt, in solitude.[24]

Here we can see a language register around the theatre space that enters the sexual realm. This is undoubtedly central, itself, to Wordsworth's juxtaposition of the vivacious life of the city with the alienation and disconnection of urban existence (in which 'men lived / Even next-door neighbours, as we say, yet still / Strangers, and knowing not each other's names'). It is also part, though, of what Geraldine Friedman calls Wordsworth's 'redemptive negation of theatricality'.[25] From 'the tide / Of pleasure', the 'beauteous dame' advancing radiantly through 'a deep recess / Of thick entangled forest', and the 'sovereign king, announced / With flourishing trumpet' who 'came in full-blown state', through the 'romping girl' to the autobiographical state of the poet who is 'passionately moved', the language here is replete with implicit *yet celebrated* sexual imagery.

As C. R. Stokes notes, the 'Residency in London' is an interesting piece for its focus on the writer's own corporeality, conditioned by space and place. This is a work 'where Wordsworth's body, and its experience of itself, is entangled in and produced by London', a work in which the writer 'struggles to explicate his own physiological reaction'—a poem of misbehaving bodies, almost akin to a subconscious sexual response.[26] It is an urban world where agency of possession is traded back and forth between the city and the author.[27] Indeed,

---

[24] Wordsworth, bk. 1850 vii.407–85.

[25] Wordsworth, bk. 1850 vii.118–120; Geraldine Friedman, 'History in the Background of Wordsworth's "Blind Beggar"', *ELH*, 56.1 (1989), 125–48 (p. 125) <https://doi.org/10.2307/2873126>. See also Bruce Mazlish, *A New Science: The Breakdown of Connections and the Birth of Sociology* (Oxford: Oxford University Press, 1989), pp. 71–7.

[26] C. R. Stokes, 'Sign, Sensation and the Body in Wordsworth's "Residence in London"', *European Romantic Review*, 23.2 (2012), 203–23 (pp. 204, 212) <https://doi.org/10.1080/10509585.2012.653281>.

[27] See, for example, John Plotz, *The Crowd: British Literature and Public Politics* (Berkeley, CA: University of California Press, 2000), p. 33.

Wordsworth creates an environment in which, following Stokes, 'the body is bound to the semiotics of the city'.[28] These passages are even more notable when one considers, as does Lawrence Kramer's psychoanalytic reading, that in the 1850 *Prelude*, 'Wordsworth cuts [many of] the passages about vivid pleasure', and particularly blunts the scene involving remembrance of a prostitute.[29] (Although it is notably the case, in both 1805 and 1850 editions that Wordsworth protests a little too much about his poor memory of this figure among 'shameless women': 'and scarcely at this time / do I remember her'/'The mother now / is fading out of memory'.)

This is all to say that there is already a long pedigree of scholarship that considers bodies, sexuality, and theatre as a nexus in Romantic poetry for discourse on and condemnation of popular urban fixation on spectacle. In the loosest of terms, this is what Sangster's map begins to show us. It does not achieve this by direct parallel. Certainly, there are serious historiographical problems aligning a list of sex workers from 1788 with geographical locations mentioned in *The Prelude* of 1850 (or even 1805). It is, as Jonathan Wordsworth notes, even 'far from clear in what order the books of *The Prelude* were composed', and Book Seven presents specific difficulties.[30] Mark L. Reed speculates, though, that Wordsworth made his first visit to London in 1788, which would mean that the description in *The Prelude* refers to 1789–90, since the 1805 edition tells us that ''Twas at least two years / Before this season when I first beheld / That mighty place'.[31] Any precise dating is further complicated by Wordsworth's processes of lifelong revision and poetic distance/reflection. The poetic licence that Wordsworth uses makes it likely that the impressionistic sweep of London that he yields is not composed of any single, 'real' visit.[32] In short, it is conceptually hazardous to compare the map data to Wordsworth's visit.

[28] Stokes, p. 217.

[29] Lawrence Kramer, 'Gender and Sexuality in *The Prelude*: The Question of Book Seven', *ELH*, 54.3 (1987), 619–37 (p. 623) <https://doi.org/10.2307/2873223>.

[30] Jonathan Wordsworth, pp. xxxiii, xxxv.

[31] Wordsworth, bk. 1805 vii.72–4; Mark L. Reed, *Wordsworth: The Chronology of the Early Years, 1770–1799* (Cambridge, MA: Harvard University Press, 2013), p. 81n <https://www.degruyter.com/view/title/321976> [accessed 28 March 2020].

[32] John T. Ogden, 'The Power of Distance in Wordsworth's *Prelude*', *PMLA*, 88.2 (1973), 246–59 <https://doi.org/10.2307/461490>.

However, I would argue that maps such as Sangster's bring para-taxis to disparate sources, which in turn permit appraisal of socially produced spaces, allowing us to focus on new and existing questions. These might include the aesthetic: does Wordsworth's language regis-ter *change* substantially as we approach theatrical venues? They might also broach the political: does taking Sangster's overlay of itinerant traders reveal a language of trade, exchange, and economy—but also of class—in particular London regions? And they might prompt fur-ther historical investigation: how had the landscape changed by the time(s) at which Wordsworth wrote and how did the produced space of London influence his poetic practice? Thus, maps, rather than just territories, can be productive sites of questioning encounter for liter-ary history and criticism.

It is this questioning and dialectical process that also informs Wordsworth's poetry. The depiction of London in *The Prelude* is one of unresolved contradictions; a battlefield of sorts. It contrasts various forms of imitative artistic representation, for instance, with reality while the battle rages between the transformational power of the poet's mind and the external assault upon his senses that the city foists. In the same way, digital maps can give us a productive foil against which to pit literary texts, with maps serving as reflexive tools for text-ual interrogation.

Questions from Grasmere

If Sangster's map takes a set of poetic London coordinates and over-lays them atop other historical references, yielding, I have argued, not a precise geography of Wordsworth's tour and its intersection with historical places and events, but rather a suggestive cartography that can refocus our attention on body language, other projects have vis-ited more traditional sites of Romantic poetry. The 'Mapping the Lakes' project, funded by the British Academy and hosted at the University of Lancaster, does, to a certain extent, what it says on the tin: it maps the Lake District of Thomas Gray and Samuel Taylor Coleridge. For me, the project highlights many of the processual advantages of conducting work with geographic information systems.[33]

---

[33] Cooper and Gregory.

By way of background description: ' "Mapping the Lakes" maps out two textual accounts of journeys through the landscape of the Lake District: Thomas Gray's tour of the region in the autumn of 1769; and Samuel Taylor Coleridge's "circumcursion" of the area in August 1802'.[34] The website that resulted from the project 'offers GIS representations of these two accounts of place and suggests ways in which the mapping process opens up spatial thinking about these geo-specific texts. The project also offers general reflections on the intersections of digital cartography and electronic textuality, paving the way for future research on the literature of landscape and environment'.[35]

In order to understand the 'Mapping the Lakes' project, one has first to grasp the aims, objectives, and underlying suppositions of the undertaking. The entire project aimed to 'construct a spatial narrative by inviting the user to move through a series of increasingly experimental and exploratory cartographies'.[36] The project then works towards a synthesis of the two narratives. For, in addition to charting the progression of Gray and Coleridge, the project seeks, in a similar way as did Sangster, to 'move beyond these single-author cartographies by highlighting the potential of layered GIS maps: maps which document the representation of place across multiple texts'. Finally, the project attempts 'to highlight the ways in which GIS technology might be used to map out more abstract, imaginative and emotional responses to landscape and environment'. These three aims bear some closer attention.

A common but erroneous criticism of digital literary projects is that they are poor at generating good, humanistic questions. Indeed, when Ted Underwood introduces *Distant Horizons* as a book about 'recent discoveries in literary history', he immediately notes that the 'word *discovery* may sound odd, because the things that matter in literary history are usually arguments, not discoveries'.[37] That is to say: there seems to be a fundamental mismatch between the expectations of

---

[34] David Cooper et al., 'Home Page', *Mapping the Lakes* <https://www.lancaster. ac.uk/mappingthelakes/index.htm> [accessed 12 March 2020].

[35] Cooper et al., 'Home Page'.

[36] David Cooper et al., 'Aims & Objectives', *Mapping the Lakes* <https://www.lancaster. ac.uk/mappingthelakes/GIS%20Aims.htm> [accessed 12 March 2020].

[37] Underwood, *Distant Horizons*, p. ix.

what literary criticism and history *are* and what digital literary studies *do*. Certainly, this is not true of 'Mapping the Lakes', which decomposes its inquiries into writer-specific, geo-specific, and theoretical topics, all of which seem to be valid fields of humanistic inquiry.[38] Examples of questions in the writer-specific domain include 'which places do both Gray and Coleridge say that they visited on their respective excursions through the Lakes?', 'do the writers name any Lake District sites which they do not actually visit?', and 'which versions of the respective texts should be used as base texts for the digital mappings?'[39] When it comes to the geo-specific questions, the project is equally as expansive: 'how do different writers define the (imaginative/ actual) boundaries of the English Lake District?', 'do different writers use similar (or contrasting) language in their respective accounts of particular locations?', and 'how do the definitions of region, suggested within the texts, correspond with the spatial boundaries imposed by the National Park Authority in the middle of the twentieth-century?'[40]

If questions are good, though, then surely answers also matter? Indeed, the authors give a set of responses to their prompts in their resulting journal article. For instance, they note that it is clear, in visual form, that Gray's 1769 tour 'moved exclusively through the eastern half of the region' while Coleridge in 1802 'focused on the more vertiginous, western fringes of the Lakes'. The geographic data they have assembled are then recombined with the already known biographical accounts, focusing on the facts that Gray's routes 'unambiguously' document a type of 'spatial mobilities of the tourist', painting a man who aestheticized his travel, carrying an artist's Claude-glass and working within (and beyond) the development of the high Picturesque of the Lake District. By contrast, Coleridge can be confirmed as an inhabitant of the region, demonstrating a 'socio-spatial insiderness'

[38] For more on ideas of decomposition, see West.

[39] David Cooper et al., 'Writer-Specific Aims: Gray & Coleridge', *Mapping the Lakes* <https://www.lancaster.ac.uk/mappingthelakes/GIS%20Writer%20Specific%20 Aims.htm> [accessed 12 March 2020].

[40] David Cooper et al., 'Geo-Specific Aims', *Mapping the Lakes* <https://www.lancaster. ac.uk/mappingthelakes/GIS%20Geo-Specific%20Aims.htm> [accessed 12 March 2020].

that informs his walking tour. The effect of the 'overarching spatial trajectories of the two journeys', as mapped in the 'Mapping the Lakes' project, is to 'reinforce the notion that Gray and Coleridge offer contrasting portraits of spatial outsiderness and insiderness'. A shocking and new observation? Perhaps not. But as the authors put it, 'the critical value of literary GIS resides in its capacity to prompt further spatial thinking about texts'.[41] This is an argument that chimes with my own provocation in this book that digital methods can bring us back to direct textual engagement.

In addition to asking questions across these domains, though, the project also has merit in the outcomes of its actual process. In the first instance, the team were frustrated by the lack of extant digital texts. Furthermore, their textual coding systems proved incredibly time consuming and it became clear to the team that their efforts could not easily grow: 'the process of digitising the primary texts involved typing up, and tagging, the respective accounts by Gray and Coleridge: a process which proved to be extremely time-consuming. Future literary GIS projects will require the development of an alternative method of textual digitisation and encoding'.[42] In addition to creating a digital textual edition here that will be of use to future scholars, this statement recognises one of the fundamental paradoxes of digital abundance thinking. Although I already highlighted this in the preceding chapter on machine-generated text, it bears repeating: while we think of the digital realm as one of digital abundance and overflow, there are hard limits placed on this abundance by the scarcity of labour provision upon which this rests.

This digital abundance thinking is exemplified in the 'Mapping the Lakes' project. For, immediately after noting the intense labour limitations that hindered the project, the team remark upon their hopes for the future expansion of their efforts: 'connected with this, the researcher will need to be able to draw upon a greater range of spatial attributes with which to tag the "data" (in other words, the primary texts). In this pilot project, each place name was given one of three

[41] Cooper and Gregory, pp. 94–8.

[42] David Cooper et al., 'Research Outcomes', *Mapping the Lakes* <https://www.lancaster.ac.uk/mappingthelakes/Research%20Outcomes.html> [accessed 12 March 2020].

attributes based upon the supposed actuality of writerly spatial experience: "visited"; "unvisited"; or "unknown". The future literary GIS, however, will need to offer a way of representing the imagined, as well as the actual, experience of place'. How, one might ask, is this to be accomplished? Resourcing for time and labour in the humanities is not set to increase. Certainly, philanthropic grant agencies continue to do much good in the world. However, it seems possible that there will *never be a time* when all materials are available digitally with comprehensively useful semantic content. Even Google, which perhaps has more resources dedicated to this than any other organization in the world, has struggled just to conduct basic digitization of all the world's texts (not least because of various copyright suit hindrances). To believe that there is some future point at which this level of digitization—or, even better, a world of semantically rich digitization—has been possible seems utopian, in the naive sense. Instead, we—and GIS projects—must acknowledge that we must *select* in the present, based on imperfect notions of canon formation, for the underlying reason that we have not sufficient labour capacity to act otherwise.

In turn, though, the shortcuts that we sometimes have to take in terms of labour time can lead to tricky elisions. In the case of 'Mapping the Lakes', this was clear in how the team created a composite version of Coleridge's tour of the Lake District. Following Roger Hudson's editorial strategy, the project conflated Coleridge's notebooks with his letters to Sara Hutchinson, creating a single text.[43] 'The creation of this composite account', however, write the project members, 'fails to acknowledge that intertextual references made in Coleridge's Notebooks (to Thomas West and William Gilpin; or to Salvator Rosa) do not feature in his letters to Sara Hutchinson'. In other words, 'the geo-specificity of these explicit references highlights how Coleridge perceives particular locations as sites of spatial intertextuality. At the same time, such discrepancies raise important questions regarding the ways in which Coleridge's articulation of his geographical experience differs across textual forms and spaces'. Participants in 'Mapping the Lakes' imagine a further, 'more comprehensive project' that 'would have to remain sensitive to these textual

[43] Roger Hudson, ed., *Coleridge Among the Lakes & Mountains* (London: Folio Society, 1991).

overlaps and intersections'. However, the question remains as to who will undertake this involved and challenging work of textual mapping and whether the payoff would be commensurate to the labour invested.

Talking Points

Thus far, I have argued that literary maps shine a spotlight on the difficult intersections between their intra-diegetic settings and the cartographic representations of the world outside. For the next section of this chapter, I would like to turn to a novel that uses cartography in exactly this way and that, thereby, is incomprehensible without an at least mental map of its landscape but also, I would argue, a tabulation of its timetable: Mark Blacklock's 2015 *I'm Jack*.[44] This is another illustration of how, following my provocation, approaches that are traditionally associated with the 'digital humanities'—building geographic coordinate systems and creating tables of (meta)data—can be a way to orient us *back* towards literary texts.

Given the particularly British context of Blacklock's novel and its relative lack of prominence, a small amount of upfront summary and historical explication is necessary. From 1975 to 1980 in Yorkshire, in the north of England, in a high-profile criminal case, Peter Sutcliffe murdered thirteen women in a a serial-killing spree. Seven other women survived Sutcliffe's attempted murders. The British tabloid press—never known for its restraint, balance, or tact—dubbed Sutcliffe the 'Yorkshire Ripper', after the famous Victorian spree-killer of prostitutes 'Jack the Ripper'. Sutcliffe was eventually apprehended and died from COVID-19 in 2020, having spent most his whole-life tariff in Broadmoor, one of three high-security psychiatric hospitals in the UK.

Blacklock's novel is bound up with the case of the Yorkshire Ripper, but it is not primarily concerned with Sutcliffe. Instead, the novel centres on one of the grimmest hoaxes of the police force in British

---

[44] Portions of this section are derived from Martin Paul Eve, 'Reading Redaction: Symptomatic Metadata, Erasure Poetry, and Mark Blacklock's *I'm Jack*', *Critique: Studies in Contemporary Fiction*, 60.3 (2019), 330–41 <https://doi.org/10.1080/00111619.2019.1568960>.

history: that of John Samuel Humble, dubbed 'Wearside Jack'. Between 1978 and 1979, Humble sent three letters to the West Yorkshire police and the newspaper the *Daily Mirror* impersonating 'the ripper' in which he accused the police of incompetence and of being unable to catch him. One of the items that Humble sent to the police was an audiotape in which he 'confessed' to the killings but told the police chief, George Oldfield, that he was unlikely ever to catch him. The letters are signed 'Jack the Ripper'. Most importantly, though, the audiotape that was sent revealed an accent from the Wearside area of Sunderland. This caused the police to divert their investigation away from the West Yorkshire area, even though they had already questioned Sutcliffe himself (who did not have a Wearside accent). In turn, Sutcliffe was then free to murder a further three women, mostly due to Humble's contamination of the investigation. Humble was eventually caught, twenty-five years after the event, in 2006, and handed an eight-year sentence for perverting the course of justice. Humble died in 2019 from heart failure.

Hence, *I'm Jack* is primarily a novel about impersonation. Re-imagining Humble's life leading up to his acts and then recounting the events via letters from prison to a (now-deceased) police chief, George Oldfield, the text itself is named after another, nonfiction book: Peter Kinsley's *I'm Jack: The Police Hunt for the Yorkshire Ripper*.[45] That is, Blacklock's novel shares its title with and usurps the title of another work. This act of archival/factual imitation sits well with the book's theme and formal mode and is itself a type of redaction; the novel quietly redacts a purported factual and historical work in favour of its own fictionalized history. For *I'm Jack* presents its fictionalized narrative through a collage of research material. Reconstructed police documents from Humble's earlier spat with the police, for example, form part of the back narrative of the text. By shadowing Kinsley's book, which is explicitly referenced in Blacklock's novel, *I'm Jack* clarifies the archival game that it is playing.[46] In many ways, of course, this is just another turn from the Hayden White school of postmodern historiography, in which the only difference between fiction and

[45] Peter Kinsley, *I'm Jack: The Police Hunt for the Yorkshire Ripper* (London: Pan, 1980).
[46] Mark Blacklock, *I'm Jack* (London: Granta, 2015), p. 107.

history is the claim to truth.[47] In another sense, though, there is a more sophisticated take at play here, since Blacklock's novel subtly but explicitly signposts its fictionality, never claiming the truth that history possesses, yet maintaining an accuracy throughout. Blacklock's work is not full of showy self-reflexive gimmicks, but is rather concerned with how narrative can emerge from the formal mechanism of documentary parataxis.

What does *I'm Jack* mean, though, to someone who has no access to the sonographic map of British accents? Blacklock himself provides some clues to a reader of the type of vocalization that a Wearside accent implies in the novel's opening pages. He there yields a stream-of-consciousness narrative in a transcription of the dialect: 'diesel greeny-bluey sheen on top uv the brown churn all flowin out tu sea all getting washed down the wiah unspoolin in the watta all the guts uv it innards out all the fish guts on the harbar the herrin guts the wifies guttin them brown loops uv it the wyrms wunda iv thes lampreys theh used tu eat them in auden days' etc.[48] Certainly this gives the reader an idea of what is meant by a Wearside accent, although the text is somewhat cryptic in refusing to say, outright, that this is a representation of that accent.

Additionally, Blacklock's use of accent is here tied to the literary precedent of Russell Hoban's seminal 1980 science fiction novel, *Riddley Walker*. That text is written entirely in a phonetic style that bears close resemblance to Blacklock's: 'on my naming day when I come 12 I gone front spear and kilt a wyld boar he parbly ben the las wyld pig on the Bundel Downs any how there hadnt ben none for a long time befor him nor I aint looking to see none agen'.[49] The difference here is that Hoban's novel is set in the distant future in Kent, after an unspecified nuclear apocalypse, whereas Blacklock's work is an epistolary historical fiction of sorts in the North East of England. Yet Hoban's future world is also regressed; its temporality is one where the time yet to come resembles the Iron Age. The novelistic world of *Riddley Walker* is, therefore, also mirrored in its linguistic regression to

[47] Hayden White, *Metahistory: Historical Imagination in Nineteenth Century Europe* (Baltimore, MD: Johns Hopkins University Press, 1975), pp. 93–7.

[48] Blacklock, p. 2.

[49] Russell Hoban, *Riddley Walker* (London: Bloomsbury, 2002), p. 1.

a transcription of a phonocentric setup where the text records the spoken dialect of the characters. In mimicking *Riddley Walker*, however, the temporality of *I'm Jack* is also affected. In Blacklock's novel, accents are not merely about place but also about time.

Yet what does it mean for the novel's plot that one can identify how an accent sounds, but perhaps not where it is placed? Initiatives such as those led by Ruth Ahnert at the Centre for Early Modern Mapping, News and Networks at Queen Mary, University of London, have done much concerning the digital visualization of 'social networks' in the early modern period, as part of what they call 'the network turn'.[50] However, the importance of space and networks to the contemporary epistolary novel remains largely uncharted.

Of course, in the case of *I'm Jack*, this narrative plotting is complicated because it is also a historical plotting; the plot points of the novel are re-imaginations of real events. Indeed, it would be tough and probably not very interesting to plot the actual metadata of the letters that Blacklock has fabricated since they almost all come from two prisons and are addressed to a single deceased man. We can plot, though, the various geometries and points of the address and time signatures of the events in the novel to more clearly see why Humble's hoax was so powerful.

The first thing to unearth here is the spatial metadata from Humble's letters, which we can make clearer with the aid of digital mapping. Ironically, these are the only addresses that do not appear in Blacklock's novelization. This is because while the prison letters contain a return address in *I'm Jack*, the original hoax letters are presented as though documentary items, in isolation and without a source or destination. In fact, apart from prison and hospital addresses, the only property listed is '26 Hawarden Crescent, Sunderland' (perhaps a joke on the part of the author, a reference to a childhood or family member's home?) In any case, when we plot Sunderland (where Humble was based) as the source of letters and tapes to the central police station in Leeds, as well as the *Daily Mirror*'s offices in Manchester,

---

[50] For more, see Ruth Ahnert et al., *The Network Turn: Changing Perspectives in the Humanities* (Cambridge: Cambridge University Press, 2020) <https://doi.org/10.1017/9781108866804>.

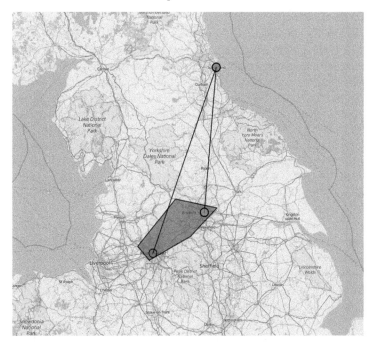

Figure 3.1 Letters and tape metadata coordination of 'Wearside Jack'. The shaded polygon represents the area in which Peter Sutcliffe was operating. Letters were sent by Humble to the two circles within the area of Sutcliffe's crimes from Sunderland. The erroneous reverse triangulation threw detectives off the case of the Yorkshire Ripper, allowing him to roam free. Map generated with Neatline. Map data copyright OpenStreetMap contributors 2015. Used under a CC BY-SA License. Image shared under CC BY-SA License.

alongside a polygonal mapping of the area in which Sutcliffe's murders were committed, it is clear why the metadata was so damaging.

Indeed, we can see in Figure 3.1 why it was such a diversion for the police and for the *Daily Mirror* to receive a letter from Sunderland. Both of the entities to which the letters were sent fall within the 'Ripper's' actual area of operation, the shaded polygon. By contrast, the letters were sent from a triangulated point some hundred miles or so north. Moreover, the voice evidence on the tape also pointed towards the Wearside area.

If the letter and tape metadata proved so crucial in terms of *place*, they were also indispensable, though, in terms of timing—a narrative element that can be better understood through a datafication method of *tabulation*. Indeed, Keith Brannen has assembled a comprehensively (some might say 'fanatically'[51]) detailed web resource about the Sutcliffe case that provides the chronological background metadata surrounding the Wearside Jack hoax.[52] The results of this, interspersed with historically accurate metadata from *I'm Jack*, can be seen in Table 3.1. In the table, lines in **bold** represent events pertaining to the hoaxer. Additional sources, beyond Brannen's site, are indicated within the table.

The crucial timings that are not wholly clear (or may be entirely fictional) are Humble's nightclub spat and his subsequent assault. I have been unable to pinpoint these outside of Blacklock's novel. Yet again, though, the chronological metadata alone here proves instructive in reading and understanding the geographic narrative flow both of history and of the novel. The most crucial interview with Sutcliffe took place on 1979-07-29 in which officers Greenwood and Laptew strongly suspected that they might be talking to the 'Ripper'. They passed on their recommendation for further investigation but this took some time to reach senior officers because of a substantial administrative backlog. By the time it had reached senior officers, the report entitled 'Murders And Assaults Upon Women In The North Of England' had been issued, which explicitly listed a criterion of a Geordie (Newcastle) accent as a necessary prerequisite for a suspect, based on Humble's tape, sent on 1979-06-17. The time signatures of

---

[51] Although Blacklock's parody of the conspiracy theorist Noel O'Gara (as 'Norris Downing' in *I'm Jack*) is more on the 'fanatical' side. Indeed, a search for Google Groups conversations on the topic will prove instructive in this regard. Furthermore, the letters that Humble writes to 'Norris Downing' are transcribed from a conspiracy theory posted on O'Gara's website. Norris O'Gara, 'John Humble', *THE REAL YORKSHIRE RIPPER STORY*, 2011 <http://www.yorkshireripper.com/2011/12/29/john-humble/> [accessed 28 December 2015].

[52] Keith Brannen, 'POLICE INTERVIEWS', *The Yorkshire Ripper*, 2015 <http://www.execulink.com/~kbrannen/intervws.htm> [accessed 28 December 2015].

Table 3.1 A chronological timeline of the investigation into John Samuel Humble and Peter Sutcliffe. Author's own.

Date (YYYY-MM-DD)	Actor(s)	Event
1977-11-02	Howard (Police), L. Smith (Police), Sutcliffe	Interview #1
1977-11-08	Police, Sutcliffe	Interview #2
1978-03-08	**Humble, Oldfield (Police)**	**Letter #1**
1978-03-13	**Humble, *Daily Mirror***	**Letter #2**
1978-08-13	P. Smith (Police), Sutcliffe	Interview #3
1978-11-23	P. Smith (Police), Sutcliffe	Interview #4
1979-03-23	**Humble, Oldfield (Police)**	**Letter #3**
1979-06-17	**Humble, Oldfield (Police)**	**Tape**
1979-07-29	Greenwood (Police), Laptew (Police), Sutcliffe	Interview #5
1979-09-13	**Police**	**Report issued: 'Murders And Assaults Upon Women In The North Of England', including elimination criterion: '(e) If his accent is dissimilar to a North Eastern (Geordie) accent'.**
1979-10-23	Police, Sutcliffe	Interview #6
1980-01-13	Police, Sutcliffe	Interview #7
1980-01-30	Police, Sutcliffe	Interview #8

Continued

Table 3.1 *Continued*

Date (YYYY-MM-DD)	Actor(s)	Event
1980-02-07	Police, Sutcliffe	Interview #9
1991	**Police, Humble**	**Humble arrested for being drunk and disorderly. Saliva swab (and DNA) stored on file.[a]**
2005-10-19/20	**Police, Humble**	**Arrest/Interview/Charge[b]**

[a] Jeremy Armstrong and Lucy Thornton, 'Yorkshire Ripper Hoaxer Wearside Jack Speaks for First Time about "prank" That Derailed Serial Killer Investigation', *Daily Mirror*, 14 July 2013 <http://www.mirror.co.uk/news/uk-news/yorkshire-ripper-hoaxer-wearside-jack-2053906> [accessed 30 December 2015].

[b] David Bruce, '"I'M JACK" HOAX – MAN CHARGED', *Yorkshire Evening Post*, 20 October 2005 <http://www.yorkshireeveningpost.co.uk/news/latest-news/top-stories/i-m-jack-hoax-man-charged-1-2135152> [accessed 28 December 2015]; Blacklock, p. 12.

the events, as well as the geographical markers, constitute important metadata for the narrative.

What begins to emerge from this plotting of temporal and spatial metadata in this text, using methods that are more usually seen in data-driven approaches, is that the unavailability of content provides an ideal space for fictional narrative. As with all geo-historical fiction, it is necessary for there to be gaps in the record that can be filled with imagined content. The metadata surrounding events provides the chronology, while the narrative provides the emplotment/history. From this, we can deduce, though, that *I'm Jack* is a (hi)story about how what is said can be, in some ways, less important than how it is said and whence it is communicated. Understanding this novel requires a comprehension of accent and sound, history and emplotment, and space and literary geography; all aspects with which a digital approach to mapping and a datafying tabulation can assist us.

Literary Geography

'What', asks Moretti, 'do literary maps allow us to see?' He provides, to his own rhetorical foil, two answers that are worth quoting in full:

First, they highlight the *ortgebunden*, place-bound nature of literary forms: each of them with its peculiar geometry, its boundaries, its spatial taboos and favorite routes. And then, maps bring to light the internal logic of narrative: the semiotic domain around which a plot coalesces and self-organizes. Literary form appears thus as the result of two conflicting, and equally significant forces: one working from the outside, and one from the inside. It is the usual, and at bottom the only real issue of literary history: society, rhetoric, and their interaction.[53]

Without some understanding of spatiality and literary geography, we have an impoverished view of what literature represents. Literary texts are set in representations of places and the logic of plot involves encounters in spaces.

So far, so obvious, even if it is a point worth restating. However, a final aspect must here be addressed: what is the role of computation in all of this? Yes, although there is debate and the 'reuse' of maps 'by critics tends to be confirmatory rather than revelatory', we can see that there might be merit in plotting literary maps in order to abet our understandings.[54] Why, though, should this distinctly be the purview of a digital humanities approach to literary studies and mapping, using computers?

The short answer is that it need not be. It is perfectly possible to conduct literary mapping exercises without the aid of a computer, as for centuries maps were drawn and produced. However, the expansion of access that computerized mapping software has brought has greatly reduced the effort involved in producing such artefacts. In addition, the existence of openly licensed global, accurate, and even historical maps provides literary cartographers with lowered barriers to geographic participation.

At the same time, this expanded accessibility brings with it fresh dangers. As more venture into the territory of literary mapping there

---

[53] Moretti, *Atlas of the European Novel*, p. 5. That said, Stefanie Markovits has questioned the extent to which the generic place-boundness is precisely not a feature of the Victorian verse-novel. Stefanie Markovits, *The Victorian Verse-Novel: Aspiring to Life* (Oxford: Oxford University Press, 2017), p. 167.

[54] Ray Davis, 'Graphs, Maps, Trees/Sets Hamper Grasp', in *Reading* Graphs, Maps and Trees: *Responses to Franco Moretti*, ed. Jonathan Goodwin and John Holbo (Anderson, SC: Parlor Press, 2011), pp. 15–30 (p. 16).

is the ever-present risk of thinking that mere plotting will yield narrative insight, when all it may actually do is to inscribe further scars on the fictional text. In fact, with the wide availability of digital maps, seemingly ready-made for literary overlay, the importance of questioning the interlink between the literary representation and the world it purportedly represents is greater than ever. Perhaps more than anything, though, digital mapping approaches demonstrate to us the problems in transposing literary texts, which use their space as narrative structuration devices, onto maps that purport to represent an extra-textual reality. Like all good humanistic inquiry, digital mapping does not simply produce positivistic answers to scientistically framed questions. Because the two—maps and reality, or mapping questions and cartographic answers—do not piece together neatly like a jigsaw. They rather sit in a relationship of mutual tension and productive questioning, like X-shaped pieces, with W-shaped holes.[55]

[55] The situation faced at the end of Georges Perec, *Life a User's Manual*, trans. David Bellos (London: Harvill, 1996), p. 497.

4

Distance and History

In the introduction to this book, I noted that, by a rough calculation, one would need to read ten novels per day, every day from age ten onwards, just to have read all English fiction published in 2015. Yet, as tempting as it is to see such proliferation as a new phenomenon, this 'overproduction', as Amy Hungerford terms it, 'has been a feature of literary history since at least the 18th century'. Following the arguments of Rita Felski in her 2008 *Uses of Literature*, Hungerford points out, with characteristic understatement, that 'overproduction at this scale makes historical approaches difficult'.[1]

The problem is no longer that there is a potentially conquerable limit of knowledge. It is not simply that an individual critic has not read sufficiently. The volume of literature produced is now so great that it is impossible for any critic ever to have read sufficiently to conduct a total and rigorous historical analysis of a literary period. This is among the reasons why Ted Underwood can note that perhaps 'the most durable' organizational principle of literary studies is 'periodization' but that we should not study why this matters, but why it 'mattered', past tense.[2] Periodization and historicism were part of a legitimating move for the discipline of literary studies when it sought professionalism. Periodization gave a sense that we were dealing with manageable scales of reading, neatly divided into sub-units such as 'Modernism'. However, the scales of literary over-production mean

---

[1] Amy Hungerford, *Making Literature Now*, Post 45 (Stanford, CA: Stanford University Press, 2016), p. 143; Rita Felski, *Uses of Literature* (Malden, MA: Blackwell Publishing, 2008), p. 10. See also Amy Hungerford, 'On the Period Formerly Known as Contemporary', *American Literary History*, 20.1–2 (2008), 410–19 <https://doi.org/10.1093/alh/ajm044>.

[2] Underwood, *Why Literary Periods Mattered*, p. 1.

that periodization is not and never has been founded on sound and comprehensive methods.

But what if you could know the contents of every literary work ever written without having to read the books themselves? (Or, if not every work, at least a much more representative and random sample of that body of work?) This is the promise of so-called 'distant reading', a term coined by Franco Moretti, but with a much longer genealogy.[3] Under such a model, the idea is that computational detection of style, theme, content, named entities, geographic place names, etc. could be discerned at scale and aggregated into a broader and continuous literary history that would not suffer from the same defects as a model that required one to read everything. At the same time, the type of pronouncements that such a literary-historical approach can make would be qualitatively different to those that we know today. Would such statistical observations even constitute a recognizable form of 'literary history'?

Distant reading, the primary focus of this chapter, is most often associated with large-scale literary history. Certainly, the case studies to which I will turn in this penultimate chapter are predominantly concerned with such a mode. However, it is essential to grasp, first, the interrelation between close and distant reading. They are not opposed to one another, despite the antonymic metaphors of their titling. As I have already noted, distant reading at the macro level depends on computational processes that can work at the micro-level and that require verification against human close reading processes. For it makes no sense to believe that a distant reading at scale can be any good unless its processes work correctly at the level of the individual texts and that it works reliably across a well-known set of extant novels or poems.

Many literary critics misunderstand this aspect of distant reading. For it is often claimed, when a digital literary studies paper proclaims that it has replicated an existing finding (i.e. the computational approach agrees with existing literary criticism), that these methods tell us nothing new. Yet this is an incremental approach to knowledge

---

[3] Moretti, *Distant Reading*; Ted Underwood, 'A Genealogy of Distant Reading', *Digital Humanities Quarterly*, 11.2 (2017) <http://www.digitalhumanities.org/dhq/vol/11/2/000317/000317.html> [accessed 21 September 2017].

that renders computational approaches compatible with extant literary criticism.[4] As Matthew L. Jockers puts it in his introductory instruction book on using the programming language *R* for text analysis: a 'good deal of computational work is specifically aimed at testing, rejecting, or reconfirming knowledge that we think we already possess'.[5]

Yet to say that such work tells us only what we already know is to miss the point. When such work confirms an existing literary-critical supposition, it adds further confirmatory evidence to that point of view. This can be especially valuable because interpretative questions in literary criticism are often pluralistic and allow for divergences of opinion. It also demonstrates that the computational method is, in some way, sound. When such approaches work across multiple texts, we can then have some confidence that they might be accurate when scaled to process texts that we have not read in advance. When a computational method works on many texts but then throws an anomaly on another, it can force a re-evaluation of the extant theories around that single text.

A second objection to digital literary methods is similar to that flagged by Andrew Elfenbein when he interacted with cognitive psychology. Namely, for literary critics what matters is the particular and the unique: the specific. However, in cognitive psychology, in Elfenbein's words, 'psychological claims depend, instead, on demonstrating that, while there are major individual differences between people, core cognitive architectures, such as memory systems or functions of executive control, have much in common'.[6] In the literary-critical field, we have learned—partially through developing literary sensibilities and partially through critical theoretical approaches that focus on the unique—'to suspect comparable psychological claims, especially about reading'.[7]

---

[4] See Andrew Piper, *Can We Be Wrong? The Problem of Textual Evidence in a Time of Data* (Cambridge: Cambridge University Press, 2020) <https://doi.org/10.1017/9781108922036> for a fascinating examination of how literary critical debate works within more scientistic ways of thinking.

[5] Matthew L. Jockers, *Text Analysis with R for Students of Literature* (New York: Springer, 2014), pp. vii–viii.

[6] Elfenbein, p. 1.   [7] Elfenbein, p. 2.

The suspicion that many literary critics have of digital methods is that they similarly reduce the specific and the unique in literary works to a type of commonality. In some senses, this is a mirror of the suspicion shared by literary critics about literary history. Certainly, history and periodization are about pattern recognition and identifying shared tropes across works, even while an approach to literary history that relies on a critic reading the texts in detail has more scope for admission of unique details. The challenge for digital methods is that this flattening of texts into constellations of relation—the knocking down of complex individual works into data points—is done without having read the originals. 'The risk', write Claire Lemercier and Claire Zalc, 'of standardization has always plagued quantitative history'.[8] For many, this appears as an abrogation of our responsibility towards literature itself; a neglect of its singularity.[9] Nonetheless, the works to which and authors to whom I turn in this chapter seek to rectify a fundamental issue in our existing ideas of canon: the 'too-much-to-read' dilemma.

Digital Material History

Before we delve into text analysis itself, another form of digital historical practice is first worth covering: digital media history. It is notable that, for nearly forty years now, almost every work has been a digital text before it has assumed any other form.[10] Those who follow Marshall McLuhan's phrasing that the medium is the message will appreciate that such a shift cannot but have profound consequences for textuality and its meanings.[11]

---

[8] Claire Lemercier and Claire Zalc, *Quantitative Methods in the Humanities: An Introduction*, trans. Arthur Goldhammer (Charlottesville, VA: University of Virginia Press, 2019), p. 3.

[9] For more on this, see Derek Attridge, *The Singularity of Literature* (London: Routledge, 2004).

[10] For more on this, see John B. Thompson, *Books in the Digital Age: The Transformation of Academic and Higher Education Publishing in Britain and the United States* (Cambridge: Polity Press, 2005).

[11] Marshall McLuhan, *Understanding Media: The Extensions of Man* (Cambridge, MA: MIT Press, 1994).

One of the most detailed and profound works to study this shift in recent years has been Matthew G. Kirschenbaum's 2016 *Track Changes: A Literary History of Word Processing*. There has long been a fascination with the material with which authors write. Kirschenbaum draws our attention to the fact that we know the make and model of typewriter on which Mark Twain composed his works, 'just as we know details of the design of the tiny table on which Jane Austen did her writing at Chawton Cottage'. Perhaps 'we don't', writes Kirschenbaum, 'know exactly why it is important to know these things, but we would rather know them than not'.[12] So why, he asks, should we not want to know on which word processors and upon which computers our contemporary writers work, even as it would be surprising if such technological intervention caused discernible inflexions within the actual writing?

There is a temptation, though, to subordinate the digital environment to the material. That is, we often like to believe that our digital interfaces are simply metaphorical recreations of physical processes and artefacts. Take the digital page, for instance—something we all take for granted. We open a word processor and what appears is a metaphorical 'representation' of a real page. Yet despite this, pages are among the 'most dramatically overlooked graphical forms' in Johanna Drucker's appraisal.[13] They are often classed as 'self-evident graphical features of any textual work'.[14] However, where they are not overlooked, there is a prevalent anti-pagination discourse that sees pages as domineering, even in the physical world of print. Pages, asserts Alberto Manguel, exert a 'tyranny' of format over the text they contain, a tyranny that must be resisted: the 'shape of a page', he writes, 'seems to cry out for counter-action'.[15] Despite the very 'idea of the book' being 'the presentation of material in relation to a fixed

---

[12] Kirschenbaum, *Track Changes*, p. 7.

[13] This section is derived from the forthcoming Martin Paul Eve, 'New Leaves: The Histories of Digital Pagination', *Book History*, 2022; Johanna Drucker, 'Graphesis', *Paj: The Journal of the Initiative for Digital Humanities, Media, and Culture*, 2.1 (2010), p. 13 <https://journals.tdl.org/paj/index.php/paj/article/view/4> [accessed 28 November 2019].

[14] Johanna Drucker, *SpecLab: Digital Aesthetics and Projects in Speculative Computing* (Chicago, IL: University of Chicago Press, 2009), p. 158.

[15] Alberto Manguel, *A Reader on Reading* (New Haven, CT: Yale University Press, 2010), p. 123.

sequence which provides access to its contents (or ideas) through some stable arrangement',[16] Henry Burton in 1636 wrote to his reader that 'the foregoing Examples are not orderly placed. Indeed it was the authors minde that they should have beene otherwise'.[17] In Shane Butler's reading, the page is 'conspicuous for the impertinence and arbitrariness with which it repeatedly barges into the text, chopping up stories, sentences, and even words where it will'.[18]

Despite the prevalence of the digital page, there has been a long-standing and concerted assault on the idea of the paginated digital document. Indeed, from the moment of the Portable Document Format (PDF)'s inception there was anxiety about enforcing the trans-medial constraints of paper on digital forms. As early as 1993, Pete Dyson, who edited an influential report in the late 1980s on the state of desktop publishing, voiced his worry: 'my biggest concern with all of these document viewers is that they start with a printed-page image. [...] I believe documents should be formatted for the medium that they are intended for'.[19] This principle is echoed in many user interface design documents, which stress that 'designers will be most effective when they design online manuals to fit the electronic medium', rather than paginating.[20]

Yet, how subordinated to the physical page is the virtual page, in reality? Our virtual pages do not behave like regular pages. Instead, they act as conjoined scrolls and re-inscriptible tablets. To begin with the scroll, as far back as 1999 Michael Heim noted that computing systems have adopted metaphors of 'scrolling' as their primary descriptions of reading, a metaphor that, for Heim, 'takes us back

[16] Johanna Drucker, *The Century of Artists' Books* (New York: Granary Books, 1995), p. 123.

[17] Henry Burton, *A Divine Tragedie Lately Acted, or A Collection of Sundry Memorable Examples of Gods Judgements upon Sabbath-Breakers, and Other like Libertines* (Amsterdam: J. F. Stam, 1636), p. H2r. Cited and further remarked upon in Helen Smith and Louise Wilson, eds., *Renaissance Paratexts* (Cambridge: Cambridge University Press, 2011).

[18] Shane Butler, *The Matter of the Page: Essays in Search of Ancient and Medieval Authors* (Madison, WI: University of Wisconsin Press, 2011), p. 10.

[19] Jeanette Borzo, 'Tools Resurrect Hope for Paperless Office Concept', *Infoworld*, 14 June 1993, 1, 24 (p. 24).

[20] Ben Shneiderman and Catherine Plaisant, *Designing the User Interface: Strategies for Effective Human-Computer Interaction*, 4th edn. (Boston, MA: Pearson, 2004), p. 540.

centuries' even as it is fused with new technologies.[21] At the same time, newer old habits die hard. Even while computer systems deploy the scroll metaphor, they also slide between this mask of unending seamless movement and that of discrete, discontinuous 'pagination'. This fusion media form parallels the earliest form of the print biblical codex, a mode that featured 'a four-column page layout resembling a section of unfurled scroll', mirroring the earlier *paginae*.[22]

Suppose, then, that the metaphorical ancestry of the digital page is diffuse and mixed, rather than a simple case of translating the physical to the virtual page. In that case, the timescale for the early adoption of read-only pagination is also out of joint with a 'path dependency' relationship. For were there a straightforward path dependency on our computing systems from printed pages, one would expect to see an enforcement of page-like representation implemented from the very outset of computing technologies. But, in actuality, it took until the 1990s for the software technology to be developed to enable this trans-media substitutability: PDF. Again, this was because early computing software technologies were specifically not designed to replicate pages between devices.

Digital pagination in the form of a PDF introduced a trans-media substitutability to malleable digital surfaces for the first time, even while it brought a read-only paradigm within the page context itself.[23] Indeed, the initial iteration of PDF, 'The Camelot Project', instigated by John E. Warnock at Adobe, specifically aimed to solve two fundamental problems in the world of computer graphics and typography:

---

[21] Michael Heim, *Electric Language: A Philosophical Study of Word Processing* (New Haven, CT: Yale University Press, 1999), p. 130.

[22] Michelle P. Brown, 'The Triumph of the Codex: The Manuscript Book before 1100', in *A Companion to the History of the Book*, ed. Simon Eliot and Jonathan Rose, Blackwell Companions to Literature and Culture, 48 (Malden, MA: Blackwell Publishers, 2007), pp. 179–93; Christopher De Hamel, *The Book: The History of the Bible* (London: Phaidon Press, 2005); Michelle P. Brown, ed., *In the Beginning: Bibles Before the Year* 1000 (Washington, DC: Freer Gallery of Art and Arthur M. Sackler Gallery, Smithsonian Institution, 2006); Bonnie Mak, *How the Page Matters*, Studies in Book and Print Culture Series (Toronto: University of Toronto Press, 2011), p. 4.

[23] For more on how, in some senses, the PDF is not even thus a digital text, see Giorgio Buccellati, *A Critique of Archaeological Reason: Structural, Digital, and Philosophical Aspects of the Excavated Record* (Cambridge: Cambridge University Press, 2017), pp. 207–8 <https://doi.org/10.1017/9781107110298>.

1. 'how to build a computer representation, in a resolution-independent way, of any printed page'; and
2. 'how to represent text, and typefaces, that are compatible with a solution to the first problem'.[24]

A critical point, however, is that it is often assumed that PDF took off immediately. In reality, it did not. John B. Thompson, for instance, notes that 'PDF quickly established itself as the de facto standard in publishing and in the graphic arts'.[25] However, in Warnock's view, PDF was widely misunderstood at the time of its inception: 'quite frankly', he writes, 'the industry "did not get it" '.[26]

Most shockingly, Warnock notes that the PDF format was not widely understood. 'I remember speaking with an analyst at the Gartner Group', notes Warnock, 'and she said: Why would anyone use this instead of just sending around "word" files and "lotus 123" files. She obviously did not understand the issues'. Warnock believes that the early problem with PDF adoption 'was to charge for the reader' instead of focusing on the consumer side. However, as compositing became a de-skilled profession[27] and with the 'explosive growth of the use of the internet', a commensurate success came to Adobe and its PDF format.[28]

The instructive lesson that we can take from the development and late adoption of the PDF format, along with the very mixed metaphors of the virtual page, is that our digital spaces are not straightforward replications of some physical environment. Instead, it is more accurate to say that they feed back into and shape that very environment as much as they are born from it. In this sense, Kirschenbaum's observations about the disciplinary nature of digital textual processing functions are astute. For the specifically gendered secretarial labour from which word processing was born 'was about making female bodies accountable, and it did so by modularizing the anatomical

[24] John E. Warnock, 'Simple Ideas That Changed Printing and Publishing', *Proceedings of the American Philosophical Society*, 156.4 (2012), 363–78 (p. 365).

[25] Thompson, p. 411.

[26] John E. Warnock, letter to Martin Paul Eve, 'The Earliest "Critique" of PDF', 24 November 2019.

[27] Thompson, p. 410.

[28] Correspondence with the author. Warnock to Eve.

functions of hand, eye, and ear'.[29] The digital media environment interacts with our physicalities in complex feedback loops that condition textual production and reception.

Indeed, digital metaphors and digital-textual/media history are perhaps better explored through the trope covered in the last chapter, which Dennis Tenen has called 'speculative formalism'.[30] This mode recognizes the mediation and friction of such metaphors, which sees the Saussurean arbitrariness of the skeuomorphic 'trash can' concerning the operations of, say, journaling file systems.[31] It is a strategy that follows in N. Katherine Hayles's footsteps, calling for analyses of 'material metaphors'.[32] Speculative formalism is a model that acknowledges that 'simulations ultimately embody specific power structures in an economy of exchange between physical and mental resources'.[33] 'What does it mean', asks Tenen, 'to turn a page in a medium that sustains neither turning nor pages?'[34]

As the prerequisite for any digital textual analysis is that the text *is digital*, it is essential always to centre the kind of media archaeological work conducted by Drucker, Hayles, Tenen, and Kirschenbaum—among many others—as a grounding for studying large-scale literary history. The media form is never neutral and engenders feedback loops with the environment within which it exists. Furthermore, as I did in the previous chapter, it is also important to consider that much work will never be available digitally and that we do not have sufficient

---

[29] Kirschenbaum, *Track Changes*, p. 147.

[30] Tenen, pp. 51–4. This is distinct from Tom Eyers's concept of the same name in Tom Eyers, *Speculative Formalism: Literature, Theory, and the Critical Present* (Evanston, IL: Northwestern University Press, 2017).

[31] Tenen, pp. 38–9.   [32] Hayles, *Writing Machines*, p. 23.

[33] Tenen, p. 53.

[34] Tenen, p. 26. That said, it is notable that one of the earliest experiments in 'realistic', or mimetic, electronic book design, conducted by the British Library in 1997, was called 'Turning the Pages' and aimed precisely to simulate this metaphor. Yi-Chun Chu et al., 'Realistic Books: A Bizarre Homage to an Obsolete Medium?', in *Proceedings of the 2004 Joint ACM/IEEE Conference on Digital Libraries—JCDL '04* (presented at the 2004 joint ACM/IEEE conference, Tucson, AZ, USA: ACM Press, 2004), p. 78 <https://doi.org/10.1145/996350.996372>; Jennifer Pearson, George Buchanan, and Harold Thimbleby, 'Designing for Digital Reading', *Synthesis Lectures on Information Concepts, Retrieval, and Services*, 5.4 (2013), 16–31 <https://doi.org/10.2200/S00539ED1V01Y201310ICR029>.

resources to bring digital versions of all texts into focus. One might also contemplate the dilemma faced by Ryan Cordell, whose article, titled 'Q i-jtb the Raven', shows us the challenges of handling 'dirty' data sources with little quality control on the optical character recognition front.[35] Certainly, the digital medium in which we operate has conditioning assumptions for our study of literary history and our study of literary history, in the future, will require knowledge of digital media.

Challenging Assumptions

Let us turn now, instead, to the application of digital methods to digital texts for literary history. One of the best things that a digital approach to literary studies can achieve is questioning existing assumptions from secondary literary criticism. This can be as 'simple' as questioning assertions of frequency in a text. For example, Erik Ketzan notes that 'Alec McHoul and David Wills write that, "Although we have not tested it empirically, we would hypothesize that, excepting routine words like 'the', 'a', etc., 'death' is the most frequently used word in *Gravity's Rainbow*." In fact, a simple query shows that death is only the 160th most frequent word in *Gravity's Rainbow*, or, if one excludes a stoplist of non-content words (as McHoul and Wills suggest), only the 61st most frequent'.[36]

Such an empirical approach that counters inaccurate assertions is of merit in its own right. If we claim that attention to the specific is an important feature of literary criticism and close reading, then any method that can correct errors can only improve our interpretations.

There have also, though, been efforts that aim to challenge more fundamental assertions of literary theory. Consider Andrew Piper's recent work in his 2018 book, *Enumerations*. Since the high point of poststructuralist theory in the 1970s, it has been a literary-philosophical

---

[35] Cordell. For another example, see Eve, 'Textual Scholarship and Contemporary Literary Studies', pp. 33–4.

[36] From the forthcoming Erik Ketzan, *Thomas Pynchon and the Digital Humanities: Computational Approaches to Style* (London: Bloomsbury, 2022). Ketzan is critiquing Alec McHoul and David Wills, *Writing Pynchon: Strategies in Fictional Analysis* (Basingstoke: Macmillan, 1990).

commonplace to state that there is no absolute difference between literary and non-literary writing. That is, there is nothing a work of fiction or nonfiction can do within its own language to persuade a reader absolutely of its factuality or fictionality. Much of the fiction of Jorge Luis Borges is premised on this type of non-distinction, yielding types of false encyclopaedic entries to the reader, as an example.

John Searle and Jacques Derrida, despite their enormous differences and arguments, have both claimed the impossibility of this distinction at various points. For Searle, for instance, the 'utterance acts of fiction are indistinguishable from the utterance acts of serious discourse' and 'there is no textual property that will identify a stretch of discourse as a work of fiction'. For Derrida, no 'exposition, no discursive form is intrinsically or essentially literary before or outside of the function it is assigned'.[37] In other words, there is a pragmatic, social, and contextual situation of a work, beyond the text itself (an ironic sentiment to ascribe to Derrida), that determines whether a work is labelled as 'fact' or 'fiction'. It is not possible, from the text alone, such a view claims, to assign a genre label of fact vs. fiction.

The only problem for such a view is that Piper shows that machine classification *can* distinguish between fact and fiction with over 95 per cent accuracy using just a 1,250-word stretch of text.[38] For the sake of clarity, this computational approach is not checking whether a text is true. It is not seeking to ascertain whether, for example, the statement 'all pandas are black and white' is an objective truth in the world. It seeks no external reference point for the truth of statements. Instead, Piper's method verifies only the work's 'intended truth claims' within language.[39] That is, contrary to dismissive claims about the intentional fallacy—that we should not attempt to ascribe intention to an author as part of our literary critical readings—texts appear to exhibit shared generic traits of whether they were supposed to be

---

[37] John R. Searle, 'The Logical Status of Fictional Discourse', in *Expression and Meaning: Studies in the Theory of Speech Acts* (Cambridge: Cambridge University Press, 1979), pp. 58–76 (p. 68); Maurice Blanchot and Jacques Derrida, *The Instant of My Death/Demeure: Fiction and Testimony*, trans. Elizabeth Rottenberg, Meridian (Stanford, CA: Stanford University Press, 2000), p. 28.

[38] Piper, *Enumerations*, pp. 94–100.   [39] Piper, *Enumerations*, p. 98.

'fact' or 'fiction'. Machines can evaluate the 'truthiness' of language in texts.

This leads Piper to some further astute questions. For instance, he asks: 'how coherent is fiction as a type of writing?' It turns out, as above, that the answer is very: 'not only are the differences between fiction and nonfiction robust across time and languages, but we can use models built in one time period to strongly predict those of another'.[40] The next, astute if foreseeable, question to which Piper turns is: 'if fiction is so predictable, what are the features that make it so?' Examining a canon of nineteenth-century novels in English, Piper ascertains that exclamation points, the uses of 'I' and 'you', the deployment of question marks, and several other features strongly distinguish fiction from nonfiction. Indeed, exclamation points are ten times more likely to appear in works of fiction than in nonfiction writing.[41] When various types of discourse are removed from novels—such as dialogue—the prevalence of third-person pronouns in fiction becomes perhaps *the* defining feature as 'there is over a threefold increase in the average number of she/he pronouns in fiction versus nonfiction outside of dialogue'.[42] For Piper, this demonstrates (perhaps not that extraordinarily) that 'imagining people *as people* may be fiction's most important role'—an element that is mirrored, linguistically, in the prevalence of third-person pronouns.[43]

Sometimes, initial exploratory digital literary work can be less efficacious in its explanatory power than in unveiling startling empirical findings. Without wishing to pick on Piper, there is a chapter of his book that I believe demonstrates this mismatch. In the section of his work on punctuation, Piper can demonstrate some alarming and strange trends in punctuation usage over the past two centuries. Explaining them is another matter, though.

Piper shows that, in the novel, since about 1800, that there has been a significantly marked increase in the use of full stops (periods) while the comma has concomitantly declined in frequency. A similar, although less marked, shift can be seen in poetry, although in general the use of *all* punctuation in poetry has markedly decreased over this time

[40] Piper, *Enumerations*, p. 105.   [41] Piper, *Enumerations*, pp. 105–7.
[42] Piper, *Enumerations*, p. 109.   [43] Piper, *Enumerations*, p. 109.

period.[44] Piper describes these findings in terms of a 'general economy' of punctuation, following Bataille but noting that computational methods may be a powerful way of studying such phenomena.

The questions that Piper poses are: 'what does the economy of the period look like in twentieth-century Anglophone poetry?' and 'where is the space of its excess and what does it say?' Perhaps one of the major challenges, though, is that while two of these questions are answerable (what does the economy look like and where is the space of its excess?), the third and final—the one that most literary scholars would like answered: 'what does it say?'—is far harder to address in aggregate. This distributional plotting, as Piper acknowledges, 'cannot tell us [...] what periods *say*'.[45]

Piper goes some way towards rectifying this by computationally examining the semantic contexts within which poetic discourses co-occur with marked punctuation increases. He can show, for instance, that '*I* and *you* are far more common in high-period poems' and that present tense and the indefinite article all likewise correlate with greater use of periods. However, in the end, Piper has to conclude from his computational approach that, 'ultimately this bird's-eye view can only tell us so much' and that 'we have to move into the poems in order to understand the way these words and features are inflected with particular meanings'.[46]

At this point in his study, Piper delves into close readings of periodicity in the poem, working on examples from Edwin Morgan, Angela Jackson, Amiri Baraka, Jackie Kay, and Kenneth McClane. For it turns out that close reading is the only way that hypotheses about punctuation frequency can really be explained in terms that make sense to us as human readers. Of course, one way of viewing this need for selective and close reading—unless it were truly randomly sampled—is that it loses many of the systematizing advantages trumpeted for the merits of computational methods. A more generous reading would posit, instead, though, that this merely shows a symbiosis between empirical computational findings and the continued need for readerly poetic engagement. It is not as though we need fear that one replaces the other. But it can instead be seen, as in Piper's

[44] Piper, *Enumerations*, p. 25.
[45] Piper, *Enumerations*, p. 31.   [46] Piper, *Enumerations*, pp. 33–4.

demonstration, that computational methods can provide unexpected hypotheses based on observation that can then bear out in, or be refuted by, sustained close readings.

Nonetheless, Piper is justified in claiming that his approach 'puts pressure on some of the more common scholarly refrains of the recent past'.[47] Computational approaches can challenge our quantitative and empirical assertions in literary studies. At the same time, they can leave difficult explanatory phenomena unspeakable without a return to the depth of close reading. It is, though, in this synthesis that we best see the merits of both approaches—of distance and of depth.

Genre and Gender

As I have already touched upon in the earlier chapter on authorship, the computation of style has a relatively long history. The notion that literary style might be measured mathematically goes back at least to 1851 when Augustus de Morgan suggested that an argument over the attribution of the epistles could be resolved by examining authors' average word lengths and comparing them against those documents known to have been written by St Paul.[48] However, it is only relatively recently that advances in machine learning and probabilistic approaches to literary *modelling* have taken off. It is to the progress made in this field that the last part of this chapter is dedicated.

What is the difference between literary statistical modelling and many of the other methods described throughout this book? Richard Jean So provides an instructive definition of a model:

Models are statistical, graphic, or physical objects, and their primary quality is that they can be manipulated. Scientists and social scientists use them to think about the social or natural worlds and to represent those worlds in a simplified manner. Statistical models, which dominate the social sciences, particularly in economics, are typically equations

---

[47] Piper, *Enumerations*, p. 99.

[48] Although, as it turns out, this is a poor method for authorship attribution. Anthony Kenny, *The Computation of Style: An Introduction to Statistics for Students of Literature and Humanities*, Pergamon International Library of Science, Technology, Engineering, & Social Studies (Oxford: Pergamon Press, 1982), p. 1.

with response and predictor variables. Specifically, a researcher seeks to understand some social phenomenon, such as the relation between students' scores on a math test and how many hours the students spent preparing for the exam. To predict or describe this relation, the researcher constructs a quantitative model with quantitative inputs (the number of hours each student spent studying) and outputs (each student's test score). The researcher hopes that the number of hours a student spent preparing for the exam will correlate with the student's score. If it does, this quantified relation can help describe the overall dynamics of test taking.[49]

As with almost every method described in this book, 'literary scholars have', writes So, 'long cast a suspicious and critical gaze toward modeling, which strikes them as offensively simpleminded and naive: models run counter to the deep and intensive reading that literary critics take pride in'.[50] If it is true that all models are, to some extent, 'wrong', though, it is also the case that the advantage of such modelling 'is that it does not present cut-and-dried results that one accepts or rejects. Built into the modeling process is a self-reflexive account of what the model has sought to measure and the limitations of its ability to produce such a measurement'.[51]

Of the works in recent years that have committed to literary statistical modelling as a technique, perhaps none has been more significant than Ted Underwood's *Distant Horizons*. The premise of Underwood's work is simple and takes the form of two challenges. The first of these challenges is to question the assumption, in a further assault on the periodicity that he unpicked in his first book, that we understand the shape of literary history. The second is to ask our discipline to think in *new terms* about how different paradigms of literary studies overlap with, rather than replace, one another. For too long, suggests Underwood, literary studies has been 'littered with terms that suggest one critical paradigm has displaced another: poststructuralism, postmodernism, New Criticism, New Historicism'. This is not the way that other disciplines work. 'Bioinformatics', writes Underwood, 'has

---

[49] Richard Jean So, 'All Models Are Wrong', *PMLA*, 132.3 (2017), 668–73 (p. 668).

[50] So, 'All Models Are Wrong', p. 668.

[51] So, 'All Models Are Wrong', p. 671.

not replaced biochemistry'. Such a model of disciplinary history, Underwood argues, with respect to digital literary studies, may have had historical merit in the contest for readerly interpretative attention, but, he argues, 'it is unreliable today'.[52]

An example of the power of Underwood's modelling is the work that he conducts upon the coherence of the genre of science fiction, touched upon earlier in this book. There are fierce debates within the study of science fiction over how the genre is constituted. As Underwood points out, for Mark Bould and Sherryl Vint, the idea of 'science fiction' is not a textual construct—it is not inherent 'in the work itself' but is instead a product of market forces and social genre contestation.[53]

Underwood can show this premise to be incorrect. While the 'dominant critical story about science fiction strongly implies that it failed to consolidate until the twentieth century', Underwood can demonstrate that science fiction coheres for a far longer period.[54] So what did Underwood do to demonstrate this? First, he took it upon himself to build a corpus of works that can be recognized as science fiction, using bibliographies by Brian Stableford, Mary Mark Ockerbloom, and others.[55] He then built a classification model that was able, with 90 per cent accuracy, correctly to assign a volume as science fiction, or otherwise.

There were some exceptions. Thomas Pynchon's *The Crying of Lot 49* (1966), for example, was classified as science fiction. Mary Shelley's *Frankenstein* (1818) was in the 'not sure' category—a determination

[52] Underwood, *Distant Horizons*, pp. 1–3.

[53] Mark Bould and Sherryl Vint, 'There Is No Such Thing as Science Fiction', in *Reading Science Fiction*, ed. James Gunn, Marleen Barr, and Matthew Candelaria (New York: Palgrave Macmillan, 2009) <https://uwe-repository.worktribe.com/output/1006830/there-is-no-such-thing-as-science-fiction> [accessed 10 April 2020].

[54] Underwood, *Distant Horizons*, p. 40.

[55] Brian Stableford, 'The Emergence of Science Fiction, 1516–1914', in *Anatomy of Wonder: A Critical Guide to Science Fiction*, ed. Neil Barron, 5th edn. (Santa Barbara, CA: Libraries Unlimited, 2004), pp. 3–22; Brian Stableford, 'Science Fiction Between the Wars, 1918–1938', in *Anatomy of Wonder*, ed. Barron, pp. 23–44; Mary Mark Ockerbloom, 'Pre-1950s Utopias and Science Fiction by Women: An Annotated Reading List of Online Editions' <https://digital.library.upenn.edu/women/_collections/utopias/utopias.html> [accessed 11 April 2020].

also present in the secondary literature given its gothic associations. In all, though, the model was pretty good.

The model also tells a different story from the traditional tale. Over a 200-year period, the model can correctly group science fictional texts while rejecting those that are ascribed to other genres. This means that the narrative of 'scientific romance' in the nineteenth century being different from 'true' science fiction in the twentieth is less plausible than previously assumed.

So what is it that is persistent in science fiction throughout its (much longer) history? Surprisingly, it is not planets or alien technologies that leap out at the computer model but a set of linguistic entities that one would not expect: a remarkable fascination with scale, for example.[56] Novels that we classify as science fictional turn out to fixate on 'invocations of scale': terms such as 'vast', 'far', 'larger', and 'infinite', but also 'tiny'. Numeric quantities (*'thousands, millions'*) also become far more prevalent than in other novel genres.[57]

This is certainly a curious observation. We might associate scale in the history of the novel with, say, Swift's 1726 *Gulliver's Travels*. In that novel, of course, the protagonist travels between worlds where his sense of scale is vastly altered against the backdrops of the resident populations. Swift's novel uses this discrepancy of scale to amplify and then critically to diminish the concerns of the environment within which it was written. Thus, scale in the novel of dislocation becomes a factor that allows for enlargement or reduction of critical concerns in the present. But this emphasis on scale is not usually thought to be a focal element for science fiction. Perhaps scale is seen more often in the SF sub-genre of utopian literature, within which we would be able to situate Swift's work. Thanks to Underwood's plotting there is, now, a new story to be told about scale in SF.

Another feature that Underwood's model discerns in SF novels that has been overlooked in the existing critical plot is the prominence of the terms 'horror', 'nightmare', and 'destruction'. Despite the aforementioned difficulty in classifying works that overlap with gothic and

[56] For more on the general place and definition of planets in the contemporary genre ecology of SF, and in particular the works of Jonathan Lethem, see Joseph Brooker, *Jonathan Lethem and the Galaxy of Writing* (London: Bloomsbury, 2020).

[57] Underwood, *Distant Horizons*, pp. 58–9.

horror, it is notable that these terms appear frequently in SF. Science fiction appears to be a more alarmist genre than its more positive incarnations, such as Star Trek, might imply.

Rounding off the list of features that occur in SF, Underwood notes the appearance of non-gendered creatures and beings, signalled using the pronoun 'its', juxtaposed to gendered humans. These references to 'unknown things', as Underwood puts it, introduce non-human actors with senses of agency and possession that add a strangely thingness to pro- and an-tagonists that is not present in other generic classifications.

Finally, some aspects feature *far less* prominently in SF novels than in a general fiction corpus. Underwood points to mentions of everyday objects—'tea' or a 'hat'—but also to days of the week as exemplary of this trend. That is, realist novels that deal with everyday situations are far less likely to exhibit this trend. That said, a well-known technique in alienating fictions is to take the quotidian and to twist it. One need only think of Orwell's 'it was a bright cold day in April, and the clocks were striking thirteen' to see how a realistic environment can be made alien.

An important point to make about Underwood's modelling is that sometimes these features co-occur. It is not that, simply, we can look for novels that feature many more instances of scale than others and say: 'that's science fiction'. Rather, the model examines the text for the correlation and collocation of these multiple vectors, the way that they come together within a text, and then assigns a probability of whether the text is science fictional. This is one of the problems of accepting the logics of statistical modelling in literary criticism. Literary criticism is good at taking a single factor and exploring it in depth. For instance, one can imagine a new literary studies monograph coming out of Underwood's work called *Fictions of Scale: SF and Size*. But this would not cover the richness of the co-occurrence and multi-dimensionality that Underwood unearths (although he remains an astute explainer of single-dimensional features where they are available and it may be that this argument about multi-dimensionality is overemphasised.) Certainly, the model has explanatory powers across single vectors for *why* a text might be classified as science fictional. But it is not that all of these lines can always be explored, in depth, in isolation. Instead, this points in some ways towards a *new type of knowledge* for literary criticism—and one that it is hard for human readers to grasp: that there may be more things in heaven and Earth, occurring side by side, at the same time, than we can hold in a single mental frame for examination. We may not yet be at the point where this is a problem, but it is a hypothetical future that we should bear in mind.

Perhaps more importantly, though, what Underwood manages to achieve in this initial work in *Distant Horizons* is to tell a story. Instead of simply feature-spotting the text, his work challenges dominant literary-historical narratives of genre and textuality. In this way, this book re-synthesizes the new types of computational knowledge into broad-scale literary-historical paradigms, even if we cannot subject the claims to the same type of conventional literary scrutiny to which we are accustomed.

I will close this chapter with an appraisal of one more aspect of work from Underwood's book. As I have already looked at his efforts in genre and fiction, I will finally turn to *gender* in fiction. Again, Underwood's work is startling: on the one hand, he can show that gendered divisions between characters in literary works have become less differentiated over the past two centuries (that is, as we move forward in time, more and more frequently the same language is used by and about characters, regardless of gender identity). On the other hand, perhaps worryingly, Underwood also finds that there is commensurately less space devoted in novels to women.[58]

Building on existing computational work on gender and fiction, with his colleagues David Bamman and Sabrina Lee, Underwood again built a model that maps out character gender and its associated traits in a text.[59] The model that they built, in this case, was less accurate than the previous genre modelling, but it still shows the aforementioned statistically significant decline in discernibility between genders throughout the twentieth century.[60] As Underwood points out, though, this is 'by no means self-evident in our critical

[58] Underwood, *Distant Horizons*, p. 114.

[59] Matthew Jockers and Gabi Kiriloff, 'Understanding Gender and Character Agency in the 19th Century Novel', *Journal of Cultural Analytics*, 1.1 (2016), 1–26 <https://doi.org/10.22148/16.010>.

[60] Underwood, *Distant Horizons*, p. 116.

narratives' as 'some stories about modernism imply that it reversed nineteenth-century progress for women; other narratives describe a significant period of backsliding in the 1940s and 1950s'.[61]

By way of upfront disclaimer: Underwood's models are, importantly, here limited. The model does not handle transgender individuals, for instance, and it works on a binary basis. Underwood presents this stance 'as a provisional simplification of public roles, not as a truth about personal identity'—but it could certainly be contested as another instance in which 'all models are wrong'.[62] This also means that the modelling may fall down when dealing with books that explicitly handle gender, and its twists, as a subject: LeGuin's *The Left Hand of Darkness* (1969) and Woolf's *Orlando* (1928) being the two canonical examples to which Underwood gestures as examples of this gender trouble.[63]

Nonetheless, for Underwood, the causes of the change that he describes are less interesting than how the shift happened. 'The underlying social forces', he writes, 'that made gender roles more flexible are not a deep mystery'.[64] What actually changes on the ground, though, is more interesting. For instance, given our knowledge of Jane Austen protagonists, we might expect that reading would be an activity particularly suited to female heroines. Not so. Underwood finds that reading within novels is undertaken almost equally by men and women over almost two centuries of fiction. Sentiment, however, exhibits a predictable pattern. Female characters earlier in the timeline more often 'felt' than their male colleagues, but the discernibility of this distinction declines as we move forward in time.

This association of terms of interior emotional sentiment with women on a declining scale over time—heart, tears, sighs, smiles, minds, and spirits—confirms, for Underwood, Nancy Armstrong's notion that 'it was at first only women who were defined in terms of

[61] Underwood, *Distant Horizons*, p. 118; Suzanne Clark, *Sentimental Modernism: Women Writers and the Revolution of the Word* (Bloomington, IN: Indiana University Press, 1991), p. 1; Gayle Greene, *Changing the Story: Feminist Fiction and the Tradition* (Bloomington, IN: Indiana University Press, 1991), pp. 39–41.

[62] Underwood, *Distant Horizons*, p. 141.

[63] Underwood, *Distant Horizons*, p. 130.

[64] Underwood, *Distant Horizons*, p. 119.

their emotional natures' in the novel form.[65] Underwood is also able to confirm, in some ways, Armstrong's contentions about the gender implications of closeted interior spaces: 'in early-nineteenth-century novels, men have houses and countries' but, conversely, 'women have private chambers and apartments inside the house'.[66]

From houses to mirth, though, some odd traits do not have an easy social explanation in Underwood's data. For, while 'women smile and laugh', notes Underwood, 'midcentury men, apparently, can only grin and chuckle'.[67] Raymond Chandler's hardboiled detectives are emblematic of this trend for Underwood—rarely smiling, frequently grinning.

Nevertheless, the second of Underwood's findings is more troubling and also hard to explain. How is it that, as Underwood shows, over the twentieth century, until about 1970, the allocated page space to female characters notably and significantly declined? One reason is, first, that the proportion of published and library-stocked authors who were women also significantly declined over this period. While well over half of all novelists were women in the early nineteenth century, this proportion fell substantially throughout the twentieth.[68] As Underwood also finds that, perhaps predictably, on the one hand 'women are consistently under-represented in books by men' while 'women writers, on the other hand, spend equal time on fictional men and fictional women', it is therefore unsurprising that we see the page space allotted to women decline over this time, in conjunction with authorship.[69]

In some senses, as he himself points out, Underwood's modelling provides the description after others—such as Tuchman and Fortin— have already given the explanation. This can feel a little like closing the stable door after the horse has bolted. Again, is it a case where

[65] Nancy Armstrong, *Desire and Domestic Fiction: A Political History of the Novel* (New York: Oxford University Press, 2006), p. 4 <https://public.ebookcentral.proquest.com/choice/publicfullrecord.aspx?p=271302> [accessed 12 April 2020].

[66] Underwood, *Distant Horizons*, p. 123.

[67] Underwood, *Distant Horizons*, p. 124.

[68] Underwood points to Gaye Tuchman and Nina E. Fortin, *Edging Women Out: Victorian Novelists, Publishers, and Social Change* (New Haven, CT: Yale University Press, 1989) as an early example of a critical narrative that recognized this decline.

[69] Underwood, *Distant Horizons*, p. 127.

digital literary studies approaches do not truly tell us anything new? I would say not: these approaches tend to bolster existing theses with new empirical data and strengthen their positions with a fresh groundedness that we would otherwise lack.

In all, though, this penultimate chapter has sought to show the potential that computational stylistic and content analysis can bring to our broader understandings of literary history. These have ranged from histories of the digital 'material' upon which our contemporary works are written and onto which our previous print structures are transposed; through the unseating of longstanding critical assumptions; up to innovative and challenging readings of textual factuality, genre, and gender.

The final aspect to which we here turned in Underwood's work—to gender—also points towards the challenges of claiming that digital humanities literary historical work is an apolitical formalism. Richard Jean So's recent work on racial inequality is also a masterclass in how digital methods can intersect with ethical studies of literature.[70] The study of gender prevalence in fiction is hardly an area devoid of political consequence. On the contrary, it is perhaps among the most important political topics that could be covered, alongside postcolonial, disability, racial, sexual, and class perspectives, highlighting, once again, the ways in which digital approaches can scarcely be said to be apolitical.

---

[70] Richard Jean So, *Redlining Culture: A Data History of Racial Inequality and Postwar Fiction* (New York: Columbia University Press, 2020).

Conclusion

Digital literary studies are not new. 'Scholars', writes Ted Underwood, have been applying computers to literary texts 'for more than fifty years'.[1] Further, as Underwood also points out, digital methods are not akin to the struggle between structuralism and poststructuralism, in which one paradigm attempted to displace the other.[2] Distant reading and close reading can exist in harmony alongside one another, although the former implies a new scale for thinking about literary history beyond extant periodizations.

The threat, then, of digital literary studies is perhaps exaggerated to some degree. However, these methods do pose challenges for those who have spent their entire careers training in periodizations. What does it mean to be a 'modernist' if a set of quantitative methods—seemingly scientific and beyond objective reproach—show that there are stylistic continuities with periodizations that appeared, previously, to be discrete? The fear of redundancy in literary studies is not just a fear among those who cannot 'do' digital humanities. It is also a fear that the very things that scholars 'are'—'modernists', 'Victorianists', 'Romanticists'—may be themselves redundant. It is not just a threat of epistemic redundancy. It is a threat of ontological redundancy.

Fortunately, the ontology of how we study literature can and should be reordered as we find new facts and interpretations on the ground. The study of literature should, surely, be ordered by truths about the literary record, rather than by institutional paradigms and pragmatics. Such a reordering will hardly happen immediately, though. Neither is it likely to happen wholesale. The conflict between institutional

---

[1] Underwood, *Distant Horizons*, p. xi.
[2] Underwood, *Distant Horizons*, pp. xvii–xviii.

pragmatics and truth is always a compromise, particularly when teaching literature to undergraduates in term-sized chunks.

Yet there are things that we can learn from digital approaches to literary studies that are valuable. For one, such methods often reintroduce empiricism to the heart of literary scholarship. That is, they can bring us back from the brink of elaborate theorization and argumentation to a focus *on the text itself*. Such methods have been united under the term 'descriptive criticism', which includes 'on the one hand, descriptive methods that extol materiality—surface reading, new materialist ecocriticism—and, on the other hand, those that extol data—distant reading, computational analysis'.[3]

Much recent debate, it seems, has attempted to make out that description and interpretation are two opposing poles that are 'somehow mutually exclusive', as Cannon Schmitt puts it.[4] However, without a focus on textual specifics—and their remediation through critical description, in data or narrative—interpretations become ungrounded. Without interpretation, though, literary-critical facts and descriptions become little more than secondary synoptic retellings. Database and narrative may be, in Lev Manovich's famous notation, opposed to one another.[5] Data and narrative need, perhaps, not be.

One of the challenges of the scale and abstraction of data-driven approaches, though, as empirical models of literary criticism, is the difficulty of its verification or disproof. Were I to write that Mrs Dalloway did not say that she would buy the flowers herself, it is easy for a critic to point to the evidence that contradicts my assertion. Factual errors at the conventional critical scale are easy to debunk. To disprove computational analysis and data collection, by contrast, requires extensive knowledge of statistical methods and computational approaches; it will generally be much harder for a conventionally trained literary critic.[6] There have even been recent philosophical

---

[3] Heather Houser, 'Shimmering Description and Descriptive Criticism', *New Literary History*, 51.1 (2020), 1–22 (p. 2) <https://doi.org/10.1353/nlh.2020.0000>.

[4] Cannon Schmitt, 'Interpret or Describe?', *Representations*, 135.1 (2016), 102–18 (p. 102) <https://doi.org/10.1525/rep.2016.135.1.102>.

[5] Lev Manovich, *The Language of New Media* (Cambridge, MA: MIT Press, 2002), chapter 5.

[6] This is the argument pursued by Da, namely that much computational criticism is, in fact, wrong.

questionings of the very ideal of causal reproducibility in computational processes, reintroducing contingency into the equation and raising the spectre of what David M. Berry has begun to call the 'explainability turn'.[7] This 'turn' represents a critical focus on the idea that we can 'explain' how algorithmic processes arrive at their judgements and what it means to have faith in such explanations.

Yet the high-profile stakes of distant reading and its verification— or otherwise—are only the most visible and contentious part of the ongoing growth of digital practices in the domain of literary studies, as I hope this book has demonstrated. From mapping to textual scholarship, digital methods can provide auxiliary modes for the understanding of literary texts. Indeed, almost all literary texts begin their lives in a virtual environment. Therefore, it is only apt that they might end their lifecycle by being studied in the same domain. Does everyone *have* to be a digital humanist now? Of course not. However, the new types of evidence that digital practices can bring to the disciplines of literary studies will become ever harder to ignore. Statistical questions will begin, over time, to enter the lexicon of feedback on literary studies papers. It would be prudent for our disciplines to begin to think about what kind of skills a new generation of scholars might need to avail themselves of such understandings.

But isn't this all very far from *reading*, the crucial reason people study literature? Does not the computational interaction with fiction take us further from, rather than closer to, books?[8] As in all literary criticism, the study of aesthetic forms, their composition, and their politics can take us away from the text. There is thus, in most literary analysis, a type of estrangement effect in which the text must be made *other* than what it was at first sight. For instance, appreciating the use of language in a text must often mean disengaging from immersive embeddedness in a fictional world. To see the text *as a text* rather than

---

[7] M. Beatrice Fazi, *Contingent Computation: Abstraction, Experience, and Indeterminacy in Computational Aesthetics* (Lanham, MD: Rowman & Littlefield, 2018); David M. Berry, 'The Explainability Turn: Critical Digital Humanities and Explanation', 2020 <https://dh2020.adho.org/wp-content/uploads/2020/07/603_TheExplainability TurnCriticalDigitalHumanitiesandExplanation.html> [accessed 2 April 2021].

[8] My elision of fiction with the book is here deliberate. For more, see Julia L. Panko, *Out of Print: Mediating Information in the Novel and the Book*, Page and Screen (Amherst, MA: University of Massachusetts Press, 2020).

as a world is part of the training of conventional close reading. Computational approaches afford us further alienation mechanisms that can allow us to understand literary works in greater detail. These methods can show us the longer-scale literary histories within which individual works are situated and tell us about those singular texts' invisible functions. Such alienation loops, though, do not detract from our engagement with fiction. Digital methods, instead, can give us a route to viewing a text anew, seeing with fresh eyes what was always there to know, just never before calculable. Digital methods give us a way to reappraise literary works. These methods allow us to appreciate texts again, in the light of new knowledge.

Bibliography

Aad, G., B. Abbott, J. Abdallah, O. Abdinov, R. Aben, M. Abolins, et al., 'Combined Measurement of the Higgs Boson Mass in p p Collisions at s = 7 and 8 TeV with the ATLAS and CMS Experiments', *Physical Review Letters*, 114.19 (2015) <https://doi.org/10.1103/PhysRevLett.114.191803>

Abbate, Janet, *Recoding Gender: Women's Changing Participation in Computing*, History of Computing (Cambridge, MA: MIT Press, 2012)

Adamo, Giuliana, 'Beginnings and Endings in Novels', *New Readings*, 1.1 (2011) <http://ojs.cf.ac.uk/index.php/newreadings/article/view/62> [accessed 30 January 2020]

Adamo, Giuliana, 'Twentieth-Century Recent Theories on Beginnings and Endings of Novels', *Annali d'Italianistica*, 18 (2000), 49–76

Adams, Tim, 'And the Pulitzer Goes To…a Computer', *The Guardian*, 28 June 2015, section Technology <https://www.theguardian.com/technology/2015/jun/28/computer-writing-journalism-artificial-intelligence> [accessed 15 April 2017]

Ahnert, Ruth, Sebastian E. Ahnert, Catherine Nicole Coleman, and Scott B. Weingart, *The Network Turn: Changing Perspectives in the Humanities* (Cambridge: Cambridge University Press, 2020) <https://doi.org/10.1017/9781108866804>

Aldridge, John W., *Talents and Technicians: Literary Chic and the New Assembly-Line Fiction* (New York: Scribner's, 1992)

Allen, Esther, 'Footnotes *sans Frontières*: Translation and Textual Scholarship', in *Perspectives on Literature and Translation: Creation, Circulation, Reception*, ed. Brian Nelson and Brigid Maher, Routledge Advances in Translation Studies, 5 (New York: Routledge, 2013), pp. 210–20

Allington, Daniel, Sarah Brouillette, and David Golumbia, 'Neoliberal Tools (and Archives): A Political History of Digital Humanities', *Los Angeles Review of Books*, 2016 <https://lareviewofbooks.org/article/neoliberal-tools-archives-political-history-digital-humanities/> [accessed 29 May 2016]

American Historical Association, 'Guidelines for the Professional Evaluation of Digital Scholarship by Historians', *American Historical Association*, 2015 <https://www.historians.org/teaching-and-learning/digital-history-resources/evaluation-of-digital-scholarship-in-history/guidelines-for-the-professional-evaluation-of-digital-scholarship-by-historians> [accessed 24 March 2017]

Ames, Christopher, 'Power and the Obscene Word: Discourses of Extremity in Thomas Pynchon's "Gravity's Rainbow"', *Contemporary Literature*, 31.2 (1990), 191–207

Argamon, S., 'Interpreting Burrows's Delta: Geometric and Probabilistic Foundations', *Literary and Linguistic Computing*, 23.2 (2007), 131–47 <https://doi.org/10.1093/llc/fqn003>

Armstrong, Jeremy, and Lucy Thornton, 'Yorkshire Ripper Hoaxer Wearside Jack Speaks for First Time about "prank" That Derailed Serial Killer Investigation', *Daily Mirror*, 14 July 2013 <http://www.mirror.co.uk/news/uk-news/yorkshire-ripper-hoaxer-wearside-jack-2053906> [accessed 30 December 2015]

Armstrong, Nancy, *Desire and Domestic Fiction: A Political History of the Novel* (New York: Oxford University Press, 2006) <https://public.ebookcentral.proquest.com/choice/publicfullrecord.aspx?p=271302> [accessed 12 April 2020]

Attridge, Derek, *The Singularity of Literature* (London: Routledge, 2004)

Babcock, C. Merton, 'Herman Melville's Whaling Vocabulary', *American Speech*, 29.3 (1954), 161–74 <https://doi.org/10.2307/454235>

Bachelard, Gaston, and Maria Jolas, *The Poetics of Space* (Boston: Beacon Press, 1994)

Bakhtin, M. M., 'Forms of Time and of the Chronotope in the Novel', in *The Dialogic Imagination: Four Essays*, ed. Michael Holquist, trans. Caryl Emerson and Michael Holquist (Austin, TX: University of Texas Press, 2006), pp. 84–258

Bann, Stephen, *Concrete Poetry: An International Anthology* (London: London Magazine Editions, 1967)

Bann, Stephen, ed., *The Tradition of Constructivism: Documents of Contemporary Art* (London: Thames and Hudson, 1974)

Baron, Dennis E., *A Better Pencil: Readers, Writers, and the Digital Revolution* (Oxford: Oxford University Press, 2009)

Barthes, Roland, 'The Death of the Author', in *Image, Music, Text*, trans. Stephen Heath (London: Fontana Press, 1987), pp. 142–8

Bartik, Jean, *Pioneer Programmer: Jean Jennings Bartik and the Computer That Changed the World*, ed. Jon T. Rickman and Kim D. Todd (Kirksville, MO: Truman State University Press, 2013)

Beardsley, Monroe C., *The Possibility of Criticism* (Detroit, MI: Wayne State University Press, 1970)

Bellin, Roger, 'Techno-Anxiety and the Middlebrow: Science-Fictionalization in the Fictional Mainstream of the Early Twenty-First Century', in *The Poetics of Genre in the Contemporary Novel*, ed. Tim Lanzendörfer (Lanham, MD: Lexington Books, 2016), pp. 115–25

Bender, Emily M., Timnit Gebru, Angelina McMillan-Major, and Shmargaret Shmitchell, 'On the Dangers of Stochastic Parrots: Can Language Models Be Too Big? 🦜 ', in *Proceedings of the 2021 ACM Conference on Fairness, Accountability, and Transparency* (presented at the FAccT '21: 2021 ACM Conference on Fairness, Accountability, and Transparency, Virtual Event Canada: ACM, 2021), pp. 610–23 <https://doi.org/10.1145/3442188.3445922>

Benedikt, Michael, ed., *Cyberspace: First Steps* (Cambridge, MA: MIT Press, 1994)

Benjamin, Ruha, *Race After Technology: Abolitionist Tools for the New Jim Code* (Medford, MA: Polity Press, 2019)

Berman, Sanford, *Prejudices and Antipathies: A Tract on the LC Subject Heads Concerning People* (Jefferson, NC: McFarland and Co., 2014)

Berry, David M., 'The Explainability Turn: Critical Digital Humanities and Explanation', 2020 <https://dh2020.adho.org/wp-content/uploads/2020/07/603_TheExplainabilityTurnCriticalDigitalHumanitiesandExplanation.html> [accessed 2 April 2021]

Berry, David M., and Anders Fagerjord, *Digital Humanities: Knowledge and Critique in a Digital Age* (Cambridge: Polity Press, 2017)

Bersani, Leo, 'Pynchon, Paranoia, and Literature', *Representations*, 25 (1989), 99–118

Biocca, Frank, 'Communication Within Virtual Reality: Creating a Space for Research', *Journal of Communication*, 42.4 (1992), 5–22 <https://doi.org/10.1111/j.1460-2466.1992.tb00810.x>

Blacklock, Mark, *I'm Jack* (London: Granta, 2015)

Blanchot, Maurice, and Jacques Derrida, *The Instant of My Death/Demeure: Fiction and Testimony*, trans. Elizabeth Rottenberg, Meridian (Stanford, CA: Stanford University Press, 2000)

Blatt, Ben, *Nabokov's Favorite Word Is Mauve: What the Numbers Reveal About the Classics, Bestsellers, and Our Own Writing* (New York: Simon & Schuster, 2017)

Bloom, Harold, 'Introduction', in *Thomas Pynchon* (Broomall, PA: Chelsea House Publishers, 2003), pp. 1–11

Bode, Katherine, 'The Equivalence of "Close" and "Distant" Reading; Or, toward a New Object for Data-Rich Literary History', *Modern Language Quarterly*, 78.1 (2017), 77–106 <https://doi.org/10.1215/00267929–3699787>

Bond, Sarah E., Hoyt Long, and Ted Underwood, ' "Digital" Is Not the Opposite of "Humanities" ', *The Chronicle of Higher Education*, 1 November 2017 <http://www.chronicle.com/article/Digital-Is-Not-the/241634> [accessed 2 November 2017]

Borzo, Jeanette, 'Tools Resurrect Hope for Paperless Office Concept', *Infoworld*, 14 June 1993, 1, 24

Bould, Mark, and Sherryl Vint, 'There Is No Such Thing as Science Fiction', in *Reading Science Fiction*, ed. James Gunn, Marleen Barr, and Matthew Candelaria (New York: Palgrave Macmillan, 2009) <https://uwe-repository.worktribe.com/output/1006830/there-is-no-such-thing-as-science-fiction> [accessed 10 April 2020]

Brannen, Keith, 'POLICE INTERVIEWS', *The Yorkshire Ripper*, 2015 <http://www.execulink.com/~kbrannen/intervws.htm> [accessed 28 December 2015]

Brennan, Michael Robert, and Rachel Greenstadt, 'Practical Attacks Against Authorship Recognition Techniques', in *IAAI*, 2009 <http://www.cs.drexel.edu/~mb553/stuff/brennan_iaai09.pdf> [accessed 1 August 2016]

Brennan, Timothy, 'The Digital-Humanities Bust', *The Chronicle of Higher Education*, 15 October 2017 <http://www.chronicle.com/article/The-Digital-Humanities-Bust/241424> [accessed 2 November 2017]

Brooker, Joseph, *Jonathan Lethem and the Galaxy of Writing* (London: Bloomsbury, 2020)

Brown, Michelle P., ed., *In the Beginning: Bibles Before the Year 1000* (Washington, DC: Freer Gallery of Art and Arthur M. Sackler Gallery, Smithsonian Institution, 2006)

Brown, Michelle P., 'The Triumph of the Codex: The Manuscript Book before 1100', in *A Companion to the History of the Book*, ed. Simon Eliot and Jonathan Rose, Blackwell Companions to Literature and Culture, 48 (Malden, MA: Blackwell Publishers, 2007), pp. 179–93

Brown, Wendy, *In the Ruins of Neoliberalism: The Rise of Antidemocratic Politics in the West*, The Wellek Library Lectures (New York: Columbia University Press, 2019)

Brown, Wendy, *Undoing the Demos: Neoliberalism's Stealth Revolution* (New York: Zone Books, 2015)

Bruce, David, '"I'M JACK" HOAX – MAN CHARGED', *Yorkshire Evening Post*, 20 October 2005 <http://www.yorkshireeveningpost.co.uk/news/latest-news/top-stories/i-m-jack-hoax-man-charged-1-2135152> [accessed 28 December 2015]

Bruhn, Jørgen, 'Between Punk and PowerPoint: Authenticity Versus Medialities in Jennifer Egan's *A Visit from the Goon Squad*', in *The Intermediality of Narrative Literature* (London: Palgrave Macmillan, 2016), pp. 103–21 <https://doi.org/10.1057/978-1-137-57841-9_6>

Buccellati, Giorgio, *A Critique of Archaeological Reason: Structural, Digital, and Philosophical Aspects of the Excavated Record* (Cambridge: Cambridge University Press, 2017) <https://doi.org/10.1017/9781107110298>

Burdick, Anne, Johanna Drucker, Peter Lunenfeld, Todd Presner, and Jeffrey Schnapp, *Digital Humanities* (Cambridge, MA: MIT Press, 2012)

Burke, Sean, *The Death and Return of the Author: Criticism and Subjectivity in Barthes, Foucault and Derrida* (Edinburgh: Edinburgh University Press, 2008)

Burrows, John, '"Delta": A Measure of Stylistic Difference and a Guide to Likely Authorship', *Literary and Linguistic Computing*, 17.3 (2002), 267–87 <https://doi.org/10.1093/llc/17.3.267>

Burton, Henry, *A Divine Tragedie Lately Acted, or A Collection of Sundry Memorable Examples of Gods Judgements upon Sabbath-Breakers, and Other like Libertines* (Amsterdam: J. F. Stam, 1636)

Butler, Shane, *The Matter of the Page: Essays in Search of Ancient and Medieval Authors* (Madison, WI: University of Wisconsin Press, 2011)

Campos, Augusto de, Decio Pignatari, and Harold de Campos, 'Pilot Plan for Concrete Poetry', in *Concrete Poetry: A World View*, ed. Mary Ellen Solt (Bloomington, IN: Indiana University Press, 1968), pp. 71–2

Canter, David, 'An Evaluation of "Cusum" Stylistic Analysis of Confessions', *Expert Evidence*, 1.2 (1992), 93–9

Catano, James V., 'Poetry and Computers: Experimenting with the Communal Text', *Computers and the Humanities*, 13.4 (1979), 269–75

Cha, Sung-Hyuk, 'Comprehensive Survey on Distance/Similarity Measures between Probability Density Functions', *International Journal of Mathematical Models and Methods in Applied Sciences*, 4.1 (2007), 300–7

Champion, Erik Malcolm, 'Digital Humanities Is Text Heavy, Visualization Light, and Simulation Poor', *Digital Scholarship in the Humanities*, 32.suppl_1 (2017), i25–32 <https://doi.org/10.1093/llc/fqw053>

Chaski, C. E., 'The Keyboard Dilemma and Forensic Authorship Attribution', *Advances in Digital Forensics*, 3 (2007)

Chaski, C. E., 'Who's at the Keyboard: Authorship Attribution in Digital Evidence Investigations', *International Journal of Digital Evidence*, 4.1 (2005)

Childs, Peter, and James Green, 'The Novels in Nine Parts', in *David Mitchell: Critical Essays*, ed. Sarah Dillon (Canterbury: Gylphi, 2011), pp. 25–47

Chu, Yi-Chun, David Bainbridge, Matt Jones, and Ian H. Witten, 'Realistic Books: A Bizarre Homage to an Obsolete Medium?', in *Proceedings of the 2004 Joint ACM/IEEE Conference on Digital Libraries—JCDL '04* (presented at the 2004 joint ACM/IEEE conference, Tucson, AZ, USA: ACM Press, 2004) <https://doi.org/10.1145/996350.996372>

Clark, Suzanne, *Sentimental Modernism: Women Writers and the Revolution of the Word* (Bloomington, IN: Indiana University Press, 1991)

Clement, Tanya E., ' "A Thing Not Beginning and Not Ending": Using Digital Tools to Distant-Read Gertrude Stein's The Making of Americans', *Literary and Linguistic Computing*, 23.3 (2008), 361–81 <https://doi.org/10.1093/llc/fqn020>

Clement, Tanya E., 'Text Analysis, Data Mining, and Visualizations in Literary Scholarship', in *Literary Studies in the Digital Age: An Evolving Anthology*, 2013 <https://dlsanthology.mla.hcommons.org/text-analysis-data-mining-and-visualizations-in-literary-scholarship/> [accessed 6 September 2017]

Clerwall, Christer, 'Enter the Robot Journalist: Users' Perceptions of Automated Content', *Journalism Practice*, 8.5 (2014), 519–31 <https://doi.org/10.1080/17512786.2014.883116>

Cooper, David, and Ian N. Gregory, 'Mapping the English Lake District: A Literary GIS', *Transactions of the Institute of British Geographers*, 36.1 (2011), 89–108

Cooper, David, Ian Gregory, Sally Bushell, and Zoe Bolton, 'Aims & Objectives', *Mapping the Lakes* <https://www.lancaster.ac.uk/mappingthelakes/GIS%20Aims.htm> [accessed 12 March 2020]

Cooper, David, Ian Gregory, Sally Bushell, and Zoe Bolton, 'Geo-Specific Aims', *Mapping the Lakes* <https://www.lancaster.ac.uk/mappingthelakes/GIS%20Geo-Specific%20Aims.htm> [accessed 12 March 2020]

Cooper, David, Ian Gregory, Sally Bushell, and Zoe Bolton, 'Home Page', *Mapping the Lakes* <https://www.lancaster.ac.uk/mappingthelakes/index.htm> [accessed 12 March 2020]

Cooper, David, Ian Gregory, Sally Bushell, and Zoe Bolton, 'Research Outcomes', *Mapping the Lakes* <https://www.lancaster.ac.uk/mappingthelakes/Research%20Outcomes.html> [accessed 12 March 2020]

Cooper, David, Ian Gregory, Sally Bushell, and Zoe Bolton, 'Writer-Specific Aims: Gray & Coleridge', *Mapping the Lakes* <https://www.lancaster.ac.uk/mappingthelakes/GIS%20Writer%20Specific%20Aims.htm> [accessed 12 March 2020]

Cordell, Ryan, ' "Q i-Jtb the Raven": Taking Dirty OCR Seriously', *Book History*, 20.1 (2017), 188–225 <https://doi.org/10.1353/bh.2017.0006>

Cosgrove, Denis E., ed., *Mappings* (London: Reaktion Books, 1999)

Court, Franklin E., *Institutionalizing English Literature: Culture and Politics of Literary Study, 1750–1900* (Stanford, CA: Stanford University Press, 1992)

Cowart, David, 'Pynchon, Genealogy, History: *Against the Day*', *Modern Philology*, 109.3 (2012), 385–407 <https://doi.org/10.1086/663688>

Cowart, David, 'Thirteen Ways of Looking: Jennifer Egan's *A Visit from the Goon Squad*', *Critique: Studies in Contemporary Fiction*, 56.3 (2015), 241–54 <https://doi.org/10.1080/00111619.2014.905448>

Culler, Jonathan, 'The Closeness of Close Reading', *ADE Bulletin*, 149 (2010), 20–5 <https://doi.org/10.1632/ade.149.20>

Da, Nan Z., 'The Computational Case against Computational Literary Studies', *Critical Inquiry*, 45.3 (2019), 601–39 <https://doi.org/10.1086/702594>

Dahl, Roald, 'The Great Automatic Grammatizator', in *Someone Like You* (Harmondsworth: Penguin, 1986), pp. 190–209

Dale, Robert, 'GPT-3: What's It Good For?', *Natural Language Engineering*, 27.1 (2021), 113–18 <https://doi.org/10.1017/S1351324920000601>

Dames, Nicholas, *The Physiology of the Novel: Reading, Neural Science, and the Form of Victorian Fiction* (Oxford: Oxford University Press, 2007)

Darnton, Robert, 'What Is the History of Books?', *Daedalus*, 111.3 (1982), 65–83

Davies, William, *The Limits of Neoliberalism: Authority, Sovereignty and the Logic of Competition* (Thousand Oaks, CA: Sage, 2014)

Davis, Ray, 'Graphs, Maps, Trees/Sets Hamper Grasp', in *Reading* Graphs, Maps and Trees*: Responses to Franco Moretti*, ed. Jonathan Goodwin and John Holbo (Anderson, SC: Parlor Press, 2011), pp. 15–30

De Boom, Cedric, Sam Leroux, Steven Bohez, Pieter Simoens, Thomas Demeester, and Bart Dhoedt, 'Efficiency Evaluation of Character-Level RNN Training Schedules', *ArXiv*, 1605.02486, 2016 <http://arxiv.org/abs/1605.02486> [accessed 17 April 2017]

De Hamel, Christopher, *The Book: The History of the Bible* (London: Phaidon Press, 2005)

Derrida, Jacques, 'The Law of Genre', trans. Avital Ronell, *Critical Inquiry*, 7.1 (1980), 55–81

Dickie, George, *Aesthetics: An Introduction* (New York: Pegasus, 1971)

D'Ignazio, Catherine, and Lauren F. Klein, *Data Feminism*, Strong Ideas Series (Cambridge, MA: MIT Press, 2020)

Dinnen, Zara, *The Digital Banal: New Media and American Literature and Culture* (New York: Columbia University Press, 2018)

Dinsman, Melissa, and Alexander R. Galloway, 'The Digital in the Humanities: An Interview with Alexander Galloway', *Los Angeles Review of Books* <https://lareviewofbooks.org/article/the-digital-in-the-humanities-an-interview-with-alexander-galloway/> [accessed 19 April 2016]

Drucker, Johanna, *Figuring the Word: Essays on Books, Writing, and Visual Poetics* (New York: Granary Books, 1998)

Drucker, Johanna, 'Graphesis', *Paj: The Journal of the Initiative for Digital Humanities, Media, and Culture*, 2.1 (2010) <https://journals.tdl.org/paj/index.php/paj/article/view/4> [accessed 28 November 2019]

Drucker, Johanna, *Graphesis: Visual Forms of Knowledge Production* (Cambridge, MA: Harvard University Press, 2014)

Drucker, Johanna, 'Humanities Approaches to Graphical Display', *Digital Humanities Quarterly*, 5.1 (2011) <http://www.digitalhumanities.org/dhq/vol/5/1/000091/000091.html>

Drucker, Johanna, *SpecLab: Digital Aesthetics and Projects in Speculative Computing* (Chicago, IL: University of Chicago Press, 2009)

Drucker, Johanna, *The Century of Artists' Books* (New York: Granary Books, 1995)

Drucker, Johanna, *The Visible World: Experimental Typography and Modern Art, 1909–1923* (Chicago, IL: University of Chicago Press, 1994)

Dunn, Sydni, 'Digital Humanists: If You Want Tenure, Do Double the Work', *Vitae*, 2014 <https://chroniclevitae.com/news/249-digital-humanists-if-you-want-tenure-do-double-the-work> [accessed 21 March 2017]

Eaglestone, Robert, 'Contemporary Fiction in the Academy: Towards a Manifesto', *Textual Practice*, 27.7 (2013), 1089–1101 <https://doi.org/10.1080/0950236X.2013.840113>

Egan, Jennifer, 'The Stylist [The New Yorker]', *The New Yorker*, 13 March 1989, 32–7

Elfenbein, Andrew, *The Gist of Reading* (Stanford, CA: Stanford University Press, 2018)

Elkins, Katherine, and Jon Chun, 'Can GPT-3 Pass a Writer's Turing Test?', *Journal of Cultural Analytics*, 2020, 17212 <https://doi.org/10.22148/001c.17212>

Elliot, W., and R. J. Valenza, 'And Then There Were None: Winnowing the Shakespeare Claimants', *Computers and the Humanities*, 30 (1996), 191–245

Elliot, W., and R. J. Valenza, 'So Many Hardballs, so Few over the Plate', *Computers and the Humanities*, 36 (2002), 455–60

Elliot, W., and R. J. Valenza, 'The Professor Doth Protest Too Much, Methinks', *Computers and the Humanities*, 32 (1998), 425–90

Ellis, J. M., 'Linguistics, Literature, and the Concept of Style', *WORD*, 26.1 (1970), 65–78 <https://doi.org/10.1080/00437956.1970.11435581>

English, James F., *The Economy of Prestige Prizes, Awards, and the Circulation of Cultural Value* (Cambridge, MA: Harvard University Press, 2005)

English, James F., 'Winning the Culture Game: Prizes, Awards, and the Rules of Art', *New Literary History*, 33.1 (2002), 109–35

Ensmenger, Nathan, *The Computer Boys Take Over: Computers, Programmers, and the Politics of Technical Expertise*, History of Computing (Cambridge, MA: MIT Press, 2010)

Eve, Martin Paul, *Close Reading With Computers: Textual Scholarship, Computational Formalism, and David Mitchell's* Cloud Atlas (Stanford, CA: Stanford University Press, 2019)

Eve, Martin Paul, 'Data Appendices for "Textual Scholarship and Contemporary Literary Studies: Jennifer Egan's Editorial Processes and the Archival Edition of *Emerald City*"', 2019 <https://doi.org/10.5281/zenodo.3253829>

Eve, Martin Paul, *Literature Against Criticism: University English and Contemporary Fiction in Conflict* (Cambridge: Open Book Publishers, 2016)

Eve, Martin Paul, 'New Leaves: The Histories of Digital Pagination', *Book History*, 2022

Eve, Martin Paul, *Open Access and the Humanities: Contexts, Controversies and the Future* (Cambridge: Cambridge University Press, 2014) <https://doi.org/10.1017/CBO9781316161012>

Eve, Martin Paul, *Pynchon and Philosophy: Wittgenstein, Foucault and Adorno* (Basingstoke: Palgrave Macmillan, 2014)

Eve, Martin Paul, 'Reading Redaction: Symptomatic Metadata, Erasure Poetry, and Mark Blacklock's *I'm Jack*', *Critique: Studies in Contemporary Fiction*, 60.3 (2019), 330–41 <https://doi.org/10.1080/00111619.2019.1568960>

Eve, Martin Paul, 'Reading Scholarship Digitally', in *Reassembling Scholarly Communications: Histories, Infrastructures, and Global Politics of Open Access*, ed. Martin Paul Eve and Jonathan Gray (Cambridge, MA: MIT Press, 2020), pp. 277–84

Eve, Martin Paul, 'SankeyTextualVariant', *GitHub*, 2015 <https://github.com/MartinPaulEve/SankeyTextualVariant> [accessed 20 December 2015]

Eve, Martin Paul, 'Scarcity and Abundance', in *The Bloomsbury Handbook of Electronic Literature*, ed. Joseph Tabbi (London: Bloomsbury, 2017), pp. 385–98

Eve, Martin Paul, ' "Structural Dissatisfaction": Academics on Safari in the Novels of Jennifer Egan', *Open Library of Humanities*, 1.1 (2015) <https://doi.org/10.16995/olh.29>

Eve, Martin Paul, 'Textual Scholarship and Contemporary Literary Studies: Jennifer Egan's Editorial Processes and the Archival Edition of *Emerald City*', *Lit: Literature Interpretation Theory*, 31.1 (2020), 25–41 <https://doi.org/10.1080/10436928.2020.1709713>

Eve, Martin Paul, 'The Great Automatic Grammatizator: Writing, Labour, Computers', *Critical Quarterly*, 59.3 (2017), 39–54 <https://doi.org/10.1111/criq.12359>

Eve, Martin Paul, *Warez: The Infrastructure and Aesthetics of Piracy* (New York: punctum books, 2022) <https://eprints.bbk.ac.uk/id/eprint/30956/> [accessed 10 April 2021]

Eve, Martin Paul, 'Violins in the Subway: Scarcity Correlations, Evaluative Cultures, and Disciplinary Authority in the Digital Humanities', in *Digital Technology and the Practices of Humanities Research*, ed. Jennifer Edmonds (Cambridge: Open Book Publishers, 2019)

Eve, Martin Paul, '"You Have to Keep Track of Your Changes": The Version Variants and Publishing History of David Mitchell's *Cloud Atlas*', *Open Library of Humanities*, 2.2 (2016), 1–34 <https://doi.org/10.16995/olh.82>

Eve, Martin Paul, Cameron Neylon, Daniel O'Donnell, Samuel Moore, Robert Gadie, Victoria Odeniyi, and others, *Reading Peer Review: PLOS ONE and Institutional Change in Academia* (Cambridge: Cambridge University Press, 2021)

Eyers, Tom, *Speculative Formalism: Literature, Theory, and the Critical Present* (Evanston, IL: Northwestern University Press, 2017)

Farringdon, J. M., *Analyzing for Authorship: A Guide to the Cusum Technique* (Cardiff: University of Wales Press, 1996)

Fazi, M. Beatrice, *Contingent Computation: Abstraction, Experience, and Indeterminacy in Computational Aesthetics* (Lanham, MD: Rowman & Littlefield, 2018)

Felperin, Howard, 'Making It "Neo": The New Historicism and Renaissance Literature', *Textual Practice*, 1.3 (1987), 262–77 <https://doi.org/10.1080/09502368708582017>

Felski, Rita, *The Limits of Critique* (Chicago, IL: University of Chicago Press, 2015)

Felski, Rita, *Uses of Literature* (Malden, MA: Blackwell Publishing, 2008)

Ferran, Bronać, *The Smell of Ink and Soil: The Story of (Edition) Hansjörg Mayer* (Cologne: Walther Koenig, 2017)

Fiormonte, Domenico, 'Towards a Cultural Critique of the Digital Humanities', *Historical Social Research/Historische Sozialforschung*, 37.3 (141) (2012), 59–76

Fitzpatrick, Kathleen, 'Do "the Risky Thing" in Digital Humanities', *The Chronicle of Higher Education*, 2011 <http://www.chronicle.com/article/Do-the-Risky-Thing-in/129132/> [accessed 21 March 2017]

Fitzpatrick, Kathleen, *Planned Obsolescence: Publishing, Technology, and the Future of the Academy* (New York: New York University Press, 2011)

Foucault, Michel, *The Birth of Biopolitics: Lectures at the Collège de France, 1978–79* (Basingstoke: Palgrave Macmillan, 2008)

Foucault, Michel, 'What Is an Author?', in *The Essential Works of Michel Foucault, 1954–1984*, 3 vols. (London: Penguin, 2000), II, 205–22

Fredner, Erik, 'How Many Novels Have Been Published in English? (An Attempt)', *Stanford Literary Lab*, 2017 <https://litlab.stanford.edu/how-many-novels-have-been-published-in-english-an-attempt/>

Friedman, Geraldine, 'History in the Background of Wordsworth's "Blind Beggar"', *ELH*, 56.1 (1989), 125–48 <https://doi.org/10.2307/2873126>

Funk, Wolfgang, 'Found Objects: Narrative (as) Reconstruction in Jennifer Egan's *A Visit from the Goon Squad*', in *The Aesthetics of Authenticity: Medial Constructions of the Real*, ed. Wolfgang Funk, Florian Groß, and Irmtraud Huber (Bielefeld: Transcript Verlag, 2012), pp. 41–61

Funk, Wolfgang, *The Literature of Reconstruction: Authentic Fiction in the New Millennium* (London: Bloomsbury Academic, 2015)

Funkhouser, Christopher, 'Digital Poetry', in *A Companion to Digital Literary Studies*, ed. Ray Siemens and Susan Schreibman, Blackwell Companions to Literature and Culture (New York: Wiley-Blackwell, 2013), pp. 318–35

Fussell, Paul, *The Great War and Modern Memory* (New York: Oxford University Press, 2000)

Galey, Alan, 'The Enkindling Reciter: E-Books in the Bibliographical Imagination', *Book History*, 15.1 (2012), 210–47 <https://doi.org/10.1353/bh.2012.0008>

Gallop, Jane, 'The Historicization of Literary Studies and the Fate of Close Reading', *Profession* (2007), 181–6 <https://doi.org/10.1632/prof.2007.2007.1.181>

Giblett, Rodney James, *Cities and Wetlands: The Return of the Repressed in Nature and Culture*, Environmental Cultures Series (London: Bloomsbury Academic, 2016)

Gitelman, Lisa, ed., *'Raw Data' Is an Oxymoron*, Infrastructures Series (Cambridge, MA: MIT Press, 2013)

Goldberg, Yoav, 'A Criticism of Stochastic Parrots', 2021 <https://gist.github.com/yoavg/9fc9be2f98b47c189a513573d902fb27> [accessed 31 March 2021]

Goldsmith, Kenneth, *Uncreative Writing* (New York: Columbia University Press, 2011)

Gottlieb, Robert, *Avid Reader: A Life* (New York: Farrar, Straus and Giroux, 2016)

Graff, Gerald, *Professing Literature: An Institutional History* (Chicago, IL: University of Chicago Press, 1989)

Grafton, Anthony, *The Footnote: A Curious History* (Cambridge, MA: Harvard University Press, 1999)

Grdseloff, Dorothee, 'A Note on the Origin of Fedallah in *Moby-Dick*', *American Literature*, 27.3 (1955), 396–403

Greenblatt, Stephen, *Renaissance Self-Fashioning: From More to Shakespeare* (Chicago, IL: University of Chicago Press, 2005)

Greene, Gayle, *Changing the Story: Feminist Fiction and the Tradition* (Bloomington, IN: Indiana University Press, 1991)

Grieve, J. W., 'Quantitative Authorship Attribution: A History and an Evaluation of Techniques' (unpublished Masters, Simon Fraser University, 2005) <http://hdl.handle.net/1892/2055>

Haffenden, John, ed., *Novelists in Interview* (London: Methuen, 1985)

Hall, Jason David, 'Popular Prosody: Spectacle and the Politics of Victorian Versification', *Nineteenth-Century Literature*, 62.2 (2007), 222–49 <https://doi.org/10.1525/ncl.2007.62.2.222>

Haraway, Donna, 'A Cyborg Manifesto: Science, Technology, and Socialist-Feminism in the Late Twentieth Century', in *Simians, Cyborgs and Women: The Reinvention of Nature* (London: Routledge, 1991), pp. 149–81

Hardcastle, R. A., 'CUSUM: A Credible Method for the Determination of Authorship?', *Science & Justice*, 37.2 (1997), 129–38 <https://doi.org/10.1016/S1355-0306(97)72158-0>

Harris-Birtill, Rose, *David Mitchell's Post-Secular World: Buddhism, Belief and the Urgency of Compassion*, New Horizons in Contemporary Writing (London: Bloomsbury, 2018)

Harrison, K. David, and Gregory Anderson, 'Review of Proposal for Encoding Warang Chiti (Ho Orthography) in Unicode', 22 April 2007 <https://www.unicode.org/L2/L2007/07137-warang-chiti-review.pdf>

Hartmann, Johanna, 'Paratextualized Forms of Fictional Self-Narration: Footnotes, Headnotes and Endnotes in Jennifer Egan's *A Visit from the Goon Squad*', in *Symbolism* 15, ed. Rüdiger Ahrens and Klaus Stierstorfer (Berlin: De Gruyter, 2015), pp. 101–20 <https://doi.org/10.1515/9783110449075-007>

HathiTrust Digital Library, 'HathiTrust Research Center Extends Non-Consumptive Research Tools to Copyrighted Materials: Expanding Research through Fair Use', *Perspectives from HathiTrust*, 2018 <https://www.hathitrust.org/blogs/perspectives-from-hathitrust/hathitrust-research-center-extends-non-consumptive-research-tools> [accessed 17 November 2018]

Hayles, N. Katherine, 'Caught in the Web: Cosmology and the Point of (No) Return in Pynchon's *Gravity's Rainbow*', in *The Cosmic Web: Scientific Field Models and Literary Strategies in the Twentieth Century*, Scientific Field Models and Literary Strategies in the Twentieth Century (Ithaca, NY: Cornell University Press, 1984), pp. 168–98 <http://www.jstor.org/stable/10.7591/j.ctt207g6gx.10> [accessed 6 April 2021]

Hayles, N. Katherine, *How We Think: Digital Media and Contemporary Technogenesis* (Chicago, IL: University of Chicago Press, 2012)

Hayles, N. Katherine, *Writing Machines*, Mediawork Pamphlet (Cambridge, MA: MIT Press, 2002)

Hebdige, Dick, *Subculture: The Meaning of Style* (London: Routledge, 1979)

Heim, Michael, *Electric Language: A Philosophical Study of Word Processing* (New Haven, CT: Yale University Press, 1999)

Heldén, Johannes, and Håkan Jonson, 'Evolution', 2014 <http://www.textevolution.net/> [accessed 15 April 2016]

Heldén, Johannes, and Håkan Jonson, *Evolution* (OEI editör, 2014)

Henrickson, Leah, *Reading Computer-Generated Texts* (Cambridge: Cambridge University Press, 2021) <https://doi.org/10.1017/9781108906463>

Herman, Luc, and John M. Krafft, 'Fast Learner: The Typescript of Pynchon's *V.* at the Harry Ransom Center in Austin', *Texas Studies in Literature and Language*, 49.1 (2007), 1–20 <https://doi.org/10.1353/tsl.2007.0005>

Hicks, Marie, *Programmed Inequality: How Britain Discarded Women Technologists and Lost Its Edge in Computing* (Cambridge, MA: MIT Press, 2018)

Hilton, M. L., 'An Assessment of Cumulative Sum Charts for Authorship Attribution', *Literary and Linguistic Computing*, 8.2 (1993), 73–80 <https://doi.org/10.1093/llc/8.2.73>

Hoban, Russell, *Riddley Walker* (London: Bloomsbury, 2002)

Holmes, David I., 'The Evolution of Stylometry in Humanities Scholarship', *Literary and Linguistic Computing*, 13.3 (1998), 111–17

Holmes, David I., and Fiona Tweedie, 'Forensic Stylometry: A Review of the Cusum Controversy', *Revue Informatique et Statistique dans les Sciences Humaines*, 31.1–4 (1995), 19–47

Holmwood, John, 'Open Access, "Publicity", and Democratic Knowledge', in *Reassembling Scholarly Communications: Histories, Infrastructures, and Global Politics of Open Access*, ed. Martin Paul Eve and Jonathan Gray (Cambridge, MA: MIT Press, 2020), pp. 181–91

Hoover, David, 'Testing Burrows's Delta', *Literary and Linguistic Computing*, 19.4 (2004), 453–75

Hopper, Keith, *Flann O'Brien: A Portrait of the Artist as a Young Post-Modernist* (Cork: Cork University Press, 2009)

Houser, Heather, 'Shimmering Description and Descriptive Criticism', *New Literary History*, 51.1 (2020), 1–22 <https://doi.org/10.1353/nlh.2020.0000>

Hudson, Roger, ed., *Coleridge Among the Lakes & Mountains* (London: Folio Society, 1991)

Hugo, François, 'The City and the Country: Books VII and VIII of Wordsworth's "The Prelude"', *Theoria: A Journal of Social and Political Theory*, 69 (1987), 1–14

Hungerford, Amy, *Making Literature Now*, Post 45 (Stanford, CA: Stanford University Press, 2016)

Hungerford, Amy, 'On the Period Formerly Known as Contemporary', *American Literary History*, 20.1–2 (2008), 410–19 <https://doi.org/10.1093/alh/ajm044>

Imam, Sharjeel, 'Digital Colonialism: 1. All Latin Alphabets and Symbols Are Denoted in Unicode by the Range of 0 to 500 in One Single Block. But Urdu-Arabic Alphabets Are Scattered in Five Different Blocks Ranging 1500 to around 64000', *@_imaams*, 2017 <https://twitter.com/_imaams/status/934109280285765632> [accessed 4 April 2019]

Jamali, Hamid R., David Nicholas, and Eti Herman, 'Scholarly Reputation in the Digital Age and the Role of Emerging Platforms and Mechanisms', *Research Evaluation*, 25.1 (2016), 37–49 <https://doi.org/10.1093/reseval/rvv032>

James, David, '"Style Is Morality"? Aesthetics and Politics in the Amis Era', *Textual Practice*, 26.1 (2012), 11–25 <https://doi.org/10.1080/0950236X.2012.638760>

Jin, Jay, 'Problems of Scale in "Close" and "Distant" Reading', *Philological Quarterly*, 96.1 (2017), 105–29

Jockers, Matthew L., 'A Novel Method for Detecting Plot', 2014 <http://www.matthewjockers.net/2014/06/05/a-novel-method-for-detecting-plot/>

Jockers, Matthew L., *Macroanalysis: Digital Methods and Literary History*, Topics in the Digital Humanities (Urbana, IL: University of Illinois Press, 2013)

Jockers, Matthew L., 'Requiem for a Low Pass Filter', 2015 <http://www.matthewjockers.net/2015/04/06/epilogue/>

Jockers, Matthew L., 'Resurrecting a Low Pass Filter (Well, Kind Of)', 2017 <http://www.matthewjockers.net/2017/01/12/resurrecting/>

Jockers, Matthew L., *Text Analysis with R for Students of Literature* (New York: Springer, 2014)

Jockers, Matthew, and Gabi Kiriloff, 'Understanding Gender and Character Agency in the 19th Century Novel', *Journal of Cultural Analytics*, 1.1 (2016), 1–26 <https://doi.org/10.22148/16.010>

Johnson, Justin, *torch-rnn*, 2016 <https://github.com/jcjohnson/torch-rnn> [accessed 17 April 2017]

Johnston, David Jhave, *Aesthetic Animism: Digital Poetry's Ontological Implications* (Cambridge, MA: MIT Press, 2016) <http://www.jstor.org/stable/j.ctt1cd0mcs> [accessed 14 April 2017]

Juhl, P. D., 'Do Computer Poems Show That an Author's Intention Is Irrelevant to the Meaning of a Literary Work?', *Critical Inquiry*, 5.3 (1979), 481–7

Juola, Patrick, 'Authorship Attribution', *Foundations and Trends® in Information Retrieval*, 1.3 (2007), 233–334 <https://doi.org/10.1561/1500000005>

Juola, Patrick, 'Stylometry and Immigration: A Case Study', *Journal of Law and Policy*, 21.2 (2012), 287–98

Kelly, Adam, 'Beginning with Postmodernism', *Twentieth Century Literature*, 57.3/4 (2011), 391–422

Kenny, Anthony, *The Computation of Style: An Introduction to Statistics for Students of Literature and Humanities*, Pergamon International Library of Science, Technology, Engineering, & Social Studies (Oxford: Pergamon Press, 1982)

Ketzan, Erik, *Thomas Pynchon and the Digital Humanities: Computational Approaches to Style* (London: Bloomsbury, 2022)

Ketzan, Erik, and Christian Schöch, 'What Changed When Andy Weir's *The Martian* Got Edited?' (presented at the Digital Humanities 2017, Montreal, 2017) <https://dh2017.adho.org/abstracts/317/317.pdf> [accessed 8 October 2017]

King, Stephen, *On Writing: A Memoir of the Craft* (London: Hodder, 2012)

King, Stephen, 'Word Processor of the Gods', in *Skeleton Crew* (London: Hodder, 2012), pp. 327–48

Kinsley, Peter, *I'm Jack: The Police Hunt for the Yorkshire Ripper* (London: Pan, 1980)

Kirby, Alan, 'Digimodern Textual Endlessness', *American Book Review*, 34.4 (2013), 12 <https://doi.org/10.1353/abr.2013.0056>

Kirschenbaum, Matthew G., 'Books.Files: Preservation of Digital Assets in the Contemporary Publishing Industry', 2020 <https://doi.org/10.13016/1i33-pl0y>

Kirschenbaum, Matthew G., 'Closing Remarks', in *Books.Files* (The Morgan Library, New York, 2018)

Kirschenbaum, Matthew G., 'Hello Worlds', *The Chronicle of Higher Education*, 23 January 2009 <https://www.chronicle.com/article/Hello-Worlds/5476> [accessed 13 April 2020]

Kirschenbaum, Matthew G., *Mechanisms: New Media and the Forensic Imagination* (Cambridge, MA: MIT Press, 2008)

Kirschenbaum, Matthew G., *Track Changes: A Literary History of Word Processing* (Cambridge, MA: The Belknap Press of Harvard University Press, 2016)

Kramer, Lawrence, 'Gender and Sexuality in *The Prelude*: The Question of Book Seven', *ELH*, 54.3 (1987), 619–37 <https://doi.org/10.2307/2873223>

Lang, Berel, ed., *The Concept of Style* (Ithaca, NY: Cornell University Press, 1987)

Latour, Bruno, 'Visualisation and Cognition: Drawing Things Together', *Knowledge and Society: Studies in the Sociology of Culture and Present*, 6 (1986), 1–33

Lemercier, Claire, and Claire Zalc, *Quantitative Methods in the Humanities: An Introduction*, trans. Arthur Goldhammer (Charlottesville, VA: University of Virginia Press, 2019)

Lerer, Seth, *Tradition: A Feeling for the Literary Past*, The Literary Agenda (Oxford: Oxford University Press, 2016)

Letzler, David, *The Cruft of Fiction: Mega-Novels and the Science of Paying Attention*, Frontiers of Narrative (Lincoln, NE: University of Nebraska Press, 2017)

Levitt, Morton P., 'Modernism Bound', *Journal of Modern Literature*, 24.3 (2001), 501–6 <https://doi.org/10.1353/jml.2001.0005>

Light, Jennifer S., 'When Computers Were Women', *Technology and Culture*, 40.3 (1999), 455–83

Liu, Alan, 'E.g. (Generic Example): "Wordsworth Uses 'joy' a Lot in Important Poems like 'Tintern Abbey'." Evidence of That Sort Underlies Much of Literary Studies, Going Back to Close Reading. Let's Compare the Statistical Validity of _that_ to DH's Attempt to Make It, If Not Right, Better', *@alanyliu*, 2019 <https://twitter.com/alanyliu/status/1106109232661725185> [accessed 17 March 2019]

Liu, Alan, 'Imagining the New Media Encounter', in *A Companion to Digital Literary Studies*, ed. Ray Siemens and Susan Schreibman, Blackwell Companions to Literature and Culture (New York: Wiley-Blackwell, 2013), pp. 3–26

Liu, Alan, *The Laws of Cool: Knowledge Work and the Culture of Information* (Chicago, IL: University of Chicago Press, 2004)

Liu, Alan, 'Where Is Cultural Criticism in the Digital Humanities?', in *Debates in the Digital Humanities*, ed. Matthew K. Gold (Minneapolis, MN: University of Minnesota Press, 2012), pp. 490–509

<https://dhdebates.gc.cuny.edu/read/untitled-88c11800-9446-469b-a3be-3fdb36bfbd1e/section/896742e7-5218-42c5-89b0-0c3c75682a2f> [accessed 14 April 2020]

Livio, Mario, *The Golden Ratio: The Story of Phi, the World's Most Astonishing Number* (New York: Broadway Books, 2003)

McCaffery, Larry, 'Introduction: The Desert of the Real', in *Storming the Reality Studio: A Casebook of Cyberpunk and Postmodern Science Fiction*, ed. Larry McCaffery (Durham, NC: Duke University Press, 1991), pp. 1–16

McClure, David, '(Mental) Maps of Texts', *David McClure*, 2014 <http://dclure.org/essays/mental-maps-of-texts/> [accessed 22 December 2018]

McGann, Jerome, *A Critique of Modern Textual Criticism* (Charlottesville, VA: University of Virginia Press, 1983)

McGann, Jerome, 'From Text to Work: Digital Tools and the Emergence of the Social Text', *Text*, 16 (2006), 49–62

McHale, Brian, 'Modernist Reading, Post-Modern Text: The Case of *Gravity's Rainbow*', *Poetics Today*, 1.1/2 (1979), 85–110

McHoul, Alec, and David Wills, *Writing Pynchon: Strategies in Fictional Analysis* (Basingstoke: Macmillan, 1990)

McIlwain, Charlton D., *Black Software: The Internet and Racial Justice, from the AfroNet to Black Lives Matter* (New York: Oxford University Press, 2020)

McLuhan, Marshall, *Understanding Media: The Extensions of Man* (Cambridge, MA: MIT Press, 1994)

McMenamin, G., 'Disputed Authorship in US Law', *International Journal of Speech, Language and the Law*, 11.1 (2004), 73–82

Mak, Bonnie, *How the Page Matters*, Studies in Book and Print Culture Series (Toronto: University of Toronto Press, 2011)

Manguel, Alberto, *A Reader on Reading* (New Haven, CT: Yale University Press, 2010)

Manovich, Lev, *The Language of New Media* (Cambridge, MA: MIT Press, 2002)

Markovits, Stefanie, *The Victorian Verse-Novel: Aspiring to Life* (Oxford: Oxford University Press, 2017)

Marquez, Antonio, 'The Cinematic Imagination in Thomas Pynchon's *Gravity's Rainbow*', *Rocky Mountain Review of Language and Literature*, 33.4 (1979), 165–79

Mazlish, Bruce, *A New Science: The Breakdown of Connections and the Birth of Sociology* (Oxford: Oxford University Press, 1989)

Melville, Herman, *Moby-Dick: An Authoritative Text, Contexts, Criticism*, ed. Hershel Parker, A Norton Critical Edition, 3rd edn. (New York: W. W. Norton, 2018)

Mendelson, Edward, 'Encyclopedic Narrative: From Dante to Pynchon', *MLN*, 91.6 (1976), 1267–75

Mitchell, David, *Cloud Atlas* (London: Sceptre, 2004)

Mitchell, David, *Cloud Atlas* (New York: Random House, 2004)

Mitchell, David, *Number9dream* (London: Sceptre, 2001)

Mitchell, David, *Number9dream* (New York: Random House, 2010)

Moholy-Nagy, László, *Vision in Motion* (Chicago, IL: P. Theobald, 1947)

Montemayor, Carlos, 'Language and Intelligence', *Daily Nous*, 2020 <https://dailynous.com/2020/07/30/philosophers-gpt-3/> [accessed 31 March 2021]

Moore, Samuel, Cameron Neylon, Martin Paul Eve, Daniel O'Donnell, and Damian Pattinson, 'Excellence R Us: University Research and the Fetishisation of Excellence', *Palgrave Communications*, 3 (2017) <https://doi.org/10.1057/palcomms.2016.105>

Moran, Alexander, 'The Genrefication of Contemporary American Fiction', *Textual Practice*, 33.2 (2019), 229–44 <https://doi.org/10.1080/0950236X.2018.1509272>

Moretti, Franco, *Atlas of the European Novel: 1800–1900* (London: Verso, 1998)

Moretti, Franco, *Distant Reading* (London: Verso, 2013)

Moretti, Franco, *Graphs, Maps, Trees: Abstract Models for Literary History* (London: Verso, 2007)

Morgan, Marcus, and Patrick Baert, *Conflict in the Academy: A Study in the Sociology of Intellectuals* (London: Palgrave Macmillan, 2015)

Moslund, Sten Pultz, 'The Presencing of Place in Literature: Toward an Embodied Topopetic Mode of Reading', in *Geocritical Explorations: Space, Place, and Mapping in Literary and Cultural Studies*, ed. Robert T. Tally (New York: Palgrave Macmillan, 2011), pp. 29–43

Mosteller, F., and D. L. Wallace, *Inference and Disputed Authorship: The Federalist* (Reading, MA: Addison-Wesley, 1964)

Muggleton, David, and Rupert Weinzierl, eds., *The Post-Subcultures Reader* (Oxford: Berg, 2003)

Muhr, Sara Louise, and Alf Rehn, 'On Gendered Technologies and Cyborg Writing', *Gender, Work & Organization*, 22.2 (2015), 129–38 <https://doi.org/10.1111/gwao.12057>

Mulhern, Francis, 'The Cambridge Affair', *Marxism Today*, March 1981, pp. 27–8

Natale, Simone, *Deceitful Media: Artificial Intelligence and Social Life after the Turing Test* (Oxford: Oxford University Press, 2021)

Nelson, Camilla, '#ThanksforTyping: The Women behind Famous Male Writers', *The Conversation*, 2017 <http://theconversation.com/thanksfortyping-the-women-behind-famous-male-writers-75770> [accessed 15 April 2017]

Niculae, Vlad, and Victoria Yaneva, 'Computational Considerations of Comparisons and Similes', in *51st Annual Meeting of the Association for Computational Linguistics Proceedings of the Student Research Workshop* (Sofia, Bulgaria: Association for Computational Linguistics, 2013), pp. 89–95 <http://www.aclweb.org/anthology/P13-3013> [accessed 16 November 2018]

Noble, Safiya Umoja, *Algorithms of Oppression: How Search Engines Reinforce Racism* (New York: New York University Press, 2018)

Nowviskie, Bethany, 'Where Credit Is Due: Preconditions for the Evaluation of Collaborative Digital Scholarship', *Profession*, 2011.1 (2011), 169–81 <https://doi.org/10.1632/prof.2011.2011.1.169>

Ockerbloom, Mary Mark, 'Pre-1950s Utopias and Science Fiction by Women: An Annotated Reading List of Online Editions' <https://digital.library.upenn.edu/women/_collections/utopias/utopias.html> [accessed 11 April 2020]

O'Gara, Norris, 'John Humble', *THE REAL YORKSHIRE RIPPER STORY*, 2011 <http://www.yorkshireripper.com/2011/12/29/john-humble/> [accessed 28 December 2015]

Ogden, John T., 'The Power of Distance in Wordsworth's *Prelude*', *PMLA*, 88.2 (1973), 246–59 <https://doi.org/10.2307/461490>

Ohge, Christopher, *Inventions of the Text: Editing, Computing, and Publishing Digital Exhibitions of Experience* (Cambridge: Cambridge University Press, 2022)

Olson, Danel, 'Renovation Is Hell, and Other Gothic Truths Deep Inside Jennifer Egan's *The Keep*', in *21st-Century Gothic: Great Gothic Novels since 2000*, ed. Danel Olson (Lanham, MD: Scarecrow Press, 2011), pp. 327–41

Olson, Hope A., 'Mapping Beyond Dewey's Boundaries: Constructing Classificatory Space for Marginalized Knowledge Domains', *Library Trends*, 47.2 (1998), 233–54

Openshaw, S., 'A View on the GIS Crisis in Geography, or, Using GIS to Put Humpty-Dumpty Back Together Again', *Environment and Planning A: Economy and Space*, 23.5 (1991), 621–8 <https://doi.org/10.1068/a230621>

Openshaw, S., 'The Truth about Ground Truth', *Transactions in GIS*, 2.1 (1997), 7–24 <https://doi.org/10.1111/j.1467–9671.1997.tb00002.x>

Osborn, Don, *African Languages in a Digital Age: Challenges and Opportunities for Indigenous Language Computing* (Cape Town: HSRC Press, 2010)

O'Sullivan, James, Katarzyna Bazarnik, Maciej Eder, and Jan Rybicki, 'Measuring Joycean Influences on Flann O'Brien', *Digital Studies / Le Champ Numérique*, 8.1 (2018), 6 <https://doi.org/10.16995/dscn.288>

Panko, Julia L., *Out of Print: Mediating Information in the Novel and the Book*, Page and Screen (Amherst, MA: University of Massachusetts Press, 2020)

Parnas, D. L., 'On the Criteria To Be Used in Decomposing Systems into Modules', *Communications of the ACM*, 15.12 (1972), 6

Paterson, Laura L., and Ian N. Gregory, 'Geographical Information Systems and Textual Sources', in *Representations of Poverty and Place* (Cham: Springer International Publishing, 2019), pp. 41–60 <https://doi.org/10.1007/978-3-319-93503-4_3>

Pearson, Jennifer, George Buchanan, and Harold Thimbleby, 'Designing for Digital Reading', *Synthesis Lectures on Information Concepts, Retrieval, and Services*, 5.4 (2013), 16–31 <https://doi.org/10.2200/S00539ED1V01Y201310ICR029>

Peet, Lisa, 'Library of Congress Drops Illegal Alien Subject Heading, Provokes Backlash Legislation', *Library Journal*, 2016 <https://www.

libraryjournal.com?detailStory=library-of-congress-drops-illegal-alien-subject-heading-provokes-backlash-legislation> [accessed 15 April 2020]

Perec, Georges, *Life a User's Manual*, trans. David Bellos (London: Harvill, 1996)

Perloff, Marjorie, *Radical Artifice: Writing Poetry in the Age of Media* (Chicago, IL: University of Chicago Press, 1991)

Perloff, Marjorie, *The Poetics of Indeterminacy: Rimbaud to Cage* (Princeton, NJ: Princeton University Press, 1981)

Perloff, Marjorie, *Unoriginal Genius: Poetry by Other Means in the New Century* (Chicago, IL: University of Chicago Press, 2010)

Pieters, Jürgen, ' "I Was Never a New Historicist": Catherine Belsey's "History at the Level of the Signifier" ', *Textual Practice*, 24.6 (2010), 1033–44 <https://doi.org/10.1080/0950236X.2010.521671>

Piper, Andrew, *Can We Be Wrong? The Problem of Textual Evidence in a Time of Data* (Cambridge: Cambridge University Press, 2020) <https://doi.org/10.1017/9781108922036>

Piper, Andrew, *Enumerations: Data and Literary Study* (Chicago, IL: University of Chicago Press, 2018)

Plato, *Phaedrus*, trans. Christopher Rowe (London: Penguin, 2005)

Plotz, John, *The Crowd: British Literature and Public Politics* (Berkeley, CA: University of California Press, 2000)

Precup, Amelia, 'The Posthuman Body in Jennifer Egan's "Black Box" ', *American, British, and Canadian Studies*, 25.1 (2015), 171–86

Pressman, Jessica, *Digital Modernism: Making It New in New Media*, Modernist Literature & Culture, 21 (New York: Oxford University Press, 2014)

Pressman, Jessica, 'House of Leaves: Reading the Networked Novel', *Studies in American Fiction*, 34.1 (2006), 107–28 <https://doi.org/10.1353/saf.2006.0015>

Prieto, Eric, 'Geocriticism, Geopoetics, Geophilosophy, and Beyond', in *Geocritical Explorations: Space, Place, and Mapping in Literary and Cultural Studies*, ed. Robert T. Tally (New York: Palgrave Macmillan, 2011), pp. 13–27

Ramsay, Stephen, *Reading Machines: Toward an Algorithmic Criticism*, Topics in the Digital Humanities (Urbana, IL: University of Illinois Press, 2011)

Rancière, Jacques, *The Politics of Aesthetics: The Distribution of the Sensible*, trans. Gabriel Rockhill (London: Bloomsbury, 2018)

Reed, Mark L., *Wordsworth: The Chronology of the Early Years*, 1770–1799 (Cambridge, MA: Harvard University Press, 2013) <https://www.degruyter.com/view/title/321976> [accessed 28 March 2020]

Reilly, Charlie, 'An Interview with Jennifer Egan', *Contemporary Literature*, 50.3 (2009), 439–60 <https://doi.org/10.1353/cli.0.0074>

Rhody, Lisa Marie, 'Beyond Darwinian Distance: Situating Distant Reading in a Feminist *Ut Pictura Poesis* Tradition', *PMLA*, 132.3 (2017), 659–67

Richards, Ivor Armstrong, *Practical Criticism: A Study of Literary Judgment* (London: Transaction Publishers, 2008)

Richards, I. A., *The Principles of Literary Criticism*, 2nd edn. (London: Routledge, 1926)

Rieder, Bernhard, and Theo Röhle, 'Digital Methods: Five Challenges', in *Understanding Digital Humanities*, ed. David M. Berry (Basingstoke: Palgrave Macmillan, 2012), pp. 67–84 <https://doi.org/10.1057/9780230371934_4>

Risam, Roopika, *New Digital Worlds: Postcolonial Digital Humanities in Theory, Praxis, and Pedagogy* (Evanston, IL: Northwestern University Press, 2018)

Roache, John, ' "The Realer, More Enduring and Sentimental Part of Him": David Foster Wallace's Personal Library and Marginalia', *Orbit: A Journal of American Literature*, 5.1 (2017) <https://doi.org/10.16995/orbit.142>

Robot Darnton, 'Book Historians Should Consider the Role of Airline Pilots in the Book Trade', *@RobotDarnton*, 2018 <https://twitter.com/RobotDarnton/status/1072470428755607552> [accessed 11 December 2018]

Rogers, Richard, *Digital Methods* (Cambridge, MA: MIT Press, 2015)

Rolls, Albert, 'The Two *V*s of Thomas Pynchon, or From Lippincott to Jonathan Cape and Beyond', *Orbit: Writing Around Pynchon*, 1.1 (2012) <https://doi.org/10.7766/orbit.v1.1.33>

Ruppert, Evelyn, John Law, and Mike Savage, 'Reassembling Social Science Methods: The Challenge of Digital Devices', *Theory, Culture & Society*, 30.4 (2013), 22–46 <https://doi.org/10.1177/0263276413484941>

Said, Edward W., *On Late Style* (London: Bloomsbury, 2006)

Sample, Mark, 'Tenure as a Risk-Taking Venture', *Journal of Digital Humanities*, 1.4 (2012) <http://journalofdigitalhumanities.org/1-4/tenure-as-a-risk-taking-venture-by-mark-sample/> [accessed 24 March 2017]

Samuels, Barney, 'I Voted Leave…But Now I've Got 10,000 SEX ARSES Stuck at Calais!', *Daily Sport*, 2 January 2021

Samuels, Lisa, and Jerome J. McGann, 'Deformance and Interpretation', *New Literary History*, 30.1 (1999), 25–56 <https://doi.org/10.1353/nlh.1999.0010>

Sangster, Matthew, 'Romantic London', 2017 <http://www.romanticlondon.org/> [accessed 24 February 2020]

Schmidt, Benjamin M., 'Do Digital Humanists Need to Understand Algorithms?', in *Debates in the Digital Humanities 2016*, ed. Matthew K. Gold and Lauren F. Klein (Minneapolis, MN: University of Minnesota Press, 2016), pp. 546–55 <http://dhdebates.gc.cuny.edu/debates/text/99>

Schmitt, Cannon, 'Interpret or Describe?', *Representations*, 135.1 (2016), 102–18 <https://doi.org/10.1525/rep.2016.135.1.102>

Searle, John R., 'The Logical Status of Fictional Discourse', in *Expression and Meaning: Studies in the Theory of Speech Acts* (Cambridge: Cambridge University Press, 1979), pp. 58–76

Seh, Suzanne Patience Mpouli Njanga, 'Automatic Annotation of Similes in Literary Texts' (unpublished Ph.D., Université Pierre et Marie Curie—Paris VI, 2016)

Shetterly, Margot Lee, *Hidden Figures: The American Dream and the Untold Story of the Black Women Mathematicians Who Helped Win the Space Race* (New York: William Morrow and Company, 2016)

Shneiderman, Ben, and Catherine Plaisant, *Designing the User Interface: Strategies for Effective Human-Computer Interaction*, 4th edn. (Boston, MA: Pearson, 2004)

Siemens, Ray, and Susan Schreibman, eds., *A Companion to Digital Literary Studies*, Blackwell Companions to Literature and Culture (New York: Wiley-Blackwell, 2013)

Skains, R. Lyle, *Digital Authorship: Publishing in the Attention Economy* (Cambridge: Cambridge University Press, 2019)

Smith, Barbara Herrnstein, 'What Was "Close Reading"? A Century of Method in Literary Studies', *The Minnesota Review*, 87 (2016), 57–75 <https://doi.org/10.1215/00265667-3630844>

Smith, David A., Ryan Cordel, Elizabeth Maddock Dillon, Nick Stramp, and John Wilkerson, 'Detecting and Modeling Local Text Reuse', in *IEEE/ACM Joint Conference on Digital Libraries* (presented at the 2014 IEEE/ACM Joint Conference on Digital Libraries (JCDL), London, United Kingdom: IEEE, 2014), pp. 183–92 <https://doi.org/10.1109/JCDL.2014.6970166>

Smith, Helen, and Louise Wilson, eds., *Renaissance Paratexts* (Cambridge: Cambridge University Press, 2011)

So, Richard Jean, 'All Models Are Wrong', *PMLA*, 132.3 (2017), 668–73

So, Richard Jean, *Redlining Culture: A Data History of Racial Inequality and Postwar Fiction* (New York: Columbia University Press, 2020)

Sokal, Alan, *Beyond the Hoax: Science, Philosophy and Culture* (Oxford: Oxford University Press, 2009)

Solt, Mary Ellen, *Concrete Poetry: A World View* (Bloomington, IN: Indiana University Press, 1970)

Stableford, Brian, 'Science Fiction Between the Wars, 1918–1938', in *Anatomy of Wonder: A Critical Guide to Science Fiction*, ed. by Neil Barron, 5th edn. (Santa Barbara, CA: Libraries Unlimited, 2004), pp. 23–44

Stableford, Brian, 'The Emergence of Science Fiction, 1516–1914', in *Anatomy of Wonder: A Critical Guide to Science Fiction*, ed. by Neil Barron, 5th edn. (Santa Barbara, CA: Libraries Unlimited, 2004), pp. 3–22

Stahl, Geoff, 'Tastefully Renovating Subcultural Theory: Making Space for a New Model', in *The Post-Subcultures Reader*, ed. David Muggleton and Rupert Weinzierl (Oxford: Berg, 2003), pp. 27–40

Staley, David J., *Computers, Visualization, and History: How New Technology Will Transform Our Understanding of the Past*, History, Humanities, and New Technology (Armonk, NY: Sharpe, 2003)

Stein, Gertrude, *The Making of Americans, Being a History of a Family's Progress* (Project Gutenberg, 2016) <http://gutenberg.net.au/ebooks16/1600671h.html> [accessed 27 November 2018]

Stein, S., and S. Argamon, 'A Mathematical Explanation of Burrows' Delta', in *Proceedings of Digital Humanities* 2006 (Paris, France, 2006)

Sterling, Bruce, 'CATSCAN 5: Slipstream', *SF Eye*, 5, 1989 <http://lib.ru/STERLINGB/catscan05.txt> [accessed 30 November 2018]

Stokes, C. R., 'Sign, Sensation and the Body in Wordsworth's "Residence in London"', *European Romantic Review*, 23.2 (2012), 203–23 <https://doi.org/10.1080/10509585.2012.653281>

Strong, Melissa J., 'Found Time: *Kairos* in *A Visit from the Goon Squad*', *Critique: Studies in Contemporary Fiction*, 59.4 (2018), 471–80 <https://doi.org/10.1080/00111619.2018.1427544>

Swafford, Annie, 'Continuing the Syuzhet Discussion', *Anglophile in Academia: Annie Swafford's Blog*, 2015 <https://annieswafford.wordpress.com/2015/03/07/continuingsyuzhet/>

Swafford, Annie, 'Why Syuzhet Doesn't Work and How We Know', *Anglophile in Academia: Annie Swafford's Blog*, 2015 <https://annieswafford.wordpress.com/2015/03/30/why-syuzhet-doesnt-work-and-how-we-know/> [accessed 17 November 2018]

Tally, Robert T., 'On Geocriticism', in *Geocritical Explorations: Space, Place, and Mapping in Literary and Cultural Studies*, ed. Robert T. Tally (New York: Palgrave Macmillan, 2011), pp. 1–9

Tenen, Dennis, *Plain Text: The Poetics of Computation* (Stanford, CA: Stanford University Press, 2017)

Terras, Melissa M., Julianne Nyhan, and Edward Vanhoutte, eds., *Defining Digital Humanities: A Reader* (Farnham: Ashgate Publishing, 2013)

Thomas, Alan, 'Here Are the First of Nan Z. Da's Suggested Guidelines for Peer Review of Computational Literary Studies, from Her Critique of the Field in @CriticalInquiry. How Realistic for Authors and Publishers?', *@alnthomas*, 2019 <https://twitter.com/alnthomas/status/1106616795534934016> [accessed 17 March 2019]

Thompson, John B., *Books in the Digital Age: The Transformation of Academic and Higher Education Publishing in Britain and the United States* (Cambridge: Polity Press, 2005)

Thornton, Sarah, *Club Cultures: Music, Media and Subcultural Capital* (Cambridge: Polity Press, 1995)

Torre, Juana T. Guerra de la, 'Fractals in Gertrude Stein's "Word-System": Natural Reality and/or Verbal Reality', *Atlantis*, 17.1/2 (1995), 89–114

Tuchman, Gaye, and Nina E. Fortin, *Edging Women Out: Victorian Novelists, Publishers, and Social Change* (New Haven, CT: Yale University Press, 1989)

Underwood, Ted, 'A Genealogy of Distant Reading', *Digital Humanities Quarterly*, 11.2 (2017) <http://www.digitalhumanities.org/dhq/vol/11/2/000317/000317.html> [accessed 21 September 2017]

Underwood, Ted, *Distant Horizons: Digital Evidence and Literary Change* (Chicago, IL: University of Chicago Press, 2019)

Underwood, Ted, 'The Life Cycles of Genres', *Journal of Cultural Analytics*, 1.1 (2016) <https://doi.org/10.22148/16.005>

Underwood, Ted, *Why Literary Periods Mattered: Historical Contrast and the Prestige of English Studies* (Stanford, CA: Stanford University Press, 2013)

Underwood, Ted, and Jordan Sellers, 'The Longue Durée of Literary Prestige', *Modern Language Quarterly*, 77.3 (2016), 321–44 <https://doi.org/10.1215/00267929-3570634>

Vee, Annette, ' "Literary Analysis by Computer" Offered at Dartmouth, Winter 1969, Working with Paradise Lost. #1960sComputing', *@anetv*, 2017 <https://twitter.com/anetv/status/919219418189660160/photo/1> [accessed 18 October 2017]

van de Velde, Danica, ' "Every Song Ends": Musical Pauses, Gendered Nostalgia, and Loss in Jennifer Egan's *A Visit from the Goon Squad*', in *Write in Tune: Contemporary Music in Fiction*, ed. Erich Hertz and Jeffrey Roessner (New York: Bloomsbury, 2014), pp. 125–35

Vonnegut, Kurt, *Palm Sunday: An Autobiographical Collage* (New York: Random House Publishing Group, 2009)

Warnock, John E., 'Simple Ideas That Changed Printing and Publishing', *Proceedings of the American Philosophical Society*, 156.4 (2012), 363–78

Warnock, John E., Letter to Martin Paul Eve, 'The Earliest "Critique" of PDF', 24 November 2019

Weisenburger, Steven, 'The End of History? Thomas Pynchon and the Uses of the Past', *Twentieth Century Literature*, 25.1 (1979), 54–72

Weisenburger, Steven, 'Thomas Pynchon at Twenty-Two: A Recovered Autobiographical Sketch', *American Literature*, 62.4 (1990), 692–7

Weiskott, Eric, 'There Is No Such Thing as "the Digital Humanities"', *The Chronicle of Higher Education*, 1 November 2017 <https://www.chronicle.com/article/There-Is-No-Such-Thing-as/241633> [accessed 17 November 2018]

West, David, *Object Thinking* (Redmond, WA: Microsoft Press, 2004)

Westphal, Bertrand, 'Foreword', in *Geocritical Explorations: Space, Place, and Mapping in Literary and Cultural Studies*, ed. Robert T. Tally (New York: Palgrave Macmillan, 2011), pp. xi–xv

White, Hayden, *Metahistory: Historical Imagination in Nineteenth Century Europe* (Baltimore, MD: Johns Hopkins University Press, 1975)

Williams, Raymond, *The Country and the City* (New York: Oxford University Press, 1975)

Winder, William, 'Writing Machines', in *A Companion to Digital Literary Studies*, ed. Ray Siemens and Susan Schreibman, Blackwell Companions to Literature and Culture (New York: Wiley-Blackwell, 2013), pp. 492–516

Wittgenstein, Ludwig, *Remarks on the Foundations of Mathematics*, 3rd edn. (Oxford: Blackwell, 1978)

Wordsworth, Jonathan, 'Introduction', in William Wordsworth, *The Prelude: The Four Texts (*1798, 1799, 1805, 1850*)*, Penguin Classics (London: Penguin Books, 1995), pp. xxv–xlvii

Wordsworth, William, *The Prelude: The Four Texts (*1798, 1799, 1805, 1850*)*, Penguin Classics (London: Penguin Books, 1995)

Zeller, Jr, Tom, 'A New Campaign Tactic: Manipulating Google Data', *The New York Times*, 26 October 2006, section U.S. <https://www.nytimes.com/2006/10/26/us/politics/26googlebomb.html> [accessed 14 April 2020]

Index

Note: italic page numbers refer to figures and tables.